AN
INNKEEPER'S
DIARY

AN INNKEEPER'S DIARY

SEPTEMBER 1996–SEPTEMBER 1997

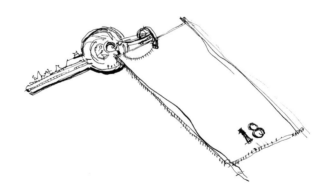

KIT CHAPMAN

WEIDENFELD & NICOLSON
LONDON

First published in Great Britain in 1999
by Weidenfeld & Nicolson

A CIP catalogue record for this book is available from the British Library
ISBN 0 297 82460 0

Art Director: David Rowley
Designer: Nigel Soper
Illustrations by Madeleine Floyd

Set in Bembo
Printed by Butler & Tanner Ltd, Frome and London

In certain instances names have been changed to protect identities

Weidenfeld & Nicolson
The Orion Publishing Group Ltd
5 Upper Saint Martin's Lane
London WC2H 9EA

In memory of my father,

PETER FRANCIS CHAPMAN, 1915-1997

CONTENTS

LIST OF ILLUSTRATIONS   VIII

FOREWORD   IX

THE SIEGE OF TAUNTON   1

RHODES AROUND TEDDINGTON   11

CAVIAR IN A CRISIS   19

A SPIDER IN THE HOUSE   25

TALES OF THE IRON LADY AND A SCARLET WOMAN 34

ST MARY'S GIRLS LOVE A GOOD RABBIT   47

WHEN IS A BROTH NOT A BROTH?   53

'ALL THE WORLD'S A STAGE'   60

DAYS OF JUDGEMENT   70

MIND GAMES AND MAGIC   79

MINSTRELS THAWS OUT   88

NO SIGN AT THE INN   94

GHOST STORY   103

NEW YEAR STING   110

FALLEN STAR   121

HAPPY BIRTHDAY FRANZ   129

THE FRIDGE   134

OF BANKERS AND BANQUETS   145

A POACHED EGG AND A CUP OF TEA   153

PAVEMENT PEOPLE   171

PIG POLITICS   181

LIBERAL TENDENCIES   190

EARLY RECOLLECTIONS   210

POKER GAME OF LIFE   233

GOODBYE ENGLAND'S ROSE   238

INDEX   251

ILLUSTRATIONS

My grandmother, Nell   x

My grandfather, Henry Prüger   ix

The principal players   xvi

My parents, Etty and
Peter Chapman   20, 21

Gastronomic evening, with guest of
honour Sir Bernard Ingham   35

Louise and me   49

The gondola dinner at
The Savoy Hotel, 30 June 1905
(Archives of The Savoy Hotel Ltd)   62

Christmas at the Castle, 1978   97

Patrick Lichfield and me   101

Mrs Jackie Ballard, MP
(Somerset County Gazette)   181

Phil Vickery, Alan Crompton, Steve
Waugh and the whortleberry pie   223

Kit and Gerald Chapman
as Tudor page boys, 1956   224

FOREWORD

THE TITLE OF THIS BOOK is taken from the same written by John Fothergill, proprietor of the Spreadeagle in Thame, Oxfordshire, and published by Chatto & Windus in 1931. I think I would have got on rather well with Fothergill. Students of this trade will be struck by the shared joys and tribulations which, each day, lift and afflict the innkeeper. *Plus ça change, plus c'est la même chose.*

Fothergill's diary is dedicated to 'Kate [his wife], too good for words; to our generous staff; and to the kind victims of our innkeeping'. I too offer mine to Louise, my wife and partner, the staff of the Castle at Taunton (unfailingly kind and generous) and to our victims (kind or otherwise). But above any other, this journal is dedicated to my dear father, Peter Chapman, who laid the foundations of the family business and rescued this hotel from dust, gloom and obscurity after the war. Without him this book could not have been written.

As I am descended from a long line of innkeepers, a brief sketch of the family may help to set the scene. My cousin Richard – a tiger hotelier on the Pacific Rim – and I represent the fourth generation. And my sons Dom (an aspiring chef in a fashionable London eaterie) and Nick (reading a degree in 'hospitality management') are likely to become the fifth.

In the 1920s, while John Fothergill was writing about life at the Spreadeagle, my paternal grandfather Henry Prüger was creating one of the grandest hotels in Europe – in Bratislava, the city of his birth. His mother, Amelia, was just eighteen when he was born on 15 September 1867 and she went on to bear eight more children for her husband, Henry Anthony Prüger. The elder Henry was a gifted chef who once ran a restaurant in Vienna, the imperial capital of Austria-Hungary, before opening a small hotel with his young wife in Bratislava – or Pressburg as the city was known until it was renamed after the collapse of the Habsburg Empire at the end of the Great War.

The family prospered and it soon became apparent that young Henry was destined to build a glittering career as an international hotelier. In 1903, aged 36, Prüger landed the job of general manager at the Savoy in London. It was here that he made his name as a brilliant host and impresario of the Edwardian age, and in

My grandmother, Nell

1911 the Emperor awarded him the Knight's Cross of the Order of Francis Joseph, entitling him to assume the style 'von Prüger', a title he never adopted. In the same year he married my grandmother Nell Chapman, thus providing the only English blood to run through my veins (my mother is Greek). Nellie was the daughter of a plumber-turned-builder from Uppingham in Rutland whom Sir George Reeves-Smith, the Savoy's managing director, appointed as the hotel's 'Lady Housekeeper'. However, by 1911 Henry and Nell had left the Savoy and my grandfather was running the RAC Club, which had just opened its stately new premises in Pall Mall. Nell bore Henry three sons: Michael, the eldest, was born at the Club and grew up to become the most famous hotelier of the fifties and sixties by making the Imperial in Torquay Britain's top resort hotel for the rich and famous. The second was Anthony and Peter, my father, was born in 1915, the Benjamin of the family.

With the relentless upward drive of his career, Prüger amassed a substantial fortune. In 1908, while he was still at the Savoy, he started to buy into a prime site in the centre of Pressburg and by 1912 the family had become the owners of a large three-storey hotel which Henry christened the Savoy-Carlton. While he pursued his work in England, Amelia – now widowed but a matriarch of indomitable standing – held sway at home. In London, Henry purchased a property in St James's, determined to build a second hotel.

With the outbreak of war in 1914, Prüger found himself in an impossible predicament. He was an enemy alien. In spite of the considerable influence of his friends at the RAC Club, he refused to accept naturalization as a British subject. His patriotism cost him dearly. He lost both his job and the property in St James's. Nevertheless, the authorities decided not to deport him and Henry spent the war years organizing food and clothing schemes for thousands of his dispossessed countrymen who had been employed in London as musicians or catering workers and now found themselves confined in British internment camps.

My grandfather, Henry Prüger

After the war, with Europe in chaos and the Empire dissolved, my grandfather returned to Pressburg – now Bratislava, capital of Slovakia and, after Prague, the second city in the new Czechoslovakia. As a staunch patriot of the old Austro-Hungarian order, he despised his new masters and they didn't care much for him. But the city grew as an industrial and commercial centre and with it the Savoy-Carlton prospered. By the mid-twenties, Henry was laying plans to double the size of his hotel to 254 bedrooms – a vast palace with its own power station, laundry and workshops; several brasseries, cafés and restaurants; a winter garden and a night club. The plans were over-ambitious and as the world descended into depression, his Slovak bankers squeezed him. On 11 July 1929, Prüger clambered into an unfinished roof-space on the seventh floor of his great hotel and took his life.

My father was fourteen when the news came through. He was coming to the end of his summer term at Dover College, where he and his brothers were pursuing a very English public school education. Eventually, the banks foreclosed and a second Prüger fortune was lost. By 1936 there was nothing left for Nell in Bratislava. She returned home to settle in a small cottage in Sussex and in May 1937 the family changed its name to Chapman, Nell's maiden name. She died in 1954.

The trauma of the family tragedy and the loss of the Savoy-Carlton made my father vow never to become an hotelier. When he left school in 1933, he joined J & P Coats, the cotton manufacturers, and two years later the company posted him to India. At the end of the war, and now a major in the Indian Army, my father landed in northern Greece, where he fell madly in love with my mother, Etty, the striking nineteen-year-old daughter of a wealthy banker from Thessalonika. They married and have remained madly in love ever since. However, England in 1946 was no petal-strewn romantic paradise, and Peter found himself broke, jobless and married to a beautiful young Greek girl pregnant with me.

Big brother Michael offered him a job in Torquay but the association ended in tears and in October 1950 my father accepted the position of manager at a decrepit pile in the centre of Taunton, Somerset's county town. We have been at the Castle Hotel ever since; and since our grim arrival it has blossomed phoenix-like into a very handsome bird. The story is picked up in more detail later in this journal with a few meandering recollections of my childhood years. My grandfather's life also continues to intrigue me, and for the past year I have been dipping into the archives at the Savoy and the RAC Club. Some of my findings are included in the narrative, revealing Henry Prüger as a most extraordinary man. He had a mind touched by moments of sheer genius but, equally, he was capable of heroic misjudgements. Ultimately, I believe my grandfather was shown to be a coward; a man with a flawed personality, so consumed by pride and vanity he was prepared to desert his wife and three teenage sons rather than face the prospect of failure.

To some degree, Prüger's achievements have been mythologized by my family who, in the end, were left with nothing. The third generation – my father and my uncle Michael – have more to show for their lives' labour. Michael mixed a sharp commercial mind with the charms of a matinée idol. He knew better than most the business potential of literally putting on the Ritz; no one played the showman like Michael Chapman. In grey, dismal post-war Britain, he wowed his punters with gaiety and gastronomy, flying Europe's top chefs in to cook their specialities over long weekends by the sea. He was spinning dreams forty years before spin doctors were invented, branding the Imperial with the shameless slogan 'The English hotel in the Mediterranean manner' and persuading the worthy aldermen of Torquay to slap the line 'The English Riviera' across all the resort's publicity. Then, in 1969, he sold his jewel to Charles Forte and made a killing. Today the Imperial has lost its seductive dazzle – a rusting cruise liner abandoned on the rocks overlooking Torbay.

Although I was immersed in hotel life from birth, like my father I fled the industry in my twenties, until the blood-line hauled me back. I was educated at Taunton School, a vile institution I thank only for equipping me with A levels in Greek, Latin and French. In 1965 these exams saw me into the University of Surrey, a free-spirited and splendid place where I took a degree in Hotel and Catering Administration. At first this was the career I wanted – only, I suspect, because my head had been turned by the glamour and fun of my uncle's gastronomic weekends at the Imperial and the sybaritic pleasures of similar watering holes to which I was taken by my parents. But I soon learned that being on the receiving end of good food and flunkies falling at your feet was very different from the business of providing the good life to others.

Disillusioned by my stints in the trade, in 1969 – the year of my graduation – I was sufficiently infused with the jargon of management theory and the sinister techniques of marketing to land a brilliant job with Grey Advertising, an international agency with an impressive client list whose London offices were situated in the heart of the West End. I loved it and for the next seven years I flogged detergent (Ariel), crisps (Smiths), cigarettes (Players), soap (Camay) and much else in a succession of smart agencies, each more eager than the last to inflate my salary by several hundred per cent. I worked hard and enjoyed life in the fast lane, especially as it allowed me to indulge my passion for good food and wine by dining my clients in all London's trendiest eateries. My expense claims were outrageous.

In December 1971 I married Louise and within four years we were a family: Dom was born in '73, Nick in '75. Then, I sense, my values began to shift and I found myself pushing a pram round Wandsworth Park questioning the game I was playing. Intellectually, the advertising business is immensely stimulating: you work alongside groups of clever, creative, talented people and, if you are any good, the money is wonderful. But, ultimately, that's all there is: money. I began to wonder how any sane and civilized human being could get excited about a bar of soap or a packet of crisps. In the end, the life of the advertising man is extraordinarily shallow: the biz has no more depth than a sheet of newsprint. Ads are ephemeral pieces of puffery. They are not designed to endure.

My epiphany came in Manchester, at a sales conference to launch a new unisex hairspray called US. I presented the advertising campaign and, come the climax of a presentation cunningly orchestrated to build up the hype, the sales director unveiled the product: screens on the stage slid aside to reveal a gigantic display of aerosol cans, laser beams pierced the darkness, Beethoven's *Ode to Joy* smacked our eardrums. As the music hit a final crescendo, the house lights were raised and an army of waiters burst through the doors of the auditorium bearing trays of champagne. On stage, the sales director lifted his glass in a Nazi salute and pronounced the toast: 'To US hairspray!'

It was time to move on. Besides, I could feel the call inside; an ancient rumble in the guts. While that infamous can of glue bombed, never to be heard of again, my future went on hold for twelve months. In 1975 my father – now sixty years old – entered a long final phase in his negotiations to buy the hotel and in February the following year the sale was completed. Two months later the prodigal son returned.

This diary – one year in the life of the Castle Hotel – is like a TV soap. It has its own thread of events, its own pulse and tone of voice, its own flashbacks and ruminations. Gradually, I hope you will come to know its dramatis personae. It is not for dipping in and out. To enjoy it, begin at the beginning. *Bon appétit.*

KIT CHAPMAN
THE CASTLE AT TAUNTON
OCTOBER 1997

The principal players (left to right, back row): Andrew Grahame, Simon Girling, Phil Vickery; (front) Kit and Louise Chapman

THE SIEGE OF TAUNTON

SATURDAY, 7 SEPTEMBER 1996

A BUSY WEEK. But then it always is. With the end of our financial year only three weeks away, we have been immersed in budgets and plans for the coming months. Although we have had a cracking year, with the promise of record profits, it's been hard going. My general manager, Andrew Grahame, has been desperately ill with cancer – non Hodgkin's lymphoma – and he has languished in hospital for most of this time. He is only thirty-four, was married last year to Cécile, a feisty raven-headed French girl, and they have a beautiful baby daughter, Chlöe. Eventually, after months of chemotherapy, he was discharged from Musgrove Park Hospital in Taunton in April with the news that his treatment had failed. Andrew was declared a terminal case. Now, five months on, he is back at work full time and firing on all cylinders. At our last board meeting, we made him a director of the family firm – he's the best general manager I've ever had.

In the dark days of last winter, I used to visit him in hospital. After a while, I could walk those long, grim corridors to Ward 9 almost blindfold. There he'd lie, pale as mist, skeletal and hairless. The food was unspeakably foul, so I'd bring him flasks of soup from the hotel and Cécile brought Marks & Spencer ready-made meals which the nurses microwaved for him. Who knows what agonies a cancer patient suffers? I don't. But I saw one man's pain and how he coped with it. From the start, he was determined to see the disease off. He had everything to live for: a young wife, a newly born baby and a job he loved. There was also his wicked sense of humour which he never lost, even in his darkest moments: 'Guaranteed free nine-month holiday with every case,' he'd quip. Andrew's sheer bravery made us all feel a little ashamed of our own feeble problems.

He still returns to Musgrove for a weekly check-up and his doctors are amazed by the extraordinary recovery he has made. There is also a mystical dimension to Andrew's condition. On his days off, he drives home to Derby to see his family and visit his uncle Arthur, a spiritual healer. I first came to hear about Arthur when Andrew was in hospital. As a teenager Andrew had suffered from a problem knee which had stopped him from playing games at school. No doctor could cure him of this debilitating ailment, but uncle Arthur did.

Of course, Louise and I still worry about Andrew but, touch wood, we've never seen him on such terrific form. Yesterday afternoon he bounced into my office to say he was going out for half an hour. 'I'm getting my first haircut,' he said proudly. 'And when they look at my head, I bet they ask "Who cut *this* last time?"'

Dear old Vickery [the Castle's chef] has been unusually good-humoured this week too. He makes his television début on Monday in *Who'll do the Pudding?* and he appears on *Ready Steady Cook* later in the autumn. But the biggest excitement in his life is his new plaything. Phil (to my absolute horror) has just taken delivery of a Suzuki 600 Bandit, a monstrous two-wheeled machine capable of 100 mph from a standing start in six-and-a-half seconds. It's dangerous and it's absurd. And I can't see any point in the thing other than as a sex substitute. But then, Chef has come through a grisly divorce this year, and only two weeks ago his girlfriend was given notice to quit and seek alternative digs. So perhaps this new toy is no coincidence, just a simple swap: the ecstasy of the bed for the thrust and throb of the open road.

I went down to the kitchen to see him.

'Chef, what's all this I hear? Aren't you going to introduce me to your new mistress?'

'Oh!' he replied, grinning all over his face. 'You've heard, have you?'

'You bet. It's today's hot gossip.' My secretary, Gill Whatmore, had briefed me only five minutes before.

We walked through the kitchen to the back door and I followed Phil into the garage. And there it was, like a tart in an Amsterdam window. He started stroking it, patting it. The make-up was pretty startling too. 'What colour's that?' I asked.

'Candy marine, bluish-green. Isn't it great? The latest colour!'

'So every time you wrap your legs round that body, it gives you an orgasm?'

'Well, I must admit I got an erection the first time I rode it,' he confessed. 'Let's go back to my office. I want to show you my leathers.'

This was getting better and better. In his office, an airless hole beneath the back stairs, all the gear was laid out, new and pristine: jet-black leather armour, black boots, black helmet.

'How much did all this set you back?' I asked.

'A thousand quid for the suit. Two hundred for the helmet,' he replied. And then, sensing my anxiety, he added, 'Don't worry. It's a powerful bike but I respect its power and I'm well protected. I promise I'll be careful.' That was good enough for me. Damn it all, I thought, the man is in his mid-thirties.

'OK, Phil,' I said. 'I believe you. But I've seen enough of hospitals for one year.'

The past three weeks have been dominated by a local furore which might loosely be described as the Siege of Taunton. The press has been full of it and the Castle is in the thick of the fray. The centre of the town is bedlam, a nightmare of diggers, trucks and Portuguese navvies who, for the past eight months, have been busy redeveloping the area in what the Council twely describes as the 'Town Centre Enhancement Scheme'. On top of all this chaos, cacophony and grime, the normally placid disposition of the good citizens of Taunton is being stirred into a frenzy of angst by a small invasion of New Age barbarians who are turning the heart of the town into an open-air squat; worse, a hostile encampment that can turn very nasty.

Some weeks ago, I'd had enough aggro and wrote to the Leader of the Council, Jefferson Horsley, with copies to the police and our local paper, the *Somerset County Gazette*.

20 August 1996

Dear Jefferson,

This morning our Reception Office was besieged by guests complaining bitterly about the rowdy and abusive behaviour of vagrants in Castle Bow. We were first made aware of the problem at about 8.30 last night and called the police who dealt with the matter. Then, later that evening, there was a serious disturbance outside the Ferret & Trouserleg [a pub adjacent to the Castle].

This latest example of loutish behaviour in the town centre is stretching our patience. The police will tell you that my managers and I have frequently called to complain about the behaviour of vagrants, beggars and drunks who now seem to have taken up residence in the town centre. As you will know, we are all in favour of the new enhancement scheme and, indeed, we are impressed with the high quality of the development which should do much to improve the attractiveness of the town centre.

However, the millions you are spending on this wonderful scheme will be rendered worthless if the town centre is going to continue to be blighted by the uncivilized behaviour of a few very unpleasant people. The new town centre should be a source of great civic pride. Unless something is done to resolve this growing problem, the centre of Taunton – supported by your ratepayers – will just become another nasty inner city ghetto.

Yours sincerely,

C H G Chapman
Managing Director

The letter hit its target. The headlines in the *Somerset County Gazette*, which is published weekly on Fridays, continue to roll off the presses.

Somerset County Gazette, 23 August 1996
Hotel Boss Joins The Protest About Drunks And Beggars…And Warns:
TOWN CENTRE IS TURNING INTO A GHETTO FOR LOUTS

Somerset County Gazette, 30 August 1996
Disabled Grandfather Speaks Of His Fears After Town Centre Attack Just
Before Noon On Sunday
I'M DEAD SCARED OF TAUNTON NOW
A grandfather has told how he was attacked near Taunton's Castle Hotel
just before midday on Sunday – only days after the hotel's managing
director called for action to control beggars, drunks and vagrants…

Somerset County Gazette, 6 September 1996
We Are Becoming 'No-Go Area' In Centre Of Taunton – County
Museum Assistant Officer Speaks Out
GANGS SCARE OFF OUR VISITORS
…Assistant county museums officer Steve Minnitt claims visitors and staff
have been harassed, threatened and intimidated by drunks using the
entrance as a public toilet… His comments also follow criticism of 'rowdy
and abusive vagrants' in the area by the Castle Hotel…

The good thing about the *Gazette* is that it is not prone to hype. Our estimable local organ faithfully records the experiences and feelings of its readers. Regrettably, this does not always apply to the reactions of our politicians, whose response to our plight has been predictably pusillanimous. Taunton's MP, the sitting Tory, David Nicholson, made much of the fact that he had spent a night on the beat with the town's police and said the streets were 'friendly, not threatening'! Pathetic. Mr Nicholson neither lives nor works in Taunton. And if I'd spent an evening on the beat protected by the police, I am sure that I would find Taunton a most agreeable place. The trouble is, when we need the police they are nowhere to be seen.

Eventually, on 2 September, I received a reply to my letter from Ol' Waffles, Jefferson Horsley.

Dear Kit,

Thank you for your letter of 20 August 1996. *[Five lines of huff, puff and heartfelt sympathy followed.]*

I am awaiting the outcome of a report by our Community Safety Officer, who is undertaking a Safety Audit of the town and this is due shortly. I believe that one of its recommendations will be for the council to examine closely the introduction of a bye-law *(sic)* banning the consumption of alcohol in public places. This is not an easy option and may well be only a deterrent. I am not sure at this moment it enjoys the support of the local Police as they have expressed in the past that they believe there are adequate laws to cover the behaviour of those who disturb the majority going about their ordinary business.

Please rest assured that I shall vigorously pursue the appropriate path to make the town centre attractive and prosperous for all who use it.

Yours sincerely,

Jefferson Horsley

Now dear Ol' Waffles is not such a bad bloke. As an earnest Lib-Dem, he means well and, after all, the Taunton Town Centre Enhancement Scheme is his great vision. The other day, he and a group of colleagues were having lunch in the hotel while I was in the far corner of the restaurant snatching a quick Caesar salad. One of Louise's large flower arrangements in the centre of the room partially screened me from their line of sight. I kept my head down, thankful to the floral veil for guarding my anonymity. But Jefferson spotted me in my safe haven. Up he bounced and lunged towards me. I groaned inwardly. Tall and thin, beak-nosed, with popping eyes, Ol' Waffles is one of those types who has the disconcerting habit of crowding you when he wants to engage in intimate dialogue. He thrusts his gawky visage within millimetres of your face and fixes you with his stare.

'Oh, hello Jeff,' I choked, my mouth half-full of Caesar salad. 'I hope you're enjoying your lunch?'

'Yes, yes,' he replied. 'Very good, very good.' He became conspiratorial, his voice almost whispering. 'Got your letter. Of course I'll be replying. But I thought you'd like to know – and this is confidential at the moment – we are in touch with the Home Office to see what powers we might have available to introduce a by-law to limit drinking in public places. But it's not easy. There are problems.'

'Yes, Jeff,' I said comfortingly. 'There will always be problems. But in the end, if the political will is there, it is amazing what you can do.'

'Of course, of course,' he replied. 'I can assure you, the political will is there. It is there. We're not going to let this one go, Kit. We're not. But there are problems.' And we left it at that.

Taunton's colony of New Age vagrants may be a menace, but the 'enhancement' contractors are also being a pain in the neck. Early on Wednesday morning, some boss-eyed navvy dug up a cable which cut off our power for three hours. At seven o'clock, Andrew Grahame walked into the hotel to find the place in semi-darkness. He telephoned the electricity board, who could not find us registered under our post code.

'Do you have a coin-operated meter system there?' asked the voice at the other end of the line.

'No,' replied Andrew. 'This is the Castle Hotel.'

'Do you have a customer reference number?'

'No,' said Andrew. 'But I do have an hotel in darkness. So please will you kindly get someone out to us as soon as possible.'

At 7.20, two suits walked in asking for breakfast. 'We rang yesterday,' said one of them. 'We were told you were quite busy and your girl advised us to come early.'

Andrew peered at them across the gloom of the reception desk. 'I'm terribly sorry but our power's down and at the moment I simply can't offer you any breakfast. To be honest, I doubt anyone's going to get breakfast this morning.'

'But we did call yesterday,' insisted the suit. 'And we were told there would be no problem.'

At this point, Andrew was getting a little exasperated. The message was not sinking in.

'Were we clairvoyant, I am sure my receptionist would not have told you that breakfast was available,' he said.

'Well, can we just have a coffee?' droned the suit.

'As I have explained, Sir, none of our equipment is functioning.'

As they left, one muttered to the other: 'Don't understand it. They can't even do a simple breakfast.'

'And we did call yesterday!' added the other.

No sooner had the businessmen gone than the telephone rang. Andrew lifted the receiver to hear a guest barking down the line from his bedroom. 'What sort of hotel has no electricity?'

'One experiencing a power cut?' suggested Andrew in despair.

The potential for disaster is high in any hotel. This is because hotels, in essence, trade in the foibles and frailties of the human condition. Ultimately, our mission is to introduce a little sunshine, a little interest, a little levity, into the stresses of people's everyday lives. We are in the happiness business and, as such, we are especially susceptible to 'Sod's Law' and the whimsy of the human being.

Yesterday I took a call from Lady Armstrong, wife of Lord Armstrong. As Mrs Thatcher's Cabinet Secretary in the eighties, Sir Robert (as he was before his elevation to the Lords) became famous for coining the expression 'being economical with the truth' when he gave evidence in the Peter Wright *Spycatcher* case in Australia. The Armstrongs keep a home in Somerset and so we are acquainted. He is a man with all the easy charm and urbanity of a senior mandarin. She is like cut glass. If she came wrapped and packaged, the box would be labelled 'HANDLE WITH CARE'.

I last saw them in February at one of our musical evenings. During the interval, I went over to greet them and commented that it had been some years since their last visit.

'Oh, indeed,' said Lady Armstrong. 'It's been six years. The last time we came, we ordered duck and it was quite inedible.'

'I'm sorry to hear that,' I replied. 'Actually, we are rather proud of our duck and coincidentally it's on tonight's menu. You'll love it! So this is our chance to restore your confidence in our kitchen.'

At dinner Louise and I were entertaining a party of eight. The Armstrongs had booked for two and were some distance from us. Come the duck – a roast breast – my knife bounced off the wretched bird. It was tough, dry and a total disaster. I felt like digging a deep hole and leaping into it. Summoning the restaurant manager, I asked him to present the Armstrongs with a half-bottle of champagne with their puddings: it was Lady A's fiftieth birthday. 'Say nothing about the duck,' I instructed. 'This is just a goodwill gesture on a special occasion.'

Later, as they came to leave, they approached our table and Lord Armstrong thanked me warmly for the fizz. I turned to Lady A and muttered an apology for the wretched duck.

'Well I'm glad you said it rather than me,' she snapped. A few days later, I received a polite thank-you note for the champagne with the codicil: 'Sadly I think that I will have to draw a veil over duck at the Castle, but the starter was delicious.'

And so yesterday, when the receptionist announced that Lady Armstrong was on the line, I was primed, alert and ready for battle. In fact, all she wanted was to reserve a table for dinner, for herself, her husband and her daughter. Now among the many things I have learned in this game, this is one: the more self-consciously grand people become, the more they feel compelled to call the *patron*, even for the simplest of requests like a table for dinner.

Before leaving, I alerted Simon Girling, my restaurant manager, and Phil Vickery. 'Beware!' I said.

This morning, as I walked into the hotel, I found Vickery, black as thunder, bending Andrew Grahame's ear.

'What's up?' I asked.

'Your Lady Armstrong,' he hissed. I groaned a baleful groan.

This time it was the starter that was wrong. She had chosen the salad of artichokes, rocket and beetroot with straw potatoes. The dish had been presented (as it always is) with a sprinkling of wild mushrooms (we dislike essays for menu descriptions and we like the element of surprise). When Girling went over to their table, he saw Lady A vigorously plucking the fungi out of her salad and depositing them on her daughter's plate. Moreover, she complained of the paucity of beetroot. Girling then explained that beetroot is not, by definition, only red, pointing to the yellow and white varieties on her plate.

I suspect we may have lost Lady Armstrong – anyway for another six years.

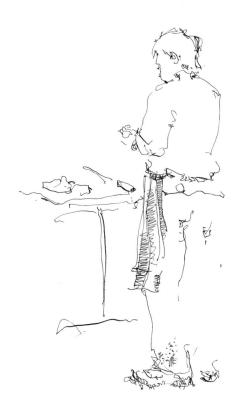

RHODES AROUND TEDDINGTON

SATURDAY, 21 SEPTEMBER 1996

I'M EXHAUSTED. One short week away – in Spain to attend a cousin's riotous wedding celebrations – and I return to a desk piled high with paper, petty staff problems and the Christmas publicity to sort out. Still, September is looking good, with occupancies topping eighty per cent, and Andrew Grahame seems on good form.

In the kitchen, Phil Vickery is stressed and touchy. He's done seventeen days and nights without a break to allow his sous-chef time off to repair the latest rupture in his marriage. Meanwhile, Phil is also being pursued by a posse of hungry TV producers who are convinced he is the new Sharon Stone of the stoves. They keep asking him for the name of his agent – so I've told him to refer them to me in future. Then I rejected his Christmas menus. 'Chef,' I scrawled across the papers, 'you've got chicken on Christmas Eve, turkey on Christmas Day and guinea fowl on Boxing Day. Give us some red meat!' That was three days ago and I'm still waiting to hear back.

We are also having endless debates about the future of Minstrels, our pub next door to the hotel. We want to revamp the menu, bring in a new chef and tart the place up a little. The exteriors need painting and the builder has proposed a pink and juniper green colour scheme. 'You wanted rock'n'roll, Mr Chapman,' he said. 'I tell you, this is the business. You'll love it. Believe me.' Well, I don't. When he showed us samples of the colours painted on blocks of wood, the tone of the green looked more excremental than juniper.

'I think I'd prefer something nearer a racing green for the doors,' I said. 'This is shit green – there's no other way to describe it. And I can't imagine what pink walls will look like in Castle Bow.'

'Racing green won't work with the pink,' insisted the builder. 'With nice brass door furniture, this'll work a treat, believe me!' he repeated.

'We could always rename Minstrels the Shit Green Shack,' suggested Andrew. The debate continues.

Yesterday was an extraordinary day, remarkable for the fact that I had been invited to join two celebrations arranged in honour of two men who, in their own different ways, had played a major part in the life of the Castle. The first was a memorial service – billed as a 'Musical Celebration' – for Ivan Sutton at St Giles' Church, Cripplegate, in the City. Ivan, who died in May, launched the Castle's annual season of musical weekends in 1977 and continued as our artistic director until his retirement three years ago, when he was succeeded by Carolyn Humphreys. He became a special friend and it is to him entirely that I owe my passion for good chamber music.

The second celebration came off another planet. I was asked to appear as a surprise guest on Michael Aspel's *This Is Your Life* – and the man he was to spring with the Big Red Book was my former head chef-turned-TV star, Gary Rhodes. Thames Television, who produce the programme for the BBC, had promised to pick me up from St Giles' at four and drive me to the studios in Teddington in time for the show at six.

I arrived in London mid-morning. The first thing I needed was a haircut and I grabbed a taxi from Paddington to Fulham for my eleven o'clock appointment. Douglas Chisholm, whose clients include luminaries like André Deutsch and Laurie Lee, has been cutting my hair for more than twenty-five years from his high-rise flat in Elm Park Gardens. It's all very casual and homely. Shampoos are conducted by kneeling on a fat cushion, bending over the bath tub. Then, hair dripping, you step across the corridor to the spare room where Douglas snips away over mugs of Nescafé and opera on the CD player. As I was early, I settled down in his sitting room while he applied the final grooming touches to a lady in her forties. Like the best in his profession, Douglas is endowed with that seductive charm which invariably elevates the hairdresser's role to that of client confessor. I have never really understood why this should be, but I suppose if you can trust a man to cut your hair, you can trust him with your deepest secrets. As I waited my turn, I picked up snatches of conversation.

Douglas: 'So are you still in love?'

Lady: 'Oh yes. Very much so.'

D: 'But you still haven't moved in with him then?'

L: ' No, no. We like our independence.'

By Douglas's standard, this exchange was pretty tame. In the past, I've heard him open with:

'So you're getting laid at last!'

'How on earth did you know?' replied the woman.

'I can see it written all over your face.'

When my turn came, the only sex talk dwelt on the hot issue of bonking bishops and the case for celibacy within the Catholic clergy. The rest of the time was spent discussing this year's mulberry harvest. Good mulberry trees are something of a rarity, but Douglas has one in his Sussex garden and his wife, Lizzie, delivered several pounds of fruit for Phil's use when she was returning Camilla, their daughter, to Millfield at the start of the autumn term. The question that arose was how best to harvest the fruit. Should one pick by hand, or lay sheets under the tree and shake the branches to allow the ripe berries to fall to the ground? We could not agree. Either way, we did agree that 1996 was a bumper harvest.

With the memorial service at three, I headed towards the City to meet my old pal Andrew Milne-Watson, who runs his publishing business out of an office in Smithfield, a short stroll from Cripplegate. Andrew and I have been serious lunching companions since our days as thrusting young advertising men in the early seventies. We had booked a table at Stephen Bull's Bistro in St John Street and for the next two hours we gossiped over a delicious lunch of crab, scallops, duck confit and roast suckling pig, the whole gently lubricated by a healthy flow of Vernaccia di San Gimignano.

Thus fortified, I was ready for church. St Giles' was packed and I found myself a seat beside Nina Cropper whose husband, Peter, is leader of the Lindsays (the Castle's 'Quartet-in-Residence'), one of the top five string quartets in the world. Indeed, the line-up of musical, theatrical and literary talent was impressive; so impressive that I suspect dear Ivan – a shy, modest man – would have been bewildered by the fuss being made over him. The service, properly high church, was led by the Bishop of Chichester. Around the prayers and hymns we had Dame Felicity Lott, our great soprano, singing Mozart and Schubert; Prunella Scales reading Ecclesiastes and Corinthians; Steven Isserlis (who performed at the Castle this year) playing Bach; David Cairns providing the gravitas and Miles Kington the levity in their respective tributes to Ivan's life; Richard Stilgoe reading his sonnet 'on a world without music'; and finally, the Lindsays with Steven Isserlis playing the second movement of Schubert's String Quintet in C.

This was a beautiful, moving and often witty memorial to a great man, the only unchoreographed moments coming from the back of the church, from where the sound of corks popping punctured the air at frequent intervals.

'Listen to it again!' whispered Nina Cropper to me. 'It's dreadful!'

'Oh, I don't know,' I whispered back. 'I think Ivan would find it terribly funny!'

I never got my glass of wine. As the service ended well after four, I rushed outside to find a grey-liveried Hertz chauffeur in a dark blue Scorpio. We set off purposefully, the driver braking and accelerating abruptly in his efforts to beat the mounting congestion. This was Friday afternoon – the start of the weekend rush – and he was clearly under orders to get his passenger to Teddington before six o'clock. He began perspiring.

At 4.40, the car phone babbled maniacally to life. Jim wrenched the receiver from its fixture on the dashboard and slammed it against his left ear. He paused to listen to the voice on the other end of the line, snarling his replies in contempt.

'A long way!'… 'How long is a piece of string? Next question!'… 'At Hyde Park Corner'… 'Depends on the traffic!'

At 5.10, the phone started warbling again… 'Hogarth Roundabout,' hissed Jim, replacing the receiver with a sharp snap. Ten minutes later, the voice from Hertz called again. This time it was more conciliatory… 'Still a long way,' said Jim. 'About a mile from Richmond. I've a feeling I'm not going to make it by six'… 'I'll try my best!'

The traffic was solid as we crawled through Richmond, crossing the river at about a quarter to six. Jim persevered. Both of us were now resigned to the impossibility of the deadline.

'Do you often do this run for Thames?' I asked.

'Oh yes,' replied Jim with a sigh. 'I've done it many times. This always happens. I don't know why they don't use a studio in central London. People are always late.'

'So what do they do? Do they delay the show?'

'Sometimes they do. Sometimes they don't. Depends how important the person is.' He paused for a moment. 'Are you important?'

'Well, I'll soon find out,' I said.

At ten past six, Jim brought the Scorpio to a final halt outside Teddington Studios. I tumbled out of the car and rushed through the doors. Clare, an assistant producer on the programme, greeted me with a harassed smile.

'Come this way,' she said. 'We're going to have to hurry. They're all waiting and you've got to do your voice-over.'

'Do you mind if I have a pee first?' I asked.

'OK,' said Clare, slowing down and pointing to the gents. 'It's just here.'

I emerged relieved and refreshed, suddenly realizing that I'd better start psyching myself up. In spite of the marathon crawl across London, Schubert was still playing sublimely in my ears. The prospect of 'Gary Rhodes – This Is Your Life' had not registered. I retuned my mindset.

'I've read the script,' I said as we dashed off towards a recording studio. 'Can I change my voice-over?'

'No,' said Clare. 'It'll throw Michael. He needs your words as scripted to cue your entrance.'

Seconds later I was seated in a cupboard in front of a microphone. I spoke my words. The technician said, 'Great. That was *great*, Kit!' And Clare dragged me off again.

Behind the set, a crowd of guests mingled, half-listening to a warm-up artist entertaining the studio audience on the other side of the screens. An electrician pounced on me, wiring my suit with a radio mike; a make-up lady dabbed powder on my nose and chin; and a floor manager with a head-set and clipboard started to drill me.

'This is where you stand for your cue,' she instructed. 'Right here, feet by the blue marker on the floor. After your voice-over, Michael will announce you and the doors will slide open. Then walk down the ramp and greet Gary.' We rehearsed the walk. The ramp, I thought, was decidedly flimsy, bouncing beneath my feet. I had visions of slipping.

'When you've greeted Gary,' continued the floor manager, 'stand here and Michael will ask you your question. But don't speak to Michael, talk directly to Gary and end with a tribute to him. You have forty seconds. Then go and sit over there.' She pointed to a curved banquette. We disappeared back up the ramp and out of sight while the warm-up artist carried on with his stock of well-worn gags.

Backstage and feeling mildly dazed by the studio lights, I looked around for a familiar face. Raymond Blanc and Glynn Christian were there – the Frenchman in pristine whites embroidered with the name of his famous *manoir*, the writer and TV chef looking frightfully dapper in an immaculate double-breasted suit. We chatted for a while.

'They've flown me over from Sydney!' said Glynn. 'When they called, I thought – gosh, Gary? He's a bit young for that!'

'I sought zee same,' said Blanc. 'But it iz all to do with zee audience – wiz zee ratings.'

A cheerful voice then called 'Hello Mr Chapman!' I turned and it was Jenny Rhodes, Gary's wife. She gave me a big hug and a kiss, and seemed genuinely pleased to see me after a lapse of more than six years. At first I was a little overcome. The warmth and spontaneity of her greeting surprised me. In the four years that Gary was my head chef, Jenny had also worked at the Castle. She was bright and very able – so much so I promoted her to restaurant manager. This turned out to be a mistake and I had no choice other than to fire her, which I did as kindly as possible over a box of Kleenex tissues. But once the deed was done, I was not exactly Jenny's favourite person.

To make matters worse, the Rhodes's departure from Taunton in 1990 was not conducted in the happiest of circumstances. Gary had done a brilliant job for me, but perhaps more importantly we had established a strong working relationship and a warm friendship. I trusted him. When he came to resign, that trust was tested. Under pressure from his new employer – who had pursued him for years – he left in some haste and did not serve out his full notice, leaving me no time to find his successor. This created chaos in my kitchen. The entire brigade quit, either to follow Gary to London, or to use the moment to find a job in another high-profile restaurant. This was my worst nightmare come true. I spent a day calling my friends in the trade asking them if they might spare one or two of their own chefs to come and help out. Richard Shepherd at Langan's Brasserie sent me one of his best. So did Michel Roux from the Waterside Inn at Bray. Roux' words to me still echo in my ears. 'Zat is zee trouble, Kit,' he said. 'You build zem up. You build zem up. And zen zey shit on you from a great height!' We survived. And as the years passed, time healed the wound – although, I suspect, Gary always harboured a nagging guilt for the way he behaved.

Now, with seconds to go before the show went live, I waited to make a very private reconciliation in front of an audience of eight million. On cue, the doors slid back and I stepped on to the ramp. Gary – hair magnificently gelled and standing provocatively erect – was gobsmacked. This was one blast from the past he was not expecting. His pleasure at seeing me was palpable and like a pair of fairies we fell into one another's arms. The producers loved it. Michael Aspel who, for all his sleek professionalism, looked bored to tears, fed me my scripted question and I told the story of Gary's arrival at the Castle: how he'd been a nouvelle cuisine artist who liked to write his menus in French and how I'd had to persuade him to start cooking honest-to-goodness English food. Gary then took up the story, telling the audience about his four-hour interview with me in a London hotel and how he'd nearly died when I'd explained that I wanted traditional dishes like Lancashire hotpot.

The demons were exorcized. We had made peace at last. I took my place on the banquette, sat back and enjoyed the rest of the show.

Part of the Rhodes persona is his passion for fast cars and later in the programme Aspel asked him what he owned: 'Two Porsches, a Mercedes and a Lotus Elan,' confessed Gary. 'But I've only got one garage!' His reply made me smile. At the Castle, he owned a second-hand Audi Coupé. When he fell into debt, we helped him clear his credit-card arrears by buying it for £5,000, and he continued to run it as a company-owned car. When he came to leave, Gary was deeply reluctant to hand back his beloved coupé, a car he wouldn't look twice at now.

Such are the fruits of fame. But watching Gary Rhodes in close-up on that set, I was struck by his easy rapport with the audience. There is no question about it. He has that elusive thing called *star quality* – bags of it.

Caviar in a Crisis

Thursday, 26 September 1996

A WEEK CONSUMED by family crisis. My father has had a stroke – his second in two years – and it is bad. 'A major set-back,' said the consultant. His speech is now so seriously impaired it is barely intelligible and he has lost the ability to swallow. His life-line is an intravenous drip.

The news arrived on Monday by answerphone – a message left by my mother which Louise picked up at six when she got home. He had been taken to the Nuffield in Taunton by ambulance. An hour and a half later I arrived at his bedside to find him frail, forlorn and frightened, his mouth gaping, eyes staring. I kissed his forehead and held his hand. My mother – stooping slightly but elegant as ever, even in a pair of jeans – wandered in a daze outside in the corridor. The consultant, David MacIver, was there and he took me into an office. We talked. He was kind but honest: we should not expect too much; my father would need special care; the quality of his life would be seriously affected; he had advised my mother to 'prepare herself'. I told MacIver that my father's quality of life was already pretty grim. In May, he had nearly died of pneumonia in Greece – only days before their golden wedding anniversary. Louise and I had planned to join the celebration; instead our holiday flights had turned into a rescue mission.

My parents as newlyweds, 1946

My father is eighty-one. My mother, who is Greek, will be seventy in October. They met at the end of the war, he a dashing Indian Army officer, she a carefree nineteen-year-old, the second daughter of a well-to-do Macedonian family living in Thessalonika. The story of their love affair is pure *Gone with the Wind*, part of the enduring mythology being that my father was parachuted into northern Greece to liberate the country from the Germans and fell into my mother's arms. The point is that theirs is an old-fashioned romance that hasn't waned. Peter is never Peter but 'my Peter'. He is her great protector and pillar. She is his little Etty: beautiful, vivacious and, even now, at the age of seventy, a woman with the energy and outlook of a twenty-year-old. My problem is that she believes he is immortal, their lives and destinies indissoluble.

After the war and back in England, my uncle Michael, who ran the Imperial Hotel in Torquay, gave his younger brother a job. Then, in 1950, my father took on the

Castle as manager. I was three. Twenty-six years later, we bought the business and Louise, our two boys, Dom and Nick, and I moved down from London. But my father – a man with an unshakeable sense of duty – never retired in the accepted meaning of that word, although eighteen months ago my parents moved out of their penthouse apartment in the hotel to live on the Blackdown Hills, south of Taunton. Even so, he kept his office and he continued to come to work each day, including a couple of hours on Sunday mornings.

This Monday he arrived at about eleven, a little later than usual. He shuffled into my office next door to his to give me some papers. He looked pale, but then, I thought, he has his good days and bad days. I asked him how he was. 'Not so bad,' he replied. But there was a strange expression in his face and I sensed something was not quite right. The telephone rang and the business of the day nudged my unease to the back of the mind. Nine hours later, I was by his hospital bed.

We didn't stay long. It was already dark and my mother was anxious to get home. My father struggled to speak to me, his face twisted with worry, his words little more than a blur. 'Look after Mummy,' he stuttered. His frantic, garbled message

My parents at home, late 1980s

was clear: she was frightened, she hated being alone in the house at night. I squeezed his hand and promised to look after her.

As I drove her back to Avon Lodge, their pretty hillside villa overlooking the Vale of Taunton Deane, she wept like a child. When we got in, I opened a bottle of Chablis and gave her a glass. She began to relax and think of supper. Taking a small jar out of the fridge, she suddenly said: 'Have some caviar!' So we sat in the kitchen and ate caviar on Ritz biscuits. For supper, she warmed up a Greek *fassoulada* she had prepared the previous day – a simple, nourishing stew of beans, tomatoes and onions. At ten we watched the news and I began to agonize about what to do. Should I stay with her for the night or leave? I decided to go home. My father, I am sure, would have wanted me to stay but, deep down, I felt this would be a mistake. I locked up, hugged her and left feeling guilty as hell. Later that night the *fassoulada* took its revenge: I woke up at three with violent flatulence.

In the morning, the telephone rang shortly after eight. It was my dear mother, wailing in the best tradition of Greek tragedy, a Euripidean chorus in full flood: 'It's unbearable! It's unbearable!' she cried. 'He's such a good man. He's a saint. It's not fair! It's not fair!' I tried to comfort her, but I was no help. I passed the receiver to Louise and left for work.

By Wednesday, there was little change in my father's condition. When I visited him at midday I found him sitting in his chair shaving, a small mirror and a plastic bowl on the table before him, his intravenous drip standing sentry at his side. For a few moments I stood and watched unseen by the door. He scraped in precise, determined strokes, concentrating on his left cheek, feeling the flesh for any rogue bristles which may have escaped his razor. When I went into the room, he looked up and smiled broadly. I sat on the edge of his bed and, as we talked, I listened intently, repeating his mangled speech to be sure that I had understood. He complained about the nurses – always a good sign – because they hadn't washed him on time. And when an auxiliary came in to remove the shaving bowl, he said, suddenly finding his voice and jabbing a finger in my direction: 'He's the only one who understands me!'

In the evening, my mother came round to us for supper. As caviar is not a staple in our household, she had to make do with Louise's excellent shepherd's pie. To my relief, Etty was on good form, adapting well to the nights alone on her hill. She was convinced he was getting better. At eight, David MacIver telephoned and I took the call next door. 'There's been a little progress,' he said, 'but there's no real change. I'm sorry. He's going to get very depressed and frustrated.' I returned to the kitchen and said nothing. Later, when my mother got home, she called to thank us for supper and say all was well.

Today I arrived at the hospital at lunchtime. My father was lying motionless on his bed, propped up by half-a-dozen pillows, drifting in and out of a sleepless dream. The effort of speech is so great that, for much of my time with him, I sit in silence just holding his hand. By his bedside, the exercise papers of the speech therapist lay untouched: 'Protrude the tongue and turn the tip upwards to the nose. Hold for two seconds and relax. Repeat slowly ten times.' 'Say la-la-la-la-la. Repeat slowly ten times.' 'Say ka-ka-ka-ka-ka. Repeat slowly ten times.' My father opened his watery eyes and smiled. His lips puckered. 'Good to see you,' he stammered. 'It's such a comfort.'

Some moments later, my mother breezed into the room wearing a smart brown trouser suit and a perky Laura Ashley flat cap. In her arms she clutched a large orange folder stuffed with correspondence, my father's diary, various papers and the hotel wine list. She decided it was time her Peter had something to do and – I discovered – earlier she had gone to Andrew Grahame for the latest business statistics. 'My husband has asked for the figures!' she announced. 'He must be kept up to date!' Andrew had been a little nonplussed by this request, wondering *what* figures exactly Mr Chapman was so anxious to see. He printed off the current occupancy report and handed it to Mrs Chapman in the hope that this would do.

I took my mother gently by the arm and we went into the corridor.

'Look,' I said, 'I really don't think he needs all this now.' She cut me short.

'It's good to keep him occupied and it's something for us to talk about,' she protested, then promptly changed the subject to tell me about some Greek ship-owning friends whom she had invited to dine with her at the Castle this evening. Ah, the wine list! I thought. She wants her Peter to choose some suitable bottles for her party. I held my peace.

Having just arrived, my mother now decided to leave. 'The car park was full,' she said, 'so I double-parked. I'll go, do some shopping and come back later.' She marched off down the corridor in the opposite direction of the hospital entrance.

I tried to call after her, but she didn't hear. At the end of the wing, she stopped, thought and turned on her heel. As she passed me, she shook her head and muttered in Greek, 'I'm going crazy!'

When I returned to my father's room, the nurses had got him out of bed and into his chair. A bowl of soup stood on the table and the auxiliary sat beside him. I sniffed. 'Asparagus,' I said. 'Smells OK!'

'Is that what it is,' said the nurse. 'Do you like asparagus soup, Mr Chapman? It smells ever so good!'

My father – a white towel draped loosely round his neck – stared vacantly at the bowl. 'Do you want me to help you?' asked Carol, waving a teaspoon. He shook his head firmly and picked up the soupspoon. I sat silently and watched, my stomach burning. My father heaved his body awkwardly towards the bowl, struggling to raise the spoon. He heaved again, determined to lift the spoon to his lips. The pale liquid spilled on to the towel. Again he tried – again, and again. Carol and I sat fixed to our chairs. As a child, one of my father's favourite parables was the story of Robert the Bruce. 'If at first you don't succeed, try, try and try again' are words that still ring in my ears. But he failed – there was no strength in his right arm. He put the spoon down for a moment, then picked it up with his left hand. Dipping his head over the bowl and opening his mouth wide, he raised the spoon up and sucked the soup over his lower lip. Down he went again, scooping the liquid up, working rhythmically like a pendulum out of control. Most of the soup ran down his chin into the towel. But he'd won. He was going to live.

A Spider in the House

Monday, 30 September 1996

MY APPEARANCE on *This Is Your Life* was not a pretty sight. The programme went out on the nation's television screens last Friday evening and I was horrified by the shape that emerged down the ramp to greet Gary Rhodes. I looked like a fat scoop of clotted cream. Louise was right: the baggy linen suit turned me into a rumpled, crumpled, anaemic blob. I should have worn dark blue.

On Saturday morning, I was met by a barrage of sniper-fire from my usually loyal management team, who had set their videos specially to record the boss's forty seconds of fame. Comments ranged from a thinly veiled sneer from Simon Girling to a neat jab below the belt from Vickery. 'My girlfriend thought you'd put on a little weight,' said Girling, grinning from ear to ear. 'I have to say that you looked rather rotund!' observed Phil.

Having run the gauntlet of my adoring fans, I arrived in my office to find a thick package on my desk. The parcel contained the 1997 edition of *The Good Food Guide*, and, on cue, this long-awaited moment induced its annual spasm of paranoia. Instantly blood rushes to the head as one expects to see one's precious baby pilloried, panned and demoted. Every word, every phrase, the nuance of every sentence is pored over and analysed. In the event, and to my great relief, we did quite well. Our grading remains at 4 (out of a maximum of 5), thus preserving our sacred position among the top thirty restaurants in Britain outside London. The write-up was pretty up-beat too, except for a couple of lines which had Vickery descend into one of his periodic bouts of artistic self-doubt. The second paragraph suggested that ours was 'classic, safe cooking' that lacked the 'adventure of British provincial cooking.'

'Look, Phil,' I said without bothering to disguise my own irritation. 'That comment is total bullshit and you know it. Number one, if British provincial cooking is alive in any real sense, which is debatable, it was never meant to be adventurous. Number two, the whole point about your cooking is that you've turned the British repertoire on its head and made it exciting.'

'Yes, but do you think our food is getting boring?' he moaned. 'Here it says our repertoire hasn't evolved significantly.'

'Who eats here more often than any other punter, Chef? I do! *Le patron mange ici*! And if *le patron* was getting bored you'd soon know about it.'

'But I'm not sure we are developing new dishes fast enough,' he persisted.

'It's fast enough for me. The *GFG*'s got it wrong. You have to keep your classics like the braised shoulder of lamb and the seared salmon because if you drop them our regulars will start complaining. These are great dishes. You *can't* ditch them. At the same time, look at the new ones that have hit the menu in the past year: the deep-fried skate wing, the smoked eel, the spiced lamb pudding and the pigs' cheeks. Terrific dishes.'

He left feeling a little happier. In the past week, both Phil and I have been the subject of a major feature in the *Independent on Sunday*, a piece in which Michael Bateman, the food writer, described us as the 'Gilbert and Sullivan of the restaurant world.' This was very flattering, but the article also contained one scurrilous paragraph that made me hopping mad and upset Phil so much he leapt on his Suzuki Bandit and raced across Somerset to our home on the Quantocks to make his peace. This is what Bateman wrote:

> Think of Vickery as your street-wise W S Gilbert, and Chapman as your lofty Arthur Sullivan, and you get the picture. Phil Vickery is only too aware of his proprietor's Arthurian aspirations. 'But I have a free hand to grow, cook and serve what I want. When Kit beats the drum for Britain we fall out. But he's brilliant at bouncing ideas around. I respect what he says. Most of the time. But sometimes I say, get stuffed.' That's no way to speak to, er, a fellow director?

This was beyond the pale and I shot off a letter.

24 September 1996

Dear Michael,

Your piece about the Castle in the *Sunday Independent* was, in many respects, very fine indeed and, of course, I am grateful to you for the interest you have shown in the work we do here.

However, I must tell you that both Phil and I were deeply distressed by some of the alleged comments which were published and which, in effect, gave a very distorted impression of our relationship.

For the record:

1. Phil and I have never fallen out on the subject of the development of a British repertoire or our culinary philosophy.

2. Phil has never ever told me to 'get stuffed'.

I believe my partnership and friendship with Phil is unique in this trade. Indeed, as you know, he is the first head chef ever to be made a director of the family company and he is now a shareholder. It is very unfortunate that, in an otherwise excellent piece, these few comments should have sent out signals which could be misconstrued.

Yours sincerely,

C H G Chapman
Managing Director

To Michael Bateman's credit, he replied immediately with a conciliatory postcard.

Dear Kit,

The reason why I always read back pieces (as I did to Phil Vickery, and as you know I tried to get you on the phone several times but we kept missing each other) is because I have no wish to misconstrue or distort or make errors of fact. The piece you read is the piece I read over to Phil before publication. Did he say 'Get stuffed'? I think so. But everything he said was in perfect good humour, and his respect for you was apparent in every way – 'brilliant', I think was one word he used to describe you. I don't argue that you have a unique partnership. The piece was surely recognisably tongue-in-cheek and a tribute to both your very great efforts!

With all my best wishes.

Michael

On Saturday evening, Louise and I drove in to the hotel for dinner. The atmosphere in the restaurant was lively, the tables humming with good humour, Simon Girling reporting all well. After a drink in the Rose Room, we wandered through to eat, greeting friends and regulars on our way to our table. David and Mai Morgan, with their two grown-up children, were seated at a round table in the centre of the room celebrating Mai's birthday.

'We've booked for your big night in a couple of weeks,' said David, a retired chartered surveyor.

'Oh, you're coming to the gastronomic,' I replied. 'Should be great fun. Chef and I were planning the menu this morning.'

'We're really looking forward to Sir Bernard Ingham,' said Mai. 'He's so good when he does the papers on the breakfast news. Can't wait to see him in the flesh.'

'I don't think you'll be disappointed,' I said. 'I've heard him speak before. His Mrs Thatcher handbag stories are hilarious.'

Later in the evening, I called Girling over and asked him to organize four glasses of champagne for the Morgans, with our compliments. We returned to the Rose Room for coffee and Mike, the barman, poured me a glass of port. Five minutes later, he reappeared.

'The O'Briens asked me to pass on their thanks for the champagne,' he said.

'The O'Briens? Who are the O'Briens?'

'The O'Briens. On table seven.'

'You mean the Morgans on table ten.'

'No, the O'Briens on table seven.'

'How many O'Briens?'

'Four.'

'Mike, I've never heard of the O'Briens. The champagne is for the Morgans. And they're on table ten.'

'Well, I couldn't see Mr Girling in the restaurant, so I assumed the champagne was for table seven.'

'Mike, you assumed wrong. Now pour out four more glasses and take them to table *ten*. Then find Mr Girling and ask him to come and see me.'

As Mike disappeared behind the bar, a group of people strolled into the room. A man came up to our corner table.

'Thanks for the champagne,' he said. 'Much appreciated.'

'It's a great pleasure, Mr O'Brien,' I replied. 'Hope we'll see you again soon.'

Eventually, Simon Girling appeared. He looked harassed. Alison, the head receptionist, had called him urgently after an American couple in a garden suite had complained about a spider in their bedroom.

'You're not serious?' said Simon in disbelief.

'Yes I am,' said Alison. 'They want you to go and remove it.'

Girling ran up the stairs to the first floor and along the corridor to the suite. He tapped on the door. A moment later, a man in pyjamas let him in.

'So you're the spider catcher,' said the American. 'Come on in. It's over there.'

The man pointed to a corner of the ceiling. Suddenly, an unseen voice screeched from the bathroom: 'Make sure you get it! Don't miss it! It's huge!…Has it gone?'

'I'm just getting it now, madam,' called Simon calmly.

Girling stepped on a chair while the pyjamas pointed frantically at the ceiling. The woman poked her head out of the bathroom door.

'Get it first time!' she screamed. 'Don't drop it and take it as far away as possible!'

'Please don't worry, madam,' said Girling quietly. 'I'll get it.'

'Have you got it?'

'Yes, I've got it.'

'Is it in your hands?'

'Yes, madam, yes. It's safe in my hands.'

'Well, get out then and take it with you.'

SATURDAY, 5 OCTOBER 1996

My mother celebrates her seventieth birthday today. Although this is hardly the moment for a party, she has much to celebrate. My father has made an extraordinary recovery – hailed by his saintly nurses as a 'miracle' – and he comes out of hospital tomorrow. In the meantime, I have been shopping for all those essentials which will now be necessary to support his care. Yesterday I called on the Red Cross in Taunton, who supplied me with a Zimmer frame. I loaded the gear into my car and returned to the Castle where Andrew, Paul Aplin, our auditor, and I were half-way through interviewing ten candidates for the post of hotel accountant.

If I learned anything yesterday, it is that shopping for Zimmer frames is a hell of a lot more exciting than interviewing accountants. At the start of the day, I decided that my ideal candidate must have the qualities of a determined ferret in addition to the obvious attributes of technical competence, honesty and reliability. As the sessions progressed, I awarded a ferret-factor to each candidate on a scale of alpha to epsilon. But as most of them were sending us to sleep, we also thought it might be worth probing for evidence of a sense of humour. This was not an easy task. One balding Spock look-alike in gold-rimmed spectacles was particularly anxious to know about the 'quality of the office environment.'

'Well, the office isn't air-conditioned, if that's what you mean,' I replied,

'But I think the window opens,' added Andrew.

The eyes behind the spectacles blinked vacantly. I awarded another epsilon and we moved on to the next candidate.

By four in the afternoon, we were almost comatose when the tenth candidate took her seat in front of us. She smiled. No wimpy-wet smile, this, but a big Colgate ring-of-confidence grin. We stirred in our chairs. Mrs Brown looked vaguely human. She started talking. For the past six years she had minded the books for a firm of solicitors in Ilminster. As she spoke enthusiastically about the responsibilities of her job, she smiled again. A bookkeeper with charm? How unusual, we thought.

'If we were to offer you the position,' I said, 'what sort of salary would you expect?'

'Well, at the moment I'm on twelve and a half thousand,' she replied.

This seemed fair enough to us. The rate we had set was thirteen to fourteen thousand.

'Fine, but what would you expect here?'

'I think I'd need a little more because it would mean a longer drive to work,' she hedged.

'OK, but what do you have in mind?'

'Eighteen thousand?' she asked, breaking into an enormous grin.

'Nice try,' I replied. 'But no chance!'

'Well, you did ask,' countered Mrs Brown. 'And if you don't ask, you don't get!' She bit her lip and blushed.

We shook hands and Andrew showed her out. When he returned, he said: 'She thinks she blew it and hasn't got a hope!'

We sat down to discuss the day and draw up a short list. It took us thirty seconds to agree two possible names – and Mrs Brown's is at the top by a long chalk.

In spite of the tedium of yesterday's interviews, it has been an unusually good week, boosted by a flurry of successes for the hotel, which always helps to lift morale. Following the publication of *The Good Food Guide*, the AA pushed out a press release to announce its restaurant awards for the year and we were all pretty chuffed to see the Castle listed in the top twenty in the country. Then one of our waiters, Christophe Lakehal, a bright young Frenchman, won a place in the final of the 'Young Waiter of the Year' competition. This is a fiercely contested annual event which carries a lot of prestige in the trade and attracts thousands of hopeful entrants. To get to the semi-finals is an achievement in itself and only eight waiters go through to the last round, which takes place in a month's time at the Berkeley Hotel in London. The semis were held on Wednesday at Ealing College, where the contestants were put through a series of rigorous tests designed as much to measure their skills and style as to catch them out with a few nasty little traps laid by the judges. Christophe was the only waiter to spot the deliberate mistake on a table of four where some clever-dick had dropped a breadcrumb in a glass of wine. Our boy was on the case. He removed the glass and replaced it with a fresh one.

But Christophe, flushed by his success, did me no favours last night. For most of the week, the hotel has been hosting a shooting party, a group of wealthy Americans led by a lady the size of a Centurion tank called 'Bill'. Bill was a real pain, driving the staff up the wall with her tiresome and trivial demands instead of allowing them to get on with the job. Before each dinner, she'd call a meeting to drill Simon Girling on the form, even though he knew perfectly well what was expected of him. On one evening, she called him up to her room and ordered him to sit on the bed while she finished a long telephone call to the States. Her room was a tip – papers, clothes and shoes strewn everywhere – and poor old Simon didn't know where to put himself. Twenty minutes later she came off the telephone and he nodded politely as she issued her instructions.

Last night – the shoot's final evening – dinner was served in the Penthouse Suite and Christophe was in charge. Louise and I were downstairs entertaining business friends in the restaurant. At eleven we moved through to the Rose Room for coffee. No sooner had we sat down when Christophe came in to announce that Bill had asked to be introduced to us.

'Where is she now?' I asked warily.

'Just outside,' he said.

I groaned.

'Fine,' I said. 'Do ask her to come in.'

In rolled the Tank, trailing voluminous folds of black silk. We stood up, shook hands and I introduced our friends. Christophe disappeared.

Bill pulled up a chair, sat down and would not be moved. It did not occur to her that Louise and I may have been entertaining important clients of our own. I switched off. And I have no recollection of the conversation. In fact there was no conversation, just an endless nauseating gush punctuated by Louise saying 'thank you!' or 'how fascinating!' or 'really!', the gist of the monologue being that Bill was pretty ecstatic with her stay and hoped to return next year.

Midnight came and went. Each time I opened an eye, Bill was still there. As I was about to nod off again, she threw me a look with her mole eyes. 'You don't talk much,' she said. Before I had time to answer, our guests stood up and announced they were going to bed. Bill got the message and waddled off to make another call to the States.

TALES OF THE IRON LADY AND
A SCARLET WOMAN

SUNDAY, 13 OCTOBER 1996

T HE DINING CLUB'S gastronomic evening on Friday was, I think, a success – just. We hold these dinners twice a year and they are one of the great highlights in our calendar. Each one follows a set format: a champagne reception, a five-course banquet with a different wine to match each dish and a guest speaker who is persuaded to forgo a fee in return for a weekend on the house. The arrangement works well and in the past the billing has included the likes of Ned Sherrin, Derek Nimmo, Maureen Lipman, Auberon Waugh, Clement Freud, John Wells, Sheridan Morley and Julian Critchley. The dinners sell out and about seventy revellers pay £62 all-in for an evening of serious feasting and jolly entertainment.

Sir Bernard Ingham, our guest on this occasion, could not spare a weekend off and came alone leaving his wife, Nancy, at home in Purley. He seems to be as busy as he was during his years at Number 10 with Mrs Thatcher. This, he told me, was his eighty-sixth speaking engagement this year and on Saturday morning he caught the 7.12 to Paddington because he was booked to dub his film on the Jarrow Marches in Soho at 9.30. So, for the first time, I agreed to pay a fee – the princely sum of £100 plus his return rail fare. I couldn't believe my luck.

The preparation for these dinners is intense, the planning minutely detailed. Phil and I agonize over a menu and, where necessary, dishes are tested and re-tested until we are satisfied. The menu is then discussed with one of my wine merchants and, eventually, a line-up of suitable wines is matched to the dishes. For Friday's dinner, I invited David Sommerfelt of Christopher Piper to present the wines and he produced some real gems.

That morning, I called a final briefing session in my office with the team: Phil and Andrew, Andrew's deputy Simon 'Tuck' Tucker-Brown, Simon Girling, and the assistant manager Alison Lock. Our agenda was a three-page memorandum I had issued earlier in the week and for the next hour we rehearsed every detail of the event: the precise timings of the service, the lay-up of the dining room, the table plan. Sir Bernard's train was due to arrive at Taunton station at 17.24. I would meet him, drive him to the hotel and hand him over to Tuck, who would escort him to

Gastronomic evening with guest of honour Sir Bernard Ingham

his suite. Bowls of fresh fruit were to be placed in Sir Bernard's room, David and Jean Sommerfelt's room and Bob and Moira Shapland's room. Bob Shapland is our new bank manager, this was his first visit to the Castle and, yes, I needed to impress him. I wrote three personal notes of welcome, sealed them in envelopes and instructed Girling to place the cards with the fruit in each VIP's suite. Andrew gallantly volunteered to organize breakfast for Bernard Ingham at 6.15 on Saturday morning and drive him to the station.

THE CASTLE DINING CLUB
GUEST OF HONOUR: SIR BERNARD INGHAM

Friday, 11 October, 1996

WINES
Presented by Mr David Sommerfelt
Christopher Piper Wines

Apéritif:
Domaine de l'Aigle Brut, N.V.
Méthode Traditionelle

Solear Manzanilla Pasada
Antonio Barbadillo

Chardonnay 1993
Beringer Vineyards

Pinot Noir 1993
Elk Cove Vineyards

St. Henri Shiraz 1990
Penfolds Wines

Muscat de Mireval,
Domaine du Moulinas

MENU

Stew of Wild Mushrooms
with Truffle Oil and Wild Rice

Smoked River Test Eel
with Horseradish Crème Fraîche
and Rocket Leaves

Roast Mallard with Beetroots,
Spring Onion Potato Cake,
Carrots and Braised Tomatoes

Lord of the Hundreds

Tilleys

Finn

Sautéed Apricots with Pistachios,
Vanilla Syrup and Mascarpone

We then turned to the menu and the wine service. The drinks party was scheduled for seven o'clock in the Monmouth Room. Dinner would be announced promptly at 7.30 by Simon Girling and as our guests moved to the dining room, a photographer would take pictures of Sir Bernard and the top table. Once everyone was seated, I would get up to introduce the menu, followed by David Sommerfelt who would speak briefly about the wines. Chef should be ready to roll with the first course by no later than 7.55 and the service paced from then on to have coffee on the tables by 10.30. The kitchen brigade, led by Phil and dressed in clean whites, would then parade smartly into the room for the traditional toast – *santé du chef* – which would be given by David. The moment the chefs had marched out, I would get up to introduce Bernard Ingham.

During this long meeting, one small detail inspired a fierce debate. Each cover (restaurant-speak for a table setting) would be laid with six glasses: five for the wines, one for water. With this quantity of glassware in front of each guest, there is always a risk of a cock-up with waiters moving round tables at speed and pouring the wrong wine into the wrong glass. Besides, this set-up can get pretty confusing for the punter. To avoid mistakes, we colour-code the bases of some glasses with sticky dots, matching the wines listed on the menu with an appropriately coloured dot. Simon Girling – who only joined us in April and who had not supervised a gastronomic before – is a bit of a purist. The idea of these coloured dots offended his higher professional instincts. In the end, we agreed a compromise. As we were serving a sherry with the wild mushrooms, followed by a Chardonnay with the smoked eel, the only wines that really needed distinguishing were the two reds, so we settled for red dots against the Shiraz.

There was another problem. By 11 am, the cheeses Phil had ordered from Neal's Yard Dairy in London had not arrived, although we were told they were on the way. This just put an irritating delay on the printing of the menus, on which the three cheeses had to be listed in the order of their eating, from the mildest to the strongest. No decision could be made until Phil and I had tasted them.

The meeting broke and I went down to the dining room to check progress on the laying-up and the positioning of the tables. The restaurant had been stripped and replaced by large five and six foot rounds to seat groups of eight or ten guests. Louise was busy arranging the flowers and, in the servery, a couple of juniors were polishing silver.

Just after 11.30, the kitchen called to say the cheeses had been delivered. I met Chef in the pastry room where the three varieties were laid out for our inspection. They were magnificent and in prime condition. Over the past fifteen years, we have seen an amazing revival in British cheesemaking. Where once there were less than a dozen worth eating, now there are hundreds. We gave up serving French cheeses at the Castle a long time ago. Phil began to cut slivers for tasting – each cheese produced on a single farm from its own unpasteurized milk – and we made our decision. Small wedges would be plated and presented from left to right, beginning with Lord of the Hundreds, a hard, ewes' milk cheese from Sussex, not unlike a good Pecorino. Next, the Tilleys, a goats' cheese made by Mary Holbrook on her farm in the Mendip Hills. And lastly, the Finn, a soft, unctuous, triple-cream cows' milk cheese from Hereford.

After a final check in the dining room, I drove home, buying a couple of rolls from the village bakery on the way and settling down to eat them in front of the one o'clock news. The Tory party conference in Bournemouth had just ended and a self-satisfied Brian Mawhinney, the party chairman, hailed the Tories' new start on the road to victory at the General Election. After the weather forecast, I took Caruso and Bollinger, our two golden retrievers, for a brisk hike across the fields and returned to my study to think about a suitable introduction to Sir Bernard Ingham. I had plenty of material, having spent the last few days reading his book *Kill the Messenger* and Robert Harris's biography *Good and Faithful Servant*. I came away gasping with admiration for the man. Two things, in particular, struck me: his fearless determination, his guts and his capacity for hard graft; and secondly, his deep love for Yorkshire and his home town, Hebden Bridge. There was also a third quality, the binding agent that seemed to lie at the very heart of his beliefs and outlook on life: an old-fashioned but instinctive conviction in the importance of loyalty – to friends, family, employer and roots. It was easy to see why he and Margaret Thatcher were such a natural match.

None of these reflections, of course, was suitable for after-dinner. Instead, I decided to give a light-hearted account of his youth in Hebden Bridge, pointing out that his home town lay uncomfortably close to the Lancashire border. And of his eleven years' service as Mrs Thatcher's press secretary, I suggested that she had summed up his unique survival when she declared: 'The thing about you and me, Bernard, is that neither of us are *smooth* people!'

At 4.30 I returned to the hotel to inspect the dining room with Simon Girling. It was gleaming and immaculate. The silver on the tables sparkled and Louise's flower arrangements were bright, fresh and beautiful. A final total of four hundred and twenty six glasses had been polished individually and now stood in platoons of six at every place setting. One long-stemmed goblet in each group bore a red dot at its base mirroring an identical spot against the Australian Shiraz on the silk-tasselled menu cards. We were ready to roll.

Before shooting off to the station, I saw Simon Tucker-Brown, who had already changed into his dinner jacket. 'I'm off to meet Sir Bernard,' I said. 'Keep an eye on the car park and have the key in your pocket so that you can take him straight up to his room.'

'I'll be waiting at the front door,' said Tuck, hair still damp, his cheeks bright as strawberries after a very hot bath.

The 15.35 out of Paddington came to a halt on platform one at exactly 17.24. I stood by the exit gazing down towards the first class carriages at the rear of the train. He was one of the last to get off and I spotted him immediately, scowling, his eyebrows like an overgrown hedgerow, the very image of his media persona. I strode down the platform to meet him. When I introduced myself, his face broke into a smile. Television and newspaper pictures never portray Bernard Ingham wearing a smile. The scowl is what had stuck in my mind. The smile was something new and it was a very warm, kind smile. He was wearing a Barbour over a blazer and grey flannel trousers, and as we walked out to the car, we chatted politely to one another, like the strangers that we were, unsure of what to say.

As soon as we had settled into the rush-hour traffic, we began to relax a little.

'Have you been to Taunton before?' I asked.

'No,' he replied. 'This is the first time. I think my agent thought it was about time I showed a face in this part of England.' He chuckled.

'Well, I've never been to Hebden Bridge,' I said rather stupidly.

'There are several Chapmans in Hebden Bridge,' he said. 'Did you know that?'

This surprising observation rather threw me and I launched into a potted history of my own family, making it pretty clear that I thought it unlikely I had any connections with the Chapmans of Hebden Bridge.

We struggled through the chaos of diggers and barricades in the town centre.

'What's going on here?' he asked.

'This,' I said, 'is what our local authority likes to call the town centre enhancement scheme. Actually, once they've finished, I think it'll probably be very nice.'

'How long have they been at it?'

'Ten months now.'

'Ten months!' he exclaimed. 'What a bloody nightmare. It's absolutely ridiculous.'

'Yes, I agree. But they're nearly done, so the council is now plastering notices all over town saying *Thank you for your patience. Only three weeks to go!*'

He laughed. Suddenly, his mobile telephone started warbling in his Barbour pocket. It was his wife calling to say that he had received an important message.

'We're driving through Taunton,' he told her. 'They're re-doing the town centre and we're just passing the Old Ale House!'

We turned into Castle Green and as we approached the hotel, he marvelled at the massive expanse of wisteria cloaking the façade.

'When does it come into bloom?' he asked.

'It's at its best in the first week of June,' I said proudly. 'You should come back next year with your wife. It really is a fantastic sight – worth the journey just to see it.'

On cue, Tuck came bouncing out to the car park. I introduced him to Sir Bernard and they disappeared inside while I turned the car and headed home to change. An hour later, Louise and I were back, primed and ready for the show to begin. Before we could swing through the revolving door, Tuck stopped us in the porch. He looked worried.

'Mr Chapman,' he said ominously, 'I'm afraid I have a confession to make.'

'What's happened?' I barked.

'Sir Bernard's in the wrong room. I just wasn't thinking. I grabbed the key to 120, Mr and Mrs Shapland's room.'

'You have to be joking! So where the hell is our dear bank manager?'

'They're in 71. Sir Bernard's suite. But don't worry, I removed Sir Bernard's envelope before they arrived. They've got the fruit but no welcome card.'

I hit the roof.

'Tuck! What the hell's the point of holding a briefing meeting if you're going to screw up on the simplest instructions? What have you done with Sir Bernard's envelope?'

'Nothing. I didn't want to disturb him.'

'But he's now sitting there with a bowl of fruit and a card addressed to the Shaplands?'

'Yes.'

'Well get upstairs, apologize for the cock-up and give him his envelope!'

Tuck went off, tail between his legs. This was a rare blunder for him. During Andrew's long illness he stepped into the breach magnificently and I had come to rely on him totally. But for the moment I was seething with fury. At the desk in the hall, Nicola, the duty receptionist, clearly decided that the boss was in need of a little motherly comfort. 'You're looking very nice this evening, Mr Chapman,' she said, smiling sweetly. It didn't help.

'Thank you, Nicola!' I replied curtly.

My next port of call was the dining room to check the PA system. Simon Girling was there casting a final look at the table plan.

'How do you switch this thing on?' I asked.

'I'm not really sure,' he said, fiddling with the knobs.

'Well, who knows how to work it?'

'Tuck and Andrew put it in, I think,' he said, sensing my agitation.

'Look, Simon, sort it out and when you have, let me know and I'll come back.'

By now, our guests were beginning to gather in the Monmouth Room and Louise was at the door welcoming them. I sprayed on an instant smile and walked in full of mine-hostly bonhomie. The curtain was up and we were on stage, my performance improving dramatically after a glass of David Sommerfelt's excellent fizz. After a while Girling called me and I returned to the restaurant to test the levels on the PA system. Moments later I was back with the party, introducing Bernard Ingham to our regulars as waiters topped up glasses and wove their way through the throng with trays of delicious canapés.

By 7.45 we were all seated and I got up to introduce the menu. Having read Bernard Ingham's memoirs, I could not resist quoting a passage about his eating habits as a child. For him, 'gastronomic perfection' was a Calder Valley delicacy called dock pudding, an extraordinary confection of sweet dock leaves, nettles, onions and oatmeal, fried and served with bacon. When he was a lad, the housewives of Hebden Bridge paid him sixpence for every carrier bag of dock leaves he harvested in the hills around the town.

Dinner proceeded. Vickery on top form. At our table we were eight: my mother, Andrew and Cécile Grahame, David and Jean Sommerfelt, Sir Bernard, Louise and me. We talked politics, the evils of the EU, Mrs Thatcher, John Major, the Party Conference and the Tories' prospects at the General Election: 'I'm glad she took my advice and went to Bournemouth,' said BI of his former employer. He was adamant that the Conservatives now had a good chance of winning the election.

After we had been served our pudding, I went down to the kitchen to congratulate Phil. A production line of chefs was still assembling the last table's plates of apricots, with Vickery at the end of the line inspecting each dish, carefully ladling on the vanilla syrup. As I watched the plates move down the hotplate, I suddenly became conscious of another onlooker, a young lady in black tights and a short red dress. I had no idea who she was although I vaguely remembered seeing her at the drinks before dinner. I thought little of it. My mind was on the speeches and, besides, Chef has his kitchen groupies whom he occasionally allows below stairs to watch the action.

I returned to our table to find Sir Bernard flicking through his notes. Coffee was served and I called Girling over to ask him if we were ready to go with the *santé du chef*.

'There you are, Mr Chapman,' he said. 'Exactly 10.30.'

I looked at my watch. 'Well done,' I replied.

Meanwhile, in the kitchen, Phil was cornered by the lady-in-red. Exhausted, he had slipped into the still-room and was sitting on the edge of a stainless steel table to catch his breath before leading his brigade into the restaurant for the toast. The lady-in-red followed him into the small room.

'Hi!' she said. 'I'm Toni with an I.'

She had seen Phil on *Ready Steady Cook* and her friends, Vicky and Helen, had spotted him near his house in Wellington. They thought he was delicious.

Toni put her hands on his thighs and nuzzled her body between his open legs.

'I want to fuck you,' she said.

'Well, I'm a bit busy at the moment,' he replied.

This intimate exchange was then interrupted by Toni's husband who burst into the still-room.

'Where the fucking hell have you been?' he shouted. 'I've been looking all over for you.'

'I've been trying to set Phil up with Vicky,' said Toni coyly.

They disappeared up the kitchen stairs and returned to their seats in the dining room.

Moments later, the chefs paraded to loud applause and, raising his glass to Phil and his team, David Sommerfelt proclaimed: 'If British food continues to improve, we won't need a tunnel!' The room cheered. The chefs marched off. And I stood up to introduce Bernard Ingham.

It was a brilliantly witty performance from a veteran of the after-dinner circuit. In his gravelled Yorkshire voice, the tales of life with Mrs T and Denis, the political anecdotes and the gags against himself poured out in a leisurely stream.

Mrs Thatcher, he said, was the most tactless woman he knew. At a dinner with her Cabinet, she was once served steak. 'And what about the vegetables?' said the waiter. 'They'll have steak too,' she replied. When she first met Mr Gorbachev, she told him bluntly that she despised communism. But as long as he kept it in his own country, that was OK.

Denis wasn't much better. When the Thatchers were in Goa, the lights went out just before an official function. At table, Denis boomed: 'This place is high on the buggeration factor!' And at a European summit, within earshot of François Mitterand and Helmut Kohl, Denis at one point bawled out 'Sod Europe!'

Working with the Thatchers, Bernard Ingham also got to know Denis's pet names for ascending volumes of drink, from a tincture, snifter and snorter to the ultimate, a snortereeno, which usually meant draining a whole bottle of Bombay gin.

During his eleven years at Number 10, Sir Bernard himself came in for some vicious criticism. John Biffen once said of him: 'He is the sewer rather than the sewage.' And Sir Edward Heath described him as a 'menace to the Constitution.' Pause. 'He should know,' growled BI.

By 11.15 the show was over. Well, not quite. Our lady-in-red, having consumed considerably more than a snortereeno, decided to join us on the top table and plonked herself next to Andrew's wife.

'Hi! I'm Toni with an I. Can I have a cigarette?' Cécile obliged as Andrew returned to reclaim the chair she had snatched.

'Hi!' she said. 'I'm Toni with an I. But I'm not interested in you. I want to talk to Sir Bernard.'

She then knocked a glass of water over, spilling most of it in Andrew's lap. Christophe, our Young Waiter of the Year finalist, leapt in with a clean napkin and laid it across the damp patch on the table.

'Why's he doing that?' asked Toni.

'It's his job,' replied Cécile.

'Oh! Really! I'll do it again then!'

'No you won't!' snapped Cécile angrily.

Toni stood up and began to make her way round the table, clutching at the backs of the chairs to prop herself up. On the other side, Bernard Ingham was chatting amiably to Brian and Eve Webb, two personal friends and great supporters of our gastronomic evenings. Cécile instantly despatched David Sommerfelt like a gunboat to the rescue.

'Excuse me! Excuse me!' bellowed Toni as she came alongside the group. (The Webbs gave way. HMS Sommerfelt stood by, alert to the danger.) 'I'm a Young Conservative and I didn't agree with quite a lot of what you said.'

'That doesn't surprise me,' said Sir Bernard politely.

'It's OK for older people, but not for us,' continued Toni, flicking cigarette ash on the carpet. 'Negative equity and all that!'

David edged a little closer and I moved in. Our guest of honour was eager for his bed and he had an early start in the morning. I escorted him out, thanked him warmly and said farewell.

When I returned to the dining room, Toni was slumped face down on her table with a bucket at her side provided thoughtfully by Christophe. At midnight, her husband and friends, encouraged by Simon Girling, carried her out. When Louise and I left a little later, we found the car park sprayed with vomit. My last (reluctant) instructions were to Bob, our night porter.

St Mary's Girls Love a Good Rabbit

Friday, 18 October 1996

SHERRIN'S YEAR, Ned's new book, was published this week, providing plenty of entertaining bedtime reading as one might expect. To my shame, I began at the back – with the index – scanning the names of all the people Ned had mentioned in his diary. I scored three entries, on a par with the Queen, Rik Mayall, Esther Rantzen and John Redwood; one entry more than Martin Amis, Jeffrey Archer and Robin Day; two more than Naomi Campbell, Albert Finney and Jeremy Paxman; and only one less than Harold Pinter and Camilla Parker-Bowles. This is, I accept, a disgraceful display of ego-masturbation, but I am told everybody does it. Sadly, I came nowhere near Alan Clark, Stephen Fry and Keith Waterhouse: respectively, twelve, thirteen and twenty-seven entries.

Ned is, of course, a Somerset man and I spent Wednesday morning with his cousin, Frances Kitchen, a well-known local cookery writer and presenter. The two of us have been roped in to a bizarre show at the Octagon Theatre in Yeovil on 22 November in aid of the BBC's *Children in Need* Appeal; the show will be broadcast live on Somerset Sound and Radio Bristol. The gig is intended to be an amateur spoof on *Ready Steady Cook*-cum-*Master Chef* with Frances and me cast in the dubious roles of Fern Britton and Loyd Grossman. British Gas is sponsoring the event and the BBC is calling it *Ready Teddy … Cook*.

I have yet to understand the significance of the teddy, but when I arrived at a press call in Yeovil on Wednesday, a man-size Rupert Bear character posed in all the photographs. For a while I thought the idea was probably for contestants to demonstrate their favourite bear recipes. This would have been a fascinating gastronomic experience as I have never tasted teddy before. But when we went inside the theatre for our official briefing, Frances and I were handed a pile of application forms to select the finalists and, to my disappointment, bear was not on the menu. Instead, three teams of two would be required to cook a couple of dishes using traditional West Country ingredients. On the whole, the recipes proposed by the eager applicants were quite disgusting but, in the end, we chose our finalists for the show. Even so, my hunch is that this thing is going to be an embarrassing farce. One of the teams is putting up a 'mackrell (*sic*) bake with Chedder (*sic*) cheese'. Revolting.

The briefing was shambolic. Dozens of volunteers gathered in groups around tables in the theatre's upstairs bar. There were spotty, anaemic students from Yeovil College, there were deep-voiced soroptimists, there were hairy radio presenters and there were a number of extraordinarily dim-witted people from British Gas who, I think, were meant to be instructing each group on their duties. When I left, one of them gave me a limp handshake and said: 'Sorry for the chaos, but it was the only way we could do it!'

One infinitely more agreeable duty this week was to welcome Philippa Davenport and her friend, Anna Del Conte, to the hotel for two nights. Philippa is one of the few cookery columnists I have time for. Her articles in the *Financial Times* are intelligent and well-written, and I am constantly ripping them out for Phil to read. She is a great source of inspiration to us both. The only other writers in her class are Rowley Leigh in the *Guardian* and, more eccentrically, Jennifer Paterson in the

Spectator. Anna is also in a league of her own and, arguably, Britain's leading authority on Italian food.

We dined with them on Tuesday evening and Louise discovered that Philippa, like her, was a product of St Mary's Ascot. I have only been to this great Catholic institution once and that was twenty-five years ago when I had just become engaged. Never have I seen a school like it. The bedrooms and furnishings are every inch as luxurious as the Savoy Hotel's, and to this day I do not understand how it is that St Mary's girls (I know dozens of them now) turn out so unspoilt, modest and charming. Louise and Philippa put it down to the nuns. I'm not so sure. They weren't very nice to me. When I was introduced to Mother Bridget (a legendary icon to old girls), she looked deeply into my eyes and said: 'So you are to be married to Louise Guiver?'

'Yes,' I said, beaming at her proudly.

'Are you a *good* Catholic?' she asked, assuming that I couldn't possibly be anything else.

'No,' I stuttered, 'I'm sort-of Church of England.'

'Oh!' said Mother Bridget, cutting me dead and turning to someone else.

In love...in Greece

St Mary's may be a closed shop but Louise was happy there. She only despised two girls, Sarah Hogg (née Boyd-Carpenter) and Marina Warner who, as prefects, forced Louise to recite long poems as penances. According to Louise, Mrs Hogg was particularly bossy.

At dinner – and talking about The Faith – I was heavily outnumbered, the more so when Philippa and Anna learned that Phil Vickery hailed from a principled Catholic family. The moment the food arrived, the subject changed. Entertaining serious cooks is a tense game: morsels of food are passed from plate to plate and one waits nervously for reactions. But I had nothing to fear. Their pleasure was spontaneous and genuine: the potted rabbit and spiced pears, the crab and saffron tart, the monkfish and the braised shoulder of lamb all scored high marks. Chef excelled himself and I slept peacefully that night.

This is just as well. For the past month, Phil's television commitments, though not excessive, have taken him away from his stoves and his absences have been a worry. Once or twice I've had to bitch about some of the food coming out of the kitchen. Given our high rankings in the guides, I am terrified of slipping. So is he, and we have now come to an amicable understanding to control the growing demands from producers and the media's voracious appetite to lionize chefs. We are now saying 'No' more often than 'Yes'.

The week also brought our search for a new hotel accountant to a final conclusion. The hour-long interviews with our two short-listed candidates were led by my chairman, Michael Blackwell, himself a retired accountant and a friend who has minded the family's affairs for at least thirty years. Regrettably, Mrs Brown – she of the wit and Colgate ring-of-confidence grin – failed to make the grade and we have decided to offer the job to a Mr Leaming of Chard, whose grasp of the nitty-gritty was superior. On second meeting, I warmed to him as a human being. In spite of his pearl grey suit, he struck us as a thoroughly decent chap. For a start he is a Catholic (another one!). Furthermore, Mr Leaming told us, he is a Catholic convert who had once been the sacristan of his church when he was living in Coventry. He is also a campanologist (lapsed), secretary of his local carnival club and the owner of three chocolate brown poodles. In addition to his evident accounting and administrative abilities, Michael and I concluded that these details made him the ideal man for the job. Mr Leaming is fifty and unmarried.

Saturday, 19 October 1996

I was hoping for a day off today. Instead, I walked into a basin full of trouble. As usual on a Saturday morning, I went to the hotel to check my post, review the arrivals and functions, and scoop up the newspapers (at weekends, I take the lot, principally to hoover my way through the food, drink, books and arts sections).

At nine o'clock, Simon Girling and Alison Lock, the assistant manager, demanded an audience to brief me on the catastrophes of the previous evening. The National Trust had held a dinner for ninety in the Monmouth Room to mark the twenty-fifth anniversary of their Quantock Centre.

The dinner opened with an impromptu firework display when one of the downlighters exploded and fell from the ceiling. The bulb bounced on a table, narrowly missing a pensioner, and was caught by another who exclaimed: 'Howzat! 200 watts!' Next, a small group of five guests at the end of one table decided to be troublesome throughout the evening. Nothing was right. Two ladies complained because we had run out of brown bread rolls. A third moaned that she had eaten her smoked salmon before we had offered her the black pepper mill. The other two didn't like their duck because it was too pink. Meanwhile, the organizer and all eighty-four other guests tucked in happily without a murmur of displeasure. Come the end, however, one of the waiters took it upon himself to drop a pot of coffee into the laps of the bread roll complainants. The duty manager was summoned. Alison Lock reported and apologized profusely, promising to pay their dry-cleaning bills and to deduct the price of dinner and wine from their bills. This was considered an inadequate response and a solicitors' letter was threatened. I have been asked to call them on Tuesday morning.

After the speeches, Simon and Alison were summoned again. This time a lady had collapsed and was lying unconscious on the floor. They called an ambulance.

By the time it arrived, the lady had recovered and was promptly taken home by her friends.

I made a few notes of the details to prepare myself for the telephone call next week and that was the end of that.

At ten o'clock, Chef stormed into my office in a rage. He had intercepted a breakfast order for 'Room 20' which read as follows:

2 x scrambled eggs
1 x poached eggs (two)
Sausages
Black pudding
Mushrooms
Sauté potatoes
Bacon (well done)
Baked beans
2 x white toast
1 x brown toast

The order was bogus, written by the breakfast supervisor and two other waiters who, it seems, were feeling a little peckish.

Phil had expressed his views in plain language to the three concerned and immediately decreed an indefinite ban on staff breakfast. Did I agree? Yes I did. Further, I instructed written warnings to those responsible.

At this point, Girling returned to my office looking pale and harassed. The couple in Room 69 had come down for a late breakfast and complained bitterly about the violent commotion they had overhead from the servery adjoining the restaurant. They were so upset they were threatening to check out. Chef agreed to see them immediately and apologize, and we decided to put a half-bottle of champagne in their room as a peace offering.

That was enough excitement for one morning. I left for home.

WHEN IS A BROTH NOT A BROTH?

FRIDAY, 25 OCTOBER 1996

ANDREW GRAHAME has had a most extraordinary experience. On Tuesday, he and Cécile returned from a week's holiday in Blackpool and the Lake District. Before they left for their break, the internal line used for his chemotherapy, drugs and blood samples began to play up, causing inflammation and some pain around his chest. This line – a long plastic tube – was implanted about a year ago when he was admitted to hospital. It was fitted surgically under anaesthetic; inserted behind the breast bone, running up to the shoulder, down into a main artery and exiting just below the chest. The line is held in place by material cuffs around the plastic tube, which grow into the skin tissue to keep it anchored. Before returning south, the Grahames went to Derby to visit the family and pick up Chlöe, their daughter. Andrew also went to see his uncle Arthur, the healer, who spent forty minutes concentrating his spiritual powers on the inflamed area. They then drove back to Taunton, a journey of about two hundred and thirty miles. As soon as they were home, Andrew discovered the line – about two feet of it – lying in a loose heap tucked inside his shirt. There was no blood to be seen anywhere. Next morning the exit hole in his chest had healed and the inflammation and soreness had gone. When he went to the hospital for his regular check-up, he presented his doctors with the tube in a paper bag. They were astonished, baffled, speechless – as I was. Andrew has now been taken off all his drugs.

As a hardened sceptic, I hesitate to comment on these mysterious events. The only earthly means of removing the line is under surgery. But then, as the Great Book tells, the blind will see and the lame will be made to walk.

And so to more temporal matters, and the frailty and vanity of the human race. First there is the case of Mr Leaming, the man Michael Blackwell and I were ready to appoint as the new hotel accountant. We boobed. Before writing a formal letter offering Mr Leaming the post, Andrew made discreet enquiries of his former employer and, as a consequence, we learned that the saintly Mr Leaming was not quite the ideal man we thought. According to his ex-boss, he is a 'psychological mess, morose, depressive, and in the habit of locking his office door and refusing to speak to anyone'. He had had 'two nervous breakdowns followed by extended periods of sick leave. After five requests for a doctor's certificate, he faced down his managing director and, with one dramatic sweep of his arm, had cleared the contents of the startled MD's desk onto the floor, calling him a "rotten bastard"'. The catalogue of horror continued; bizarrely, Mr Leaming was prone to writing spurious letters of resignation on behalf of other members of staff and forging their signatures. We let the problem rest for twenty-four hours and we have now decided to recall Mrs Brown for a third interview, having first run a check on her. To our relief, her principal referee gave her a clean bill of health.

Then there is the case of Mr Lynn, whose wife suffered the indignity of a pot of coffee in her lap at last week's National Trust do. I telephoned the aggrieved husband on Tuesday morning in the hope that the weekend might have cooled his militancy. Fat chance! Mr Lynn wants blood. We had ruined their evening. Covering the cost of dry-cleaning and the dinner was inadequate compensation.

'What would you suggest as fair compensation, Mr Lynn?' I enquired.

'£150,' he replied.

Big deal, I thought, but refused to be budged. Mr Lynn then played the 'solicitors' card, and I decided to call his bluff, resisting the temptation of pointing out that a solicitors' letter would cost him more than the price of dinner at the Castle. I wrote to Mr Lynn in the following terms:

23 October 1996

Dear Mr Lynn,

WITHOUT PREJUDICE

Following our telephone conversation yesterday morning, I do want to apologise once again for the unfortunate incident at the Castle last Friday evening on the occasion of the National Trust dinner. I am sure you will understand that this was an accident and I was so pleased to hear that your wife was unhurt. In addition, I note that you had no complaints otherwise about the service or dinner.

In the light of the action you now intend taking, I am afraid that you leave me no alternative other than to withdraw my offer, made in good faith, to pay for your wife's dry-cleaning and to reimburse you for the dinner and wine. I shall now wait to receive the letter from your solicitors and respond accordingly.

Yours sincerely,

C H G Chapman
Managing Director

Nothing concentrates the mind of an hotelier more than a visit by his peers. Forget the guide books (perhaps not – inspectors make us equally paranoid), welcoming one's fellows puts us on our guard. Hoteliers – even one's dearest friends – are the severest critics and they are accomplished gossips. On Monday a small delegation of the good and the great descended on us with a bevy of senior lieutenants from the British Tourist Authority and, for good measure, the chief honchos of the AA Guide and the Michelin Red Guide. We were sixteen in all. The purpose of this tryst was to discuss a major promotion in the United States next year called *Jewels of Britain* – the 'Jewels' of the title being the finest hotels in the land, about a hundred and twenty of thezm, irrespective of their star classification, be they one star or five. In the AA Guide, for example, these gems are designated by the colour red. Black stars are the proles. We reds, the aristocracy.

Imagine then, the frenzy of preparation in advance of this nobility's progress to Taunton. There is much scrubbing and burnishing; planning and rehearsal; setting and re-setting; checking and re-checking; etc., etc. Nothing is left to chance. Everything must be perfect. One's pride and reputation are on the line.

Among those present at this august gathering were three particular friends, themselves leading lights of the industry, arbiters of good taste and fierce custodians of 'standards'. (Innkeepers of this ilk are constantly beating the drum for 'standards'.) Highest in this galaxy was Martin Skan, whose Chewton Glen in Hampshire glitters with five red stars. At the Rolls Royce end of the tourism market, Martin is our senior statesman, our principal ambassador. His hotel in the New Forest is matchless, its grandeur softened by the homeliness and individuality of its furnishings. Even the ghastly Michael Winner couldn't find much to whinge about in his *Sunday Times* column when he stayed at Chewton Glen two weeks ago. Well, there was one thing. Mr Winner moaned bitterly about the wooden duck in his bathroom. It wouldn't float properly. Indeed, it sank – very irritating.

It was also good to see George Goring again. Our families have been friends for almost ninety years and George's grandfather, Otto – who founded the Goring Hotel in London (four red stars) – was my father's godfather. George is an hotelier of the old school and something of an eccentric. At work he is formal, polite, correct; he still wears stiff detachable collars. At play he is a clown and often breaks into song after dinner. This is all very well except that George's voice makes the wail of a police siren sound positively mellifluous by comparison. At one party Louise and I went to in a private room at the Goring, George ordered a waiter to place a life-size china greyhound in the middle of the table after dinner. He then balanced a sugar lump on the dog's snout and invited us to fire sugar lumps at it for a prize of a bottle of champagne to the first person who scored a direct hit. Some of us still bear the scars from the crossfire.

The third hotelier chum at the meeting was my old pal Paul Henderson, the owner of Gidleigh Park in Devon (three red stars). Gidleigh is divine. There is no place on earth like it. It is the most beautiful, the most peaceful, the most exquisite country house hotel in Britain. The proprietor – if you are fortunate enough to know him – is the kindest, most generous host I know. He is also the rudest man I know. How Paul has succeeded in this trade is a total mystery to me. But he is American and I guess we tolerant Brits have learned to live with him, much as Manchester United fans have learned to live with Eric Cantona.

The meeting got under way, led by the urbane Julian Younger, a British Tourist Authority old hand and our man in Los Angeles. The morning session went smoothly enough, but in spite of a convivial lunch the atmosphere in the afternoon turned chilly as the hoteliers lined up against the BTA to condemn the design proposals for the *Jewels of Britain* brochure. When Martin Skan introduced his own design expert, who had been sitting quietly at his side, the atmosphere descended to freezing point. The young usurper, wearing a diamond stud in his left ear lobe, made a brilliant presentation. There was no contest.

But for me, of course, the main event was lunch. With both the AA Man and the Michelin Man present, as well as this crowd of starry hoteliers, the menu had to be a showcase for the Castle and all good things British. Vickery delivered: smoked haddock and oyster broth, followed by a spiced lamb pudding with braised cabbage and mash and, to finish, a delicate vanilla blancmange with rose petal syrup. The food – with wines to match – was faultless. I was pleased. Paul Henderson, however, decided to pick a fight; the more poignant for the fact that our argument was conducted across the Michelin Man, Derek Bulmer, who sat between us. First off, Henderson contended that the broth was not a broth but a soup. I tried to explain to him that this was most definitely a broth and he should not be deceived by the fact that the liquid had been finished off with a drop of cream. The debate was further complicated by another's suggestion that the dish was neither a soup nor a broth but a chowder, because there were pieces of haddock floating in the bowls. This was, perhaps, nearer the mark but I stood firm, arguing that chowders were Anglo-Indian, a gastronomic legacy of the Raj.

Come the main course, Henderson started up again. The spiced lamb pudding was not a pudding but a raviolo. The Michelin Man stayed mum, relishing the argument as much as his lunch. Eventually, Paul shut up when I told him that he had obviously never tasted good suet paste. Undeterred, when the blancmange was served, he accused me of lapsing into unnecessary kitchen French.

Next day, I received a fax from Gidleigh Park with the Concise Oxford Dictionary's definitions of 'soup', 'broth' and 'chowder' which, anyway by my interpretation, vindicated the menu's nomenclature. But, it seems, I was wrong about the derivation of 'chowder'. Its origins are French: '*faire la chaudière* supply a pot etc. for cooking a stew of fish etc. (*chaudière* pot, CAULDRON)'.

Work has at last begun on the redecoration of the exterior of Minstrels, our pub in Castle Bow. The argument over the colour scheme – pink and juniper green – has been endless and Louise has not exactly hit it off with the builder, John Lock, who now refers to Mrs C as 'Her Indoors!' Louise, meanwhile, was determined to find an alternative to the excremental hue called 'Juniper' and produced two possibles – 'Beetle' and 'Buckingham'. Broad swathes of these three shades of green were duly splashed on to the walls beside strips of pink. And there they remain for the time being until 'Her Indoors' confesses to the obvious and admits that Mr Lock's judgement was right from the beginning.

On a more harmonious chord, this week Louise and I said our fond farewells to the Tucker-Browns – Simon and his wife, Katerina, who has been my sales and marketing manager for the past two-and-a-half years. Next week Tuck takes up his new post as general manager of the venerable Feathers Hotel in Ludlow. It is very rare for me to make much of a fuss of a departing manager, but Tuck did so well deputizing during Andrew's long absence that we decided to take them out to dinner on Wednesday evening.

I booked a table at Lettonie, a Michelin two-star restaurant near Bristol owned by Martin and Sian Blunos, where he cooks and she fronts. The 1996 Michelin

Guide lists seven two-star and four three-star restaurants in Britain. This puts Lettonie right at the top of the pile – and deservedly so. It is brilliant, the food top-of-the-range French haute cuisine, with an unusual political twist. Martin insists on describing himself as a Bristolian and he is not a little upset with me for omitting him from my last book, *Great British Chefs 2*. But although he was born in Bath and raised in Bristol, both his parents are Latvian. Innocent visitors to Lettonie almost certainly miss the connection. The place is heavy with Latvian nationalist symbolism. For a start, *Lettonie* is French for Latvia. The menu is maroon and white – the colours of the Latvian flag – and the cover features an illustration of the statue in Riga of 'Mother Latvia', mourning the death of her sons who fought for the country's freedom. On the back of the card are three words in bold capitals: TEVZEMEI UN BRIVIBAI, 'For Freedom and the Motherland.' Martin's family is a tragic reminder of the history of the Baltic States. His father was conscripted into the German army during the war and fought on the Russian front while his uncle, his father's elder brother, was drafted into the Russian army. Brother fought against brother. After the war, Martin's father was captured by the Americans and ended up in England. His uncle still lives in Latvia.

For all its Francophilia, the menu is threaded with the ethnicity of the chef. One of the most delicious dishes we tasted was a bortsch terrine served with pirogues, egg-shaped yeast dough breads stuffed with onion and caraway, similar to Russian piroshki. Eastern Europe is not noted for its cuisine, but Martin learned well by his mother's side and the Michelin Guide, notorious for its chauvinism in these matters, has showered its honours on him. Perhaps it is time I tempered my own hard line and included him in the next edition of *Great British Chefs*.

'All The World's A Stage'

Wednesday, 30 October 1996

I N LONDON on Monday, first to continue my research into the life of my grandfather, Henry Prüger, who ran the Savoy from 1903 to 1909, then to meet Sheridan Morley and his wife, Ruth Leon, to discuss a Noël Coward entertainment I want to present over the Easter weekend next March.

When the weather changes (some overnight wind and rain, that's all!) our rail system cracks up. Privatization has done nothing to improve punctuality and my train rolled into Paddington half an hour late. I took a taxi to One Savoy Hill, the offices of the Savoy Group, where I met the company's archivist, Susan Scott. After

a morning I spent in the Edwardian splendour of the RAC Club's library in Pall
Mall two months earlier (Prüger was the Club's first manager in 1911), this was a
little different. The Savoy's archives are held in an airless, windowless hole not much
larger than a broom cupboard. Ms Scott, a young lady in black, was very
accommodating in spite of an unnerving habit of staring intently at me as I worked
at the tiny desk next to hers. When I was seated, she began reciting the rule book:
no eating, no drinks (I was panting for a coffee), no smoking and no pens or biros;
only pencils, of which Ms Scott had a large supply. Ms Scott then took exception
to my purple socks.

'Oh! I'm sorry about that,' I muttered defensively. 'I'm rather fond of them.'

'They clash with your tie,' she said, pointing at the salmon and cucumber
colours of the Garrick Club.

'Well, I like the odd clashing colour,' I replied firmly.

'I suppose it makes no odds when you're standing up,' she continued, 'but I
did six months at the Courtauld Institute, so I suppose I'm sensitive to these
things.'

We got to work. About ten years ago, before Ms Scott's time, my father unearthed
a lot of material about his father from these archives. My purpose was to search for
more and I was not disappointed. With Susan Scott's help, I pulled out dusty
volumes of press cuttings, advertising and correspondence which I hadn't seen.
Books about the Savoy describe Henry Prüger as 'volatile and imaginative'. He
was a great pioneering hotelier who seemed to capture the spirit of the age by
throwing the most outrageously extravagant parties for his wealthy clients. The
most famous was the 'Gondola Dinner' on 30 June 1905 for George Kessler, the
Wall Street financier, and two dozen of his friends. My grandfather flooded a
courtyard in the hotel, dyeing the water blue and re-creating the scene of a Venetian
lagoon. The *Hello!* magazine of the time, the society publication *Cartons Mondains*,
reported the occasion in rather obsequious and inflated prose:

'... the miracle was accomplished by a magician named Prüger who kills
time by managing the Savoy. And he put live swans in the pond, live ducks,
salmon trout, whitebait, and in the middle a floating dining room in the shape
of a huge Venetian gondola.

*The gondola dinner at the Savoy on 30 June 1905. My grandfather, Henry Prüger,
sitting on the left in the small 'service gondola', keeps a close eye on the party.
This photograph was published in* Cartons Mondains *on 15 August 1905.
Picture courtesy of the archives of The Savoy Hotel Ltd.*

'The waiters each had his gondola, swiftly carrying the dainty dishes to the
favoured twenty-four.

'… Then, as in an enchanted dream, on the still, balmy atmosphere rose the
rich mellow tones of the divine Caruso's voice …

'The moon was shining brightly, by order of Mr Geo. A. Kessler, for the
American Nabob would have the illusion of Venice complete, and, after
improvising the lagoon below, created an electrically ornamented
firmament above …

'Then I caught sight of … *Jumbo Junior* [a baby elephant] carrying to the
guests … a cake, a *sweety* five feet high studded all over with electric
diamonds and revolving all the time producing the most dazzling effect.

'The floral decorations included: 12,000 choice carnations; 2,000
Malmaison carnations; 17,000 roses …

'One hundred white doves fluttered over the scene, and the lighting up
comprised no less than four hundred Venetian lamps.'

The bill for this intimate soirée came to £3,000, which in today's money, the Bank of England tells me, would equate to a little over £144,000. But what the author of this ponderous article omitted to report was that the blue dye in the water poisoned the fish and killed off the swans.

My search through these archives also revealed my grandfather as a clever marketing man and a brilliant self-publicist. On 27 September 1905, he took a full-page advertisement in the *New York Herald*, which he signed at the bottom in bold type, 'HENRI PRUGER, General Manager'. The advert was contrived to achieve two ends: firstly, to present himself as a world class hotelier, and secondly, to pander shamelessly to the snobbery of New York society. The opening paragraph read:

'In May 1904, the extensions and improvements to the Savoy Hotel were completed. Never in the history of hotel life in any country has the appreciation of the public of the comfort and luxury provided for them been shown in more substantial form. The best travellers from the Continent of Europe and America have pronounced the magnificent suites of rooms with bathrooms to be unrivalled; and their recommendation to friends has resulted in the large increase in business of 1904 over 1903 being greatly exceeded in the present year, thus showing that the more the public become familiar with the comforts and luxury of the hotel the greater is its popularity.'

[My grandfather then published his occupancy figures!]

	1903	1904	1905
MAY	4,428	4,478	8,074
JUNE	4,695	6,033	10,131
JULY	2,779	5,921	9,681

These statements and statistics took up about a quarter of the advertisement. The rest of the page was devoted to a listing of the Savoy's most notable patrons – several hundred of them – beginning with the names of nineteen Royals: one Queen

(Saxony), two Imperial Highnesses (Japan and Russia), one Sultan (Zanzibar), and a whole variety of Royal Highnesses and Serene Highnesses. Below these came the small print: hundreds of Dukes, Earls, Counts, Barons, Lords, Knights and the odd General.

In 1909, four years after this advertisement appeared, my grandfather left the Savoy to take on the management of a glittering new restaurant in New York called the *Café de l'Opéra*. The appointment carried a salary of £10,000 – or £452,400 today! However, the volatile Mr Prüger fell out with the New York unions and a year later he was back in London to open the new premises of the RAC in Pall Mall.

By one o'clock, I had barely scratched the surface but it was time to leave and, besides, I think the solicitous Ms Scott had had enough of me. Volumes of letters and memos to Prüger from Sir George Reeves-Smith, the Savoy's Managing Director, will have to wait for a return visit. Before leaving the hotel, I went via the Savoy's gents for a scrub. I was filthy. Some of these archives haven't been opened in decades.

At ten past one I walked into the bar at the Garrick where I ran into Frank Moat, a barrister, and Keith Jeffery, a retired Arts Council director who now travels the world to sit on a variety of grand committees, judging arts prizes and organizing festivals. Soon after, Sheridan and Ruth arrived and we went to our table in the Milne Room, where we sat beneath the huge portrait of Gladys Cooper, Sheridan's grandmother. To family and friends she was always known as 'G' – never Gladys, because by the 1930s 'Gladys' had acquired its distinctly lower-class association! We ordered our food and Sheridan gave me a copy of his new book on Dirk Bogarde, which he signed. Ruth promptly ticked him off for excluding Louise, so Sheridan squeezed her name in at the top of the page, making it look like an obvious afterthought.

Over an excellent lunch – wild duck terrine, Dover sole, cheese – we discussed Easter and the Noël Coward entertainment. Sheridan would present it under Ruth's direction and they needed to find an actress and a pianist. I told them that, as a first choice, I wanted Patricia Hodge, with whom I was deeply in love (artistically). I then broached the sensitive matter of artists' fees, which Sheridan gamely waived in return for the Castle's hospitality. He told me that his father, Robert Morley, was never paid a fee by British Airways in twenty years of recording voice-overs for commercials. Instead, he flew the world's favourite airline for free.

Later in the afternoon, I returned to Paddington to find the platforms absent of trains and the concourse a crush of bewildered commuters. At two-minute intervals, a nerdish announcer droned the same message: that Great Western were '*very, very* sorry for the considerable delays … due to a vehicle that had crashed into a railway bridge near Swindon' etc., etc. I ate a Cheddar, mozzarella and pesto baguette (which tasted better than it sounds) and read Sheridan's biography of Bogarde. Home by 10.30.

SUNDAY, 3 NOVEMBER 1996

A week of odds, sods and silliness; too much time wasted putting out fires. On Wednesday, a couple of maids chucked some food out of a third floor bedroom window, scoring a direct hit on a passer-by. The incident was witnessed by a flower seller in Castle Bow. Police action was threatened and narrowly averted. On Thursday morning, Andrew fired Les, the gardener. Weeping and pleading for a second chance, he was reinstated by Louise in the afternoon. I was not pleased and had a monumental row with Louise. On Friday, Mrs Brown called to say that, after all, she was not interested in pursuing the hotel accountant's job, thus wiping out our short list. Mercifully, we had taken the precaution of keeping one name on a reserve list, a Mr Lumley – but he is on holiday in Hawaii at the moment.

Sheridan Morley telephoned to say Patricia Hodge would be in Spain over Easter next year and suggested Rosie Ash, the original star in *Phantom of the Opera*, for the Noël Coward weekend. A perfect choice. I also took a call from the producer of the BBC's *Food and Drink* programme, who wanted Phil to present a couple of short film slots for the show. The idea was so asinine, I said no: a 'blind date' dinner for 350 students at Durham University.

'How's Baz?' I asked, enquiring after Peter Bazalgette, boss of Bazal Productions, the makers of the programme.

'Couldn't be better,' said the producer. 'Counting his money upstairs at the moment. And he hasn't finished!'

'The company's doing very well,' I said. 'You've got a lot of productions on air at the moment.'

'You ain't seen nothing. Baz is aiming to be bigger than Jimmy Goldsmith.'

I couldn't quite grasp the connection but I caught the general drift.

'Now I'm obliged to tell you this – but I expect you know anyway,' continued the producer.

'What's that?' I enquired.

'Well, I have to tell you that *Food and Drink* got over five million viewers last year.'

'Yes, I know that,' I said, even more determined to say 'no' to the silly idea.

Yesterday, Louise and I drove to Plymouth to view an exhibition of twenty new watercolours by the Devonian artist Karen Burgess, whose husband, Philip, is head chef at the Arundell Arms at Lifton. We are redecorating the restaurant this winter and Louise wants to replace some perfectly good but rather dull paintings with something more modern and engaging. Karen's exhibition, at the offices of the solicitors Bond Pearce, was billed 'The Kitchen Garden', which seemed appropriate. We persuaded Francis, the owner of the White Lane Gallery, where Karen normally exhibits her work, to meet us on Saturday morning for a private view. The weather was foul, so we arrived late, but Francis was there waiting patiently in the foyer of the office block and a security man let us in to see the paintings.

We were there an hour – and for most of it argued furiously! Francis, a gentle, mild-mannered soul, stood back blinking in horror. The debate was not about the quality of the work, which we loved, nor was it about our choice of paintings. The point of contention was where to hang them.

'They're beautiful. Brilliant!' I said. 'But totally inappropriate for the restaurant.'

'Rubbish'! replied Louise. 'We wanted a food theme. That's what we're about and they'll work very well in that room.'

'I don't think so. These are subtle watercolours; perfect for our bedrooms, not the restaurant. We need pictures that are bigger and bolder.'

'No way, Kit,' she snapped. 'I know exactly where to hang them and we want paintings that are soft and subtle to go with the scheme. I don't want a load of brash pictures.'

'Listen, Louise. These are gentle still-life studies full of intriguing, imaginative detail. You need the peace and quiet of a bedroom to appreciate them. In the restaurant they'll be lost. They'll make no impression whatsoever. I want something more vibrant, more powerful.'

'You just want to be like everybody else!' she said, aiming below the belt.

'No I don't! I just don't think these'll work.'

'Yes you do. And yes they will work – I know they will. Besides, I've got nothing in my budget for pictures in the bedrooms. I need them for the restaurant.'

'The budget's got nothing to do with it …'

Eventually, to Francis's relief, we agreed to reserve two paintings, *Landscove turnips* and *Peter's grapes*, and we put options on two more, *Winter leeks* and *Asparagus and ferns*.

Outside it was still raining. We said farewell to a grateful but shell-shocked Francis and returned to the car. It was time for a spot of lunch. I had thought of Chez Nous, but as we have eaten there before, we decided to take Francis's suggestion and try Piermasters in the Barbican. It was a good choice; a friendly, quayside bistro run by Stephen Williams, a garrulous and dishevelled character who reminded me of Desperate Dan. We ate a proper Provençal fish soup and some excellent sea bass, all perfectly lubricated by a crisp and fragrant bottle of Ménétou-Salon. With espressos and mineral water, the bill came to just over £50 which, we thought, was extremely good value.

Feeling mellow and at peace, we wandered down the quayside in the drizzle until we came to an art gallery advertising the work of R O Lenkiewicz, a portrait painter whom I had heard of but did not know. No sooner were we inside than this extraordinary figure appeared. Tall, mesmeric, bearded and with a thick mane of ludicrously long grey hair, I thought I'd run into the Neptune of Plymouth Dock. This was Mr Lenkiewicz. Dressed in a thick black smock with a large floppy collar, black silk scarf and black track suit bottoms tucked into black rubber-soled shoes, I was struck by a spectre that was either divine or diabolic, but I couldn't decide which. Anyway, Mr Lenkiewicz, speaking to us in a soft seductive voice, was most charming. He explained that the pictures in the gallery were painted twenty or thirty years ago, and he invited us to come to his studio a few doors further down the quay. The portraits in the gallery were vast canvases of very old men, one a low-slung nude of a bloke wearing one sock. The paintings, to my eye, were remarkable because they seemed to come from another age; dark backgrounds infused with intense contrasts of light and shade; there was a strange, biblical renaissance quality to the works. Louise hated them.

We left to seek out Mr Lenkiewicz's studio. Above the ground floor window was a painted sign that read: *The aim of these premises is to present large scale projects on the human condition. This studio is non-commercial and presents information for philosophical purposes only.* Displayed in the window were several enormous bound volumes of R O Lenkiewicz's studies into the 'human condition', the largest by far entitled *Orgasm*. We entered by a side door that led into a narrow passageway and up a steep staircase past a series of libraries stacked with antiquarian books. At the top we were met by a Pre-Raphaelite nymph called Jane who turned out to be R O L's 'secretary'. Jane also wore black and was also most charming. She invited us to wander round the studio, a vast, theatrically-lit cavern with a number of smaller rooms leading off the main area. Meanwhile, 'Robert', as Jane called her master, glided serenely in and out the shadows of his domain looking divine, beautiful, poetic, philosophical, artistic, etc.

There were hundreds – no, thousands – of canvases crammed into these spaces; some ugly, some beautiful. Louise pointed to one stunning portrait of a young woman.

'Who's that,' she asked Jane.

'It's me,' replied the nymph.

One figure recurred again and again. Wherever we looked, there he was; dozens, perhaps hundreds of visions of the magus himself – alone or in the company of maidens – and always looking serene, divine, beautiful, poetic, etc. He had had two self-portraits printed as postcards, which Jane sold at a strictly 'non-commercial' charge of 25p each: the one entitled *The painter holding himself when ninety – Project 10: Self-portrait (300 paintings)*; the other *Painter in the Wind / 3.50 AM*.

The last room we entered was the painter's bedroom, dominated by a vast, ancient, canopied bed the size of a tennis court. Learned books and pamphlets were scattered (terribly neatly) everywhere – most prominently, Einstein's theory of relativity. Aha! So this is what he likes to go to bed with. And tucked away in a dark corner of the room was a large television screen surrounded by high piles of video cassettes. I did not look too closely at their titles. I was far too engrossed in the artist's philosophical bedtime reading matter.

In the main studio, we got talking, Robert, Louise and I. I was hooked. It's not every day you get to meet a genius. I began by asking him what price for a nice portrait of Louise. £4,000, he said. But the master wasn't interested in discussing the vain request of a passing tourist. He wanted to talk about his latest project: a study of human obsessions – eight hundred portraits to be exhibited in Chicago next year –was I interested? Quite how he concluded that I was a suitable subject, I can't imagine. It may have been Louise's doing, when she said I was serious about good food and wine.

While Jane sold me some postcards, Mr Lenkiewicz invited Louise to inspect his library. Moments later, she returned.

'What's the matter?' I whispered.

'He's on to witchcraft and the occult,' she hissed.

'OK, OK!' I said, tripping down the stairs behind her.

We talked for a while, admiring his great collection of rare books. 200,000 he said. The largest private library in Britain.

We hurried home. In time for the Lottery and a poached egg.

Days of Judgement

Friday, 8 November 1996

I should be feeling rather pleased with myself: we picked up *two* industry
awards this week. Instead I'm staring out of my study window at home feeling
glum. Death on my mind. On Monday, I spent an hour with my solicitor revising
my will (I've planned a gastronomic wake and put Vickery in charge). And yesterday
was the birthday of my brother Gerald, who died nine years ago of Aids. He would
have been forty-seven and I still miss him terribly. It was only when my parents,

Louise and I were in New York for his funeral in late September 1987 that we discovered how famous and admired he had become. *The New York Times* published a substantial obituary and there were long eulogies in the deaths' columns from his friends and colleagues at the Dramatists' Guild.

Gerald first made his name as director of the Young People's Theatre Scheme and the annual Young Writers' Festival at the Royal Court in London. He was spotted by Stephen Sondheim, who invited him to found and direct a similar scheme in New York in 1980. Three years later, Gerald's festival won a Drama Critics award and his success initiated similar projects in other parts of the United States and as far away as Australia. In 1985 he was a guest director at the International Young Playwrights Festival in Sydney. At the time of his death, he had almost completed his book *Teaching Young Playwrights*, which was eventually published in 1991 and has since been acknowledged as a seminal work.

In its own wonderfully peculiar way, the hotel industry is no more than a branch of show business. Like the theatre and the movies, we love our award ceremonies. Last Monday, Andrew and Cécile attended a big bash at the Dorchester at which the Castle was declared 1996 'City Hotel of the Year' by Johansens, a thick glossy annual which lists 450 hotels of 'diversity and excellence for the discerning traveller'. A framed certificate now joins a number of other plates and plaques disguising the blemishes on our ancient walls in the hall.

On Wednesday, I went up to London for the finals of the 'Young Chef' and 'Young Waiter' of the Year competition. Our boy, Christophe Lakehal, was one of the eight contestants in the waiting category and I was invited to make up a table of 'guests' for lunch in the training restaurant of Westminster College in Vincent Square, followed by the prize-giving at the Berkeley that evening.

My train pulled into Paddington at 11.15, which gave me an hour before I was expected at the college. Time enough to buy myself some new socks which I badly needed. For the best hosiery in town there is only one place and that's Turnbull & Asser in Jermyn Street. Their range of colours is fabulous; so are their prices. At

£18 the pair, it is a silly sum to pay for socks, but we all have our vices and I bought five pairs, one each in green, burgundy, lilac, aquamarine and cerise pink.

'Do I get a discount on a bulk purchase?' I asked the assistant.

'No sir!' said the man sneeringly. 'You could buy a hundred pairs and you would still pay the full price.'

After that I needed to catch my breath. It was a beautiful autumn morning and I decided to walk through St James's Park, surely the prettiest of the London parks. As I crossed Birdcage Walk it began to rain and I took a taxi the rest of the way to Vincent Square. The training restaurant at Westminster College is not untypical of its kind: a great barn of a room furnished in a style of circa 1950. While the young chefs did their stuff in the kitchen, the eight waiters – each with a number stuck to their lapels – circled the room pouring Veuve Clicquot champagne and offering plates of very dull canapés. Christophe was number seven. It was a jolly party – good too to meet old friends and colleagues from the trade whom I had not seen for a while. Jeremy King, who with Christopher Corbin owns the Ivy and the Caprice, led the proceedings as chairman of the waiting judges. His panel included Nick Smallwood (Kensington Place) and the delicious Marianne Scrutton, who runs the Avenue. Matthew Fort from the *Guardian* was there and I had long chats with Sally Clarke, who was judging the chefs, and Patrick Gwynn-Jones (Pomegranates) who told me he made the best steak tartare in the world. It's years since I last ate at Patrick's place and I promised to return sometime. Meanwhile, if I want a good tartare I go to the Ivy or the Caprice. They also do the best *frites* in London – no one to touch them.

At one, Jeremy called us to order. Our name badges were numbered to coincide with our waiter and table allocation. Mine was number five and I took my seat with my fellow 'table guests': a talkative Jane Fonda look-alike from American Express, one of the sponsors of the competition; a plummy wine merchant who provided the Veuve Clicquot and the wines with lunch; and a city restaurateur called François. Our young waiter was perfectly nice but painfully gauche, spreading his charm like treacle – and, poor chap, he fell foul of the judges from the start by recommending our wines before telling us what we were going to eat.

Having sorted that little problem, we chose a Sancerre for our first course of red mullet. No sooner had he left to open the bottle than he returned to explain that the wine was not a Sancerre but a Sauvignon Blanc from the cellars of Baron Philippe de Rothschild. From that moment the prospects of contestant number five were doomed as error followed error and, to add to the young man's unhappiness, the Merlot we chose for the main course (braised beef) was corked. Not his fault, but a problem he could have done without.

Both the red mullet, which was served with an aromatic olive oil dressing, and the braised beef, which came with endives, cabbage and mash, were outstanding. 'I hope you enjoy the beef as much as you enjoyed the fish,' droned our waiter as he put down the main course. The young chef cooking for our table, we learned, was a junior from Le Gavroche, no less. The pudding, however, was disastrous: a banana soufflé that refused to soufflé and tasted disgusting.

With coffee, the judges placed a questionnaire on each table and asked us to record our impressions of the service. This had to be completed by the table 'host' – Jane Fonda in our case – who duly catalogued the accumulated failings of our young contestant and then went off to join Jeremy King and his panel to review the performances of all eight finalists. As Christophe had been serving a table on the far side of the room, I had hardly noticed him, but before leaving we spoke briefly. He was relaxed, smiling and confident. 'I'll see you at the Berkeley tonight,' I said, and left to find a cab.

I now needed a couple of hours to myself to catch up on my notes and to edit Gill's latest batch of typed drafts (PCs and lap-tops are beyond my ken. This diary comes hand-written on yellow American 'Legal Pads'). I headed for the Garrick and, in the peace of the Club's library, ordered a pot of Earl Grey and settled down to work.

By 6.30 I was done and on my way to the awards presentation. The taxi dropped me off at the Berkeley's ballroom entrance opposite the church in Wilton Place. As I walked in I was handed another glass of Veuve Clicquot. In the darkened ballroom, Mike Gottlieb, the chairman of the Restaurateurs' Association, had already started to deliver the opening speech from a brightly lit stage at the far end.

Behind him, an enormous split screen displayed his name and title, the competition graphics and the logos of all the sponsors. I picked my way carefully through the gloom, over cables, around light stands, and eventually found an empty chair at the end of the second row. Looking round in the darkness, I spotted Simon Girling nearby. He caught my eye and waved a nervous salute.

The speeches went on a bit. Everyone had their say. After Gottlieb came Michael Edwards of American Express. Then Neville Abraham, the chairman of the competition. Then the chairmen of the two judging panels: Paul Heathcote for the chefs, Jeremy King for the waiters. On the split screen we watched a video depicting highlights of the competition in a rapid succession of stills set to deafeningly loud dance music. Finally, we had to suffer an extremely dull speech from Ms Angela Browning MP, Minister of Food, who spoke to us like a smug headmistress on parents' day.

Only then did we get round to the prize-giving. And oh, what fun it was! The tension, the razzmatazz, the music. The amplified sound of envelopes being torn open. The pregnant pause, getting more pregnant with each new announcement, beginning with third place and ending with first. The cheers from supporters as the lucky young chefs and waiters collected their cheques and prizes from proud Mistress Browning. And, yes, our boy Christophe scooped the top award: a cheque for £1,500; one week's work experience at Daniels, a famous Manhattan restaurant; a three-day sightseeing holiday in New York; and a Methuselah of Veuve Clicquot (a gigantic bottle of champagne equivalent to eight in volume). I nearly fell off my chair with exhaustion and behind me Girling yelped with joy as his protégé mounted the stage.

The presentations over, the scene descended into anarchy as friends and colleagues rushed the stage to embrace the winners. I congratulated Christophe before he was swept away to be photographed and interviewed by the press. And after another swift glass of fizz, I shot off to Simpson's-in-the-Strand where my former publishers were throwing a joint book launch for Sonia Stevenson's *A Fresh Look at Fish* and Joanna Simon's *Wine with Food*.

Friday, 15 November 1996

Jim Ainsworth, editor of *The Good Food Guide*, descended on us for lunch yesterday – a visit intended to be 'incognito' but wasn't. The bush telegraph works well in the West Country and my old pal Henderson at Gidleigh Park called on Tuesday to alert me of an imminent inspection. 'He's heading in your direction,' he warned. 'And he'll probably be coming with Tom Jaine.' A high-powered delegation, I thought. Jaine, himself an eminent food writer, lives in Devon and was Ainsworth's predecessor on the Guide. Two great palates at one table – this was serious stuff.

As soon as they were settled in the Rose Room with their drinks, Simon Girling tipped me off and I wandered casually in to greet them. 'Well, isn't this a surprise!' I said with a grin and sat down to join them. Side by side on a sofa in the centre of the room, the two Great Palates composed a mildly eccentric cameo: Jim with his shock of horizontal hair and goatee; Tom, expertly rolling his own cigarettes, looking more madly donnish than ever. Jim, the quieter, more reflective character, sat back as Tom lunged at me.

'You weren't at the last meeting,' he said quizzically, referring to a working party of foodies set up by the National Farmers' Union to promote West Country produce and the region's cooking traditions.

'No,' I replied, 'I couldn't make it because my father had just had a stroke.'

'Oh dear! How awful! Is he all right?'

'Yes, he's fine now. Made an extraordinary recovery. Tell me about the meeting.'

'It was a disaster. An absolute disaster!'

'Why? Michael Raffael called me afterwards and told me you'd made good progress.'

'No! The whole show was hijacked by Henrietta Green and her cleavage. You should have seen it! Michael fell headlong between them! And that's not all. She brought her dog with her.'

'Henrietta always travels with her dog,' I said. 'She adores the little beast.'

'I'll tell you who else is into dogs in a big way, and I mean BIG,' added Tom, his voice rising to a crescendo, 'and that's Emily Green. She gave up men for dogs four years ago!'

Girling arrived with the menus and the Palates paused to study the day's offerings.

'Oysters!' exclaimed Tom. 'Do they sell?'

'Yes, we shift quite a few,' I replied. 'They're Pacifics, not Natives.'

'That's all right. Sally and I threw a party at home for seventy-five people and no one touched them. I ate as many as I could and had to chuck the rest out.'

Between the two of them, they ordered nine dishes: four starters (seared salmon with a spice crust, glazed crab and saffron tart, sea bream and leek terrine, and the oysters); two main courses (braised shoulder of lamb with thyme and garlic, and braised ox tongue with gherkins and mash); and three puddings (steamed jam roll, vanilla blancmange with saffron syrup, and baked egg custard tart with nutmeg ice cream). I left them to it. Half-way through lunch, I went down to the kitchen to see Chef.

'How's it going?' I asked.

'Fine,' replied Phil. 'But they're not messing around, are they? I mean look at their order!'

Later we joined the two Great Palates for coffee, anxious for their verdict. I think we passed muster. Jim did not say much but looked mellow and satisfied, nodding approval. Tom raved about the saffron syrup with his blancmange. It was gone four when they left.

Apart from this bright interlude, it has been a frustrating week – principally because Gill, my sainted secretary, has taken a week's holiday. And when Gill's away I never seem to get anything worthwhile done. Still, the hotel has been screamingly busy with meetings, dinners and a rather tiresome shooting party. Occupancies have touched 100 per cent and the latest figures have broken new records. Mustn't complain. Only a few years ago – in the pit of the recession – I'd drive to work and find our car park empty. Now I'm lucky to find a space.

John Lock, the builder, has finished the work on Minstrels and both he and 'Her Indoors' have ended up the best of friends. We are all agreed that the pink and juniper green scheme is very fetching. Louise has also completed the first of her winter crop of bedroom refurbishments. The new-look Room 65 is back in commission and seems to have caused a stir with the staff, who always look forward to inspecting Louise's new interiors and never shy from passing judgement. In the case of Room 65, the choice of wallpaper in the bathroom has been declared – pretty well unanimously as far as I can make out – ghastly. It is certainly 'different', which probably explains the shock-horror reverberating around the corridors, serveries and offices. The offending paper is a rich and exotic design of tropical fish. Future residents of Room 65 are unlikely to forget it – either in love or in hate. I love it. And if people choose to hate it that's fine by me. I'd rather be remembered than forgotten.

The other great work to have reached completion this week (at last) is the town centre enhancement scheme. Opinion has been no less controversial than Room 65. The correspondence columns of the *Somerset County Gazette* today are full of hate-mail. Once again, Louise and I seem to be in the minority. We approve – and I wrote to Ol'Waffles to pat him on the back.

11 November 1996

Dear Jefferson,

TOWN CENTRE ENHANCEMENT

No – this is not a complaint!
I am so impressed with the 'new look' town centre that I feel moved to write to tell you so. I think it is beautiful – indeed, much more attractive than I ever expected or the plans indicated.
Warmest congratulations to you and your great vision.
With my very best wishes.

Yours sincerely,

C H G Chapman
Managing Director

Saturday, 16 November 1996

An entertaining news story appeared on the front page of today's *Daily Telegraph* under the headline 'COLLEGE'S BLACK-TIE TV DINNER CAUSES OUTBREAK OF RED FACES'

> A university college has been hit by an outbreak of acute embarrassment – and dozens of students and staff by gastro-enteritis – shortly after the BBC's Food and Drink programme cooked a three-course dinner there. Dr Geoffrey Welsh, of Durham University health centre, said he had had many cases of stomach upsets since the meal on Tuesday...
> Some suspect the oyster soup, chosen to fuel the libidos of the students whose names had been put into a hat and then paired off with a blind date for the meal, the theme of which was 'romance'.
> James Martin, chef at the Hotel du Vin and Bistro in Winchester, Hants, chose the menu for the black-tie dinner...
> Mr Martin, one of Britain's best up-and-coming chefs, insisted yesterday that the oysters were innocent...
> The college of St Hild and St Bede hosted the meal in its dining hall and it was filmed for television...
> Peter Bazalgette, the executive producer of the series, said: 'I've been assured by the university that some students not at the meal have gone down with the bug so I'm sure it can't have been the oysters. I think they're being rather over-sensitive about the whole thing.'

The ridiculous producer I spoke to two weeks ago has had his comeuppance.

MIND GAMES AND MAGIC

SUNDAY, 24 NOVEMBER 1996

W E SEEM TO BE a target for hotel inspectors at the moment: last week *The Good Food Guide* and on Tuesday evening a visit by Malcolm Gage, the RAC's chief scout. My relations with these people have never been easy and occasionally they become quite turbulent. At some point in my long life at the Castle I have waged war with each one of them. Earlier this year it was the turn of the RAC, who decided to strip us of our Blue Ribbon: a prestigious badge, similar to the AA's red stars, awarded to a select collection of the best hotels within their star classification.

Too often hotels – particularly ones with established track records – fall foul of dumb inquisitors who are content to write-off a place on the strength of one, maybe two, random visits based on shallow judgements which betray all grasp of the nature of the beast they are charged with assessing. In the case of our precious Blue Ribbon, judge, jury and executioner came in the shape of a Mr McKenzie, a 'senior inspector', who condemned us in a report he filed after a visit in March. When I was notified of our fall from grace, I appealed to the RAC's chairman, Jeffrey Rose, who has known the Castle for many years.

28 March 1996

Dear Jeffrey,

BLUE RIBBON

… I feel compelled to write following the visit of one of your senior inspectors, Mr McKenzie … overall, his comments were a catalogue of quibbles and nit-picks which clearly betray an ignorance of what the Castle Hotel is about and what we stand for … let me give you some examples of what I mean:

1. A porter carried his bags but failed to carry Mr McKenzie's briefcase!
2. There was no personalised letter of welcome.
3. We did not provide fruit, mineral water or flowers in the room.
4. There were no canapés offered with his pre-dinner drink.
5. His bread and butter pudding was 'flavourless and soggy'.

The Castle is not a bijou country house hotel. We are a town centre hotel and from Monday to Thursday our clients tend to be businessmen/women. This should not preclude us from Blue Ribbon status, but, inevitably, we do tailor our service to the businessman/woman during week days. It seems to me that Mr McKenzie should be assessing the Castle more in the context of the needs and demands of our clientele. So, in response to the above I would comment as follows:

1. We carried Mr McKenzie's bags but we find that most businessmen prefer to hang on to their own briefcases.
2. Most of the best hotels in the world do **not** provide 'personalised' letters of welcome in their bedrooms. To do so for the 36 rooms at the Castle

would be utterly impractical.

3. To my certain knowledge, the Savoy, Claridges, the Berkeley and the Connaught do not put personalised letters in their rooms. Neither do these hotels provide fruit and flowers automatically.

4. Correct. We do not provide canapés on week days but do so on Friday and Saturday evenings. However, all our guests are offered almonds (roasted with sea salt and honey) and luxury olives with their pre-dinner drinks. In the Cocktail Bars of the Savoy Company, you are offered homemade crisps (if you want canapés you order them and pay for them).

5. As you know, I eat lunch or dinner at the Castle almost every day. ('*Le patron mange ici*!') Bread and butter pudding happens to be a particular favourite of mine. To describe it as 'flavourless and soggy' is inaccurate to put it mildly! Our B and B wobbles – shimmering sensually on the plate – oozing creaminess and a hint of nutmeg. There is no better in the land.

On a more positive note, may I now list what we have done at the Castle over the past 15 months:

1. 16 bedrooms have been completely refurbished.

2. We have opened our new Penthouse Suite and Roof Garden. It is magnificent. The views to the Quantock Hills impressive. You can even see the scoreboard at the County Cricket Ground.

3. All our bedrooms are now equipped with satellite television.

4. Our Rose Room is being completely refurbished in the first two weeks of April.

5. I have hired a new restaurant manager (at some considerable cost!), so that in future Mr McKenzie will get his toothpick if he asks for one! (Yes, on the evening of 12 March, we failed him miserably on this point!) Our new man starts on 10 April and his CV is peppered with stints at five-star hotels and Michelin-rosetted restaurants.

In short, we are making huge efforts to win back our Blue Ribbon – but, if Mr McKenzie's report is anything to go by, it is unlikely that we shall ever satisfy the RAC.

I am sorry to sound so grumpy about your inspectors but sometimes I despair of them!

With my best wishes,
Ever hopeful.

C H G Chapman
Managing Director

Jeffrey Rose's reply was suitably sympathetic and conciliatory. Although there was nothing he could do about our Blue Ribbon, he promised to arrange a meeting between me and his chief inspector. And so, on Wednesday morning, I met Mr Gage. Inevitably, I had prepared myself for a difficult interview, but when we shook hands, he took the wind out of my sails. Munching his bacon and egg in the dining room, Mr Gage rose to his feet as I approached his table and disarmed me instantly with a warm avuncular smile. I had barely introduced myself and he was pumping my hand. 'Perfect,' exclaimed the chief inspector. 'It's been a lovely stay. Your staff are so charming and helpful. And dinner last night was superb. My goodness you've got a good chef.' Such enthusiasm – so early in the morning – took me by surprise. I thanked him and we agreed to meet at half-past nine.

The outcome of our tête-à-tête could not have been happier. Mr Gage assured me that he had no hesitation in recommending the restoration of our Blue Ribbon in the 1998 edition of his guide. Although this now means a year in the wilderness, honour has been done and we are friends again. What a game! And all as a consequence of one over-zealous, power-mad inspector who struck us off for not carrying his briefcase and failing to provide him with a toothpick.

Yet this is the game any ambitious hotel has to play these days. Our clients are getting more demanding and difficult, not less. *Attention to detail* is the mantra we chant and success relies on our ability to respond to their wishes. Even when we do, it may not be enough. A carefully planned, well organized, perfectly executed party is no guarantee of a satisfied customer. Any number of complex human ingredients may intervene: mood, prejudice, fear, personal taste, class snobbery, social inadequacy, megalomania, a row with the wife, the death of a pet. Take your pick, mix any cocktail of human nature you like, call it emotional baggage and we have to deal with it. Worse still, as likely as not our dear client often won't really know what he wants. Even if he thinks he does, his instructions to us will not always be in the best interests of his guests, in spite of our advice and polite warnings. A bloody-minded host or party organizer can be a menace and if things go wrong, we take the rap.

A month after the event, I have at last discovered the real cause of the trouble at that one table at the National Trust dinner when five guests spent much of the evening complaining, ending with the pot of coffee in Mrs Lynn's lap. I have now heard from Mr Lynn whose solicitors, he tells me, have advised him not to take any action as 'the matter would not be justified in view of the costs involved.' I would have thought he could have worked that one out for himself. Mr Lynn goes on to say: 'With regard to the incident, I feel that the table was overcrowded, due to eleven people on one side, and this did not help the person serving coffee.' In my reply to his letter, I sympathized with Mr Lynn's comment. Far too many people *were* crammed on to his table. We knew perfectly well the seating arrangements would be uncomfortable and we told the organizer. But the organizer knew better and refused to change the table plan.

The trick, of course, is to win the confidence of the host. To do that it helps to understand the customer and sometimes that can be like reading tea leaves. Any company or organization throwing a party in a smart hotel is doing it to impress and to influence. Pleasure is, hopefully, the pay-off the guest enjoys – but it is not the reason for the occasion. Our job then is to make the client look good and to fill his guests with a warm glow so that at the end of the evening everyone trips off to bed feeling happy and thinking wonderful thoughts about the host and his firm. So what does that make us? What do we have to be to make it happen? Not just efficient, caring, sensitive managers. We're in the mind game – part psychology, part clairvoyance. We're in the business of making magic.

Last Wednesday, the Western Provident Association held its annual Chairman's Dinner, an important do for thirty-six local hot-shots and, to us, a big deal for a number of reasons. WPA is a major account, one of our most valuable clients, worth thousands and never easily pleased. The key man is the Association's chief executive, Julian Stainton, a tough customer whom the tabloid press once exposed as the 'boss from hell' because of the unusual demands he inflicts on his employees. Among his more eccentric obsessions is an aversion to potted plants in the workplace, which he regards as a dangerous distraction. To this end, when WPA's new offices were built on the fringes of Taunton, horizontal window ledges were banned in favour of 45 degree surfaces. Mr Stainton, then, is a very particular man and, love him or hate him, he runs a highly successful business.

This year's Chairman's Dinner was particularly tricky because a new man had been appointed to the post: a distinguished general no less, Sir John Wilsey, the Commander-in-Chief of UK Land Forces based in Wiltshire. Unlike his predecessor, who enjoyed his visits to the Castle, Sir John is a man who prefers to avoid hotel beds if he can reasonably return to his own. And as he invariably travels by helicopter, this is normally the case. Nevertheless, there was a suggestion that this year's dinner might take place at an hotel nearer his home as on this occasion he was being accompanied by his wife. But Julian Stainton – good man – persuaded him in favour of the Castle in spite of the journey. We were delighted but, equally, the unspoken signals flying out of Julian's office were crystal clear. We decoded them and went on red alert.

Planning this dinner began in September, but after a series of meetings we realized that our biggest problem was neither the food nor the service but the room in which the party was to be held. The Monmouth works well for large dinners of eighty or ninety people, but for thirty-six it is like a draughty barn. As our other private dining rooms are too small, there was no choice and we were faced with the challenge of creating a sense of intimacy in an impossibly large room, the more imposing for its tall ceiling.

There are many subtle, complex variables that conspire to make a successful dinner party: the food, the wine, the service, the company, the atmosphere. Except for the company, an hotel controls them all – indeed, if you get these elements right and strike the right balance, even the dullest gathering of guests can be made to sparkle. Our problem with the WPA dinner was the atmosphere. Get that wrong and we were dead. Somehow we had to transform the Monmouth Room into a space that deceived reality, that engaged a mood of good cheer and well-being. Bluntly, we needed to conjure an atmosphere which incited people to have a good time. And, not least, we needed to make Julian Stainton look good in the presence of his new chairman.

So how did we do it? Part of the answer was to reduce the impression of size by scattering furniture taken from other parts of the hotel around the perimeter of the room. This drew in the walls and softened the edges. But the real focus was on the long table down the centre. We needed to create an illusion of intimacy by diverting attention away from the high ceiling. To achieve this, the only answer was candlelight – lots of it. Louise and I raided the family silver and adorned the table with six candelabra, each piece fixed with three tall candles. The effect was stunning.

Come the evening, the guests gathered in the Penthouse for their drinks. I arrived at about a quarter to eight but before going upstairs to greet everyone, my first instinct, as always, was to double-check a number of small details. The first is to study the guest list and the table plan. I have terrible difficulty remembering the names of people I am expected to know and with whom I am usually supposed to be on first-name terms. For all the bluffing I do, it is still a problem and it has landed me in trouble in the past. Inevitably, WPA's guest list included a host of acquaintances and local customers who would expect to be recognized. A quick glance at the seating plan just saves me from the wag who fixes me with a stare and brays, 'You've forgotten who I am! Haven't you?'

In the Monmouth Room I walked slowly round the table checking each place setting. I picked up a menu card. Suddenly, reading down the list of dishes, alarm bells started ringing inside my head. The main course was roast spiced duck breast with apricots and green peppercorns. The ghost of Lady Armstrong and her disastrous experiences with our roast duck returned to haunt me. Whenever I see it on a function menu, I tremble with paranoia – and this week Phil was away shooting in Yorkshire. I went straight to the kitchen to see his sous-chef, Keith Short.

'What are the ducks like?' I asked.

'Beautiful,' he replied. 'No problem.'

'How are you cooking them? On or off the bone?'

'Off the bone,' he said defensively, sensing my agitation. 'I discussed it with Chef and that's how he told me to do it, because it's a big party.'

'OK!' I said. 'If that's what Chef told you, that's what you do. But for God's sake don't undercook those breasts – just a hint of pink – and make sure they are well rested.'

I turned on my heel and leapt up the kitchen stairs, leaving poor Keith stunned by my injunctions. I hate these birds being roasted off the bone, and Phil knows it. I just happen to believe it's wrong – but for a large party it would be impractical to cook them any other way.

By now it was nearly eight o'clock – time to show my face in the Penthouse. I paused before going in to get an instant reading on the noise level. A strange thing to do, perhaps, but like sniffing a wine before drinking it, you get a pretty good impression of the character and mood of a party just by putting an ear to the door. The noise coming out of the drawing room was fruity, full-bodied and lively. When I went in Julian greeted me like a best friend and introduced me to his new Chairman and Lady Wilsey. A waiter handed me a drink and I worked my way round the room. At 8.15 Simon Girling announced dinner and the guests made their way downstairs to the Monmouth Room. The table looked fantastic – festooned with flowers, the silver glittering in the reflected candlelight. The pleasure on people's faces was palpable and I knew we had cracked it … Save for the duck. I had to check the duck! Back in the kitchen, the breasts were all laid out on trays resting. I asked Keith to carve me a sliver to taste. It was perfect. Cooked *à point*, it was moist, tender and packed with flavour. If I had a complaint, I felt that the nutmeg in the spicing was a little overwhelming, but that didn't bother me. The British palate enjoys well spiced food and I was confident the party would love it.

On Friday, I received a letter from Julian. '… a quite remarkable evening,' he wrote. '… the time and effort invested in creating the appropriate atmosphere in the Monmouth Room was very much appreciated.' We had read the signals and delivered. But what the 'boss from hell' failed to notice was the potted plants gracing the corners of the room.

Friday was also the moment I was required to do my good turn for the BBC's *Children in Need* Appeal at the Octagon Theatre in Yeovil, Frances Kitchen and I acting as host-cum-judges in the *Ready Teddy … Cook* competition. In spite of my earlier misgivings, I rather enjoyed it, persuading myself to go with the flow and ignore the shambolic organization which was none of my business anyway. It also dawned on me that the yellow teddy at the press call in October was not Rupert Bear but a character called Pudsey, the Appeal's cuddly mascot.

The show was scheduled to go out live on the BBC's regional radio network at 10.30 in the morning. I arrived in Yeovil in good time only to find the theatre car park jammed with coaches and minibuses disgorging schoolchildren and old people with their minders. Eventually, I was so desperate I took the last space in the Manor Hotel's car park nearby – a rude practice we discourage at the Castle by clamping non-patrons and fining them fifteen pounds.

Back stage I met Frances, who introduced me to the nervous contestants – three teams of two: a pair of schoolboys, two schoolgirls and a middle-aged couple wearing the green and white strip of Yeovil Town Football Club. One small detail seemed to have escaped the organizers. There was only one mike. So when the curtain rose I hitched myself to Frances's apron strings and for the next hour we paraded about the set like inseparable lovers. As the contestants assembled their dishes, we picked and tasted and enthused about the deliciousness of the food. How we sustained this endless, breathless banter and culinary repartee for so long is beyond me. It was a relief when time was called. Then, in the semi-darkness of the wings, we conferred over the finished plates and decided to award first prize to the Yeovil Town soccer fans for their salad of Dorset blue cheese, pears and walnuts, and their apple and cider brandy tarts. In a gesture of political generosity, we declared the schoolchildren equal second. When we announced the results, Pudsey Bear – sweating pints inside his hairy costume – hugged the winners and we all went home feeling very satisfied.

Minstrels Thaws Out

Saturday, 7 December 1996

RESPLENDENT IN ITS NEW exterior livery, Minstrels was relaunched this week. Our estimable local organ, the *Somerset County Gazette*, heralded the event with a whole page of editorial supported by advertisements placed by our suppliers. We announced the appointment of a new chef, an enthusiastic young talent called Simon Garbutt, and we published Phil Vickery's new bistro-style menu, branding it boldly with his credentials as head chef at the Castle and culinary idol of the small screen.

For me, the revamp of our pub strikes an ironic note, revealing an embarrassing flaw (until now) in my own beliefs about 'good food'. For the last twenty years – since I joined the family firm in 1976 – Minstrels has been the Cinderella of our business. We've milked it for all its worth as a town centre boozer while most of the love and effort was lavished on the hotel. Gastronomically, Minstrels had become a dinosaur. Much of the catering relied on Brake Bros, well known purveyors of the frozen, the packaged and the microwavable. Nasty, acidic sauces came pre-packaged in little sachets which exploded all over your fingers. Star turns included deep-frozen breaded fillets of plaice served with (frozen) 'French fries' a pair of grotesque sausages suffering from terminal anaemia, a chicken curry, that ubiquitous pub staple the 'ploughman's platter, and a range of mean, soggy sandwiches as predictable as tinned tuna. The menu, offered only at lunchtime, was dirt cheap, and our punters – shoppers and pensioners mostly – were faithful and uncomplaining. Given the great gastronomic endeavour next door, I confess that our attitude to the food we dished up was shamefully cynical. But we prospered, happy to leave well alone. Besides, the real money was made in 'wet sales', particularly at night when the youth of the town pile in like canned sardines to have their ear-drums hammered by live bands. Ideas of serving food in the evenings have long since been abandoned. After dark the big attraction is the crush, the noise and the throb of testosterone. But while the gigs continue to fuel liquor sales, over the past year our lunch trade has wilted. And not before time. One of the most exciting trends of the nineties has been the rise of the pub-restaurant: the local where a decent plate of food matters as much as a decent pint of beer. Minstrels had become a gasping relic of the old, complacent pub culture.

Now, there is a poignant tale in this re-fashioning of Minstrels. Coincidentally, this has also been the week Louise and I celebrated twenty-five years of marriage, one of those startling moments in life when the passage of time suddenly hits you and inspires a need for reflection and reminiscence. Do you remember how it was?, we asked ourselves. And at the Castle Hotel, how it was pretty much like Minstrels except with posher accents. On one side of the wall, the kitchen changed radically – we modernized, won laurels, became famous – while on the other side the old formula stuck, grew tired and eventually decomposed.

When Louise and I got engaged we both lived and worked in London. She had never been to Taunton and on her first visit – to meet my parents in the spring of 1971 – dinner on the Friday of our arrival was an experience she will never forget. The memory of it makes me groan, but twenty-five years ago the Castle's restaurant was pretty much the standard in most respectable provincial hotel dining rooms. In other words, the food was unremarkable – even for those days – and we fell in and out of *The Good Food Guide* with nervous regularity. For my father, the cellar was far more important than the kitchen. As a young advertising man who ran up the most outrageous expenses eating in London's best restaurants, I never understood how he could match his magnificent wine list with the dismal menus of his chefs. But then the chefs were not necessarily responsible for the cooking. This was the age of the *flambé*, the silver lamp with the fierce blue flame that gave you steak Diane and crêpes Suzette. The age of the pan-wielding *maître d'hôtel* who'd thrill you by setting the place on fire. The age when chefs were skivvies not celebrities.

On that Friday evening in 1971, the *maître d'hôtel* at the Castle was fat John, an Irish rogue whose black tails and breath reeked of tobacco and beer. His staff were a gaggle of middle-aged housewives in black skirts, white pinnies and starched caps. The room was brown and every table was numbered with a little plastic tent. 'What is this place?' thought Louise. 'Whom am I marrying?' Fat John rolled into view clutching his pad in his podgy fingers. My fiancée, wisely, decided to keep it simple and chose from the grills: lamb cutlets, tomato, mushrooms. I, less wisely, ordered an *escalope de veau Holstein*, a banal assembly of breaded veal and ham topped with a fried egg. My father ordered a bottle of claret. When the food arrived the tips of the bones on Louise's desiccated cutlets were wrapped in dainty paper frills and the edges of the fried egg on my escalope were singed to a crisp.

Five years later, when we moved to Somerset, I was set to sweep all this ghastliness into the swill bin. But it took time – far longer than I expected – and I was still a novice in the trade, innocent of the complexities of running an ambitious restaurant. Arthur Mansfield, the chef at the time, was an idle slob whom I fired. He took me to an industrial tribunal and, to my immense pleasure, lost his case. The next incumbent couldn't stand the heat in a kitchen aiming for the stars and he had to go. The third chef, an Anton Mosimann protégé from the Dorchester, showed great promise but the man drank. On New Year's Eve, he head-butted his sous-chef, so I fired him too. It was not until 1983 that I got the hang of this game and, eventually, made my first successful appointment in Chris Oakes. The following year we won our precious Michelin star, which Gary Rhodes inherited and held when he succeeded Oakes in 1986. Then, in 1990, came Vickery and, in spite of the painful years of recession, we now seem to have matured into a self-confident restaurant which has, at last, established an easy rapport with a growing and more sophisticated clientele.

It has taken me twenty years to arrive at this state of grace. But the real irony, the real twist to this tale, is not that we changed the culinary ethos of the Castle's kitchen while ignoring the food in Minstrels. No, no. I was right to leave Minstrels alone and commercially foolish to re-cast the menus in the restaurant. For all the accolades we won – in Michelin, *The Good Food Guide*, Egon Ronay and the AA – for all the publicity these awards attracted, they did nothing for the business (nor the wages bill) of a provincial town centre hotel whose punters would have been much happier tucking into avocado prawns, a steak and crêpes Suzette on a Saturday night. So why did I do it? Vanity, pride, ego – all those things – but most of all because life for me would have been soulless if I couldn't enjoy the food of my own restaurant.

We were ahead of our time. But time had caught up. And what we began to do twenty years ago in the hotel will be translated more easily in Minstrels. The new menu has only been running six days, too early to arrive at any firm conclusions, but the week's results look promising and, predictably, first reactions have been mixed. On the one hand, sales have leapt by over 40 per cent (averaging eighty to a hundred covers a day) and on the other, I have received a flurry of complaints (the first in twenty years!) mourning the passing of the old menu. A letter from a Mrs Irene Warner of Eastgate Gardens, Taunton, was typical: '*Dear Mr Chapman,*' she wrote. '*It was with great sadness that my friend and I said Goodbye to the Minstrels Restaurant today. We are two elderly ladies who have had lunch there most Tuesdays for the last three years. I admit we are conservative in our tastes so were totally unprepared for your new menu. My friend enjoys salads – but not Caesars …. My deep-fried gurnard was not a patch on my normal plaice and the thin chips left much to be desired. Whilst I can understand your desire to introduce new dishes I feel you would be well advised to stick to some of the old ones. We were not the only diners who said we would not be coming back … Thank you for the last 3 years – we shall now look for somewhere else to eat on Tuesdays.'*

My reply to Mrs Warner was properly solicitous but I doubt I brought her much comfort. Her comment about the gurnard is a classic illustration of the state of the British palate, at least as it was until a younger middle class discovered real food with the help of Delia and Sainsbury's. But for Mrs Warner and her friend, there was no contest between a fresh gurnard and a frozen plaice, real chips and industrialized 'fries'. Years of Birdseye bliss had seduced their taste-buds into accepting the frozen pap as the real thing. As for gurnard, what's a gurnard when it's at home? Weeks before, when Phil and I discussed the menu, we debated the wisdom of being too up-front with our menu nomenclature. Unfamiliar beasts like gurnard and pollack will be a turn-off, I argued. Let's not confuse them. After all, fish'n'chips is fish'n'chips and fishcakes is fishcakes. In the end honesty and principle prevailed – and, so far, the evidence suggests we were right not to fudge the issue on the menu. These two items are among the top sellers of the week, along with the braised shin of beef and the spicy sausages, onion rings and mash. The results, however, confirm the Tauntonian's innate conservatism and lingering xenophobia. While the beef sales show that no one round here gives a toss about BSE, Mrs Warner's friend was not alone in giving the Caesar salad the thumbs down. We sold two portions in six days, the other major failures being the chorizo sausage (eight portions) and the gravadlax (three portions). The only 'foreigner' to find any favour with our dear locals was the pasta dish (twenty-one portions) which, at least, suggests that the Italomania sweeping across Britain at the moment has not completely bypassed Taunton.

All-in-all not a bad start; the figures look good but in the coming weeks I suspect we shall have to tweak the menu. Vickery agrees. Indeed, the only argument we have had is over the style of his *frites*. He has this obsession about leaving the skins on the potatoes, which lends a slightly bitter taste to the chips and gives them a grubby appearance when they should look pale gold. 'Minstrels is a pub,' he says. 'The chips are gorgeous! And it saves us money doing them this way.'

'Yes, yes,' I say. 'Just add 10p to the price and give me chips like the Ivy. It'll make all the difference and we'll sell more.'

The only other problem that bothers me is a hard core of regular drinkers who sit nursing their pints when the tables could be used for lunchers. Like the pensioners, they will have to move on. That's the price of change.

NO SIGN AT THE INN

CHRISTMAS – or what this pagan age numbingly calls the 'festive season' – is upon us. Its approach is like a stalking vampire and as the final days close in, the dread of it – there poised to draw blood – consumes us with a strange, irrational madness. I hate it for all its bogusness and even our bleating tills, calling up loadsa money we wouldn't otherwise earn, are no palliative. For this hotel, and any other I guess, Christmas is a season of frenzy and stress through which we are obliged to wear a mask of comfort and joy. For that is our duty. You pays your money, you gets your dose of goodwill. But behind the green baize door, there is a weird pathology that seems to grip us at this time of year; a subversive syndrome that only surfaces at Christmas, that is triggered by Christmas, that is utterly alien to the spirit of Christmas. Demons that lie dormant all year rise up and cause terrible mischief. Mild, inconsequent irritations inflate like balloons and explode into rows. Obedient computers misbehave. Nasty viruses strike down key staff on the busiest nights. Jealousies rage. Sexual indiscretion is rife. Humanity is pottier than at any other time.

At this particular moment, as I write these words hidden away in my attic study at home, Louise is below me in her studio quietly tying dozens of red and gold butterfly bows for the hotel's Christmas tree. This twenty foot monster – to be erected tomorrow – will reach up the stairwell from the hall to the first floor. It is a wondrous sight and over the years it has become a local legend. Every Christmas the citizens of Taunton, those who would not otherwise set foot in the place, come in to gawp, pass judgement and pass away until another year. It is a tradition. For the moment – half past eight in the evening – we are at peace, each one at our work benches sipping a glass of wine and doing our thing. Tomorrow will be different. Tomorrow will be a day of frantic activity as the Castle Hotel casts off its mufti and dresses for the festive pantomime. The revolving doors will be unhinged and a small platoon of porters will bear in the great tree to plant it in a dustbin, leaving Louise to hang her ribbons, beads and ornaments while others wreathe the prickly conifer with a chain of starry illuminations. This annual ritual may sound straightforward – but it isn't.

Louise has her method and each year she selects her helpers, usually from the housekeeping department. There are no special qualifications demanded in this selection process other than a simple requirement that the chosen individuals be companionable. Let it not be said that Louise has her favourites. She just finds some members of staff more agreeable than others – a perfectly good reason, it seems to me, for choosing her helpers. Besides, as it takes the best part of a day to dress the tree and decorate the hotel, someone has to cover the cleaning and servicing of the bedrooms. Nevertheless, this momentary state of domestic apartheid whips up a squall upstairs and the decision on who will or will not be seconded to tree duty is only resolved after a tense negotiation between Louise and Alison Brown, the head housekeeper.

This year, however, and long before the day set for the grand ceremonial of our Christmas illumination, there was another problem. As I have said, the Castle Hotel's tree has acquired a special place in the hearts of the townspeople. Like a much-loved local landmark, they have made it their own and, as such, we are honour bound to uphold the tradition. We cannot disappoint. The big problem this year was not in the decorating arrangements for tomorrow, but in finding a decent tree to erect at all: one of the right height, width, shape and bushiness. So, six weeks ago, Louise put in her order with Monkton Elm, a garden centre just outside Taunton, leaving the manager a precise specification of the tree she wanted. On Sunday, she went to Monkton Elm to inspect the goods. To her horror, she found no tree and an unapologetic manager whose story was that his supplier had failed to deliver. All he could offer was a tree 'round the back'. When Louise set eyes on it, she blew. The man had been given plenty of notice to find our tree and now he was demanding £150 for a forlorn and withered specimen in an advanced stage of mange.

With three days to go, we were now in a state of crisis. Large Christmas trees of the quality we need do not, well, fall off trees. The manager knew it and decided to push his luck. 'Do you want to pull out of the deal?' he challenged. Louise was so enraged by the cheek of the man, she told him what he could do with his tree and made off to St John's, the only other garden centre in the area of any consequence. As she drove in, panic welling up inside her, she spotted a trailer bearing *the perfect tree*. Better still, it was still for sale. And, best of all, the asking price was a modest £50.

WEDNESDAY, 11 DECEMBER 1996

The work is done. But not without incident. Worse, it did not take us long to fall foul of our duty as innkeepers where – let us remind ourselves – 'hospitality' might pass as a secular expression of the Christmas message. Giving? Goodwill? These virtues were in short supply this morning. Mind you, they weren't that evident two thousand years ago and ever since the curmudgeonly innkeeper has received a bad press.

Christmas at the Castle, 1978. Three generations of Chapmans

All was going swimmingly until about nine o'clock, when the progress of the great tree into the hall and its erection up the stairwell coincided with the arrival of thirty-odd delegates for a management seminar in the Monmouth Room. The organizer of the seminar – as we soon discovered – was a precise and humourless man who took his job with a grim earnestness. Years of experience had taught him that the first thing delegates want when they arrive at an hotel is a large sign with a large arrow pointing the way to the seminar room. The size, the style and the atmosphere of the hotel make no difference. That the Castle is small and personal, the Monmouth Room no more than a hop and skip up one flight of stairs, were aspects of today's 'venue' that did not mitigate his tubular vision on this matter. But the truth of today was also that Mr Seminar was our *guest* – and, for a moment, we wilfully abandoned a cardinal virtue of our trade by forgetting just that.

The trouble began when Mr Seminar decided that there was only one place for his signpost: at the foot of the staircase right in front of the Christmas tree. I loathe these notices at the best of times. We are not a Hilton or a Posthouse where displays of this kind are a useful embellishment to their stark and sterile foyers. Corporate logos in our antique and gracious hall are, for me, worse than graffiti. But I've learned to be tolerant – that is until today. The sheer crassness of Mr Seminar's gesture went beyond my tolerance and, besides, the position of the sign made it impossible for Louise to decorate the tree. So she told him to remove it.

Half-an-hour later word filtered back that our guest was a deeply unhappy man. 'I don't feel welcome in this place,' he grumbled to Martin, the porter. 'It's going down in my report to Head Office.' I decided to intercede on Louise's behalf.

'I'm terribly sorry, sir,' I pleaded, trying to sound conciliatory. 'The last thing we want is to make you feel unwelcome but, as you can see, my wife is decorating the Christmas tree this morning.'

Mr Seminar then gave me the benefit of his long experience on the importance of signposting but he accepted my apology and promised to omit any reference to his unfriendly reception from his report. I then made the mistake of trying to humour him. 'I've told my wife that I'll divorce her if she does it again,' I said flippantly.

Shortly after, Louise went to see him to make her peace. 'Oh yes,' he said sympathetically. 'Don't worry, I quite understand. I didn't mean to come between you and your husband. But if he's divorcing you, my sister's a good lawyer if you need one!'

WEDNESDAY, 18 DECEMBER 1996

The Christmas carousel spins on, faster and faster. I'm dizzy with the effort and the angst – and the irritation of time wasted dealing with sack-loads of Christmas cards from people I don't know, people on the make and people with indecipherable signatures. I suppose I must have received over three hundred so far, of which perhaps a couple of dozen are from family and friends. Meanwhile, the hotel is vibrating deafeningly to the throb of private parties and corporate schmooze. And then poor Andrew went down with flu, which laid him out for three days (rekindling dreadful, unspoken fears of a return of his disease), but the staff have been commendably cheerful under the strain. Still, with a week to go, the pressure is beginning to show and this is when things can go wrong.

Sometimes I wish I were a soap manufacturer; so much easier to control the quality of the 'product'. How, I ask myself, do you control the quality of the hospitality 'product'? 'Training' cry the pundits; you've got to 'invest in people'. Trite phrases like 'skills development' and 'customer care' have become a huge growth industry. These notions may be very worthy but they have their limitations. Machines are designed to do what they are told but human beings in the happiness trade are not a production line. How do you program humans in the art of *savoir faire*? How do you train people in 'customer care' to cover every tiny 'interface' (ghastly word) that may arise? You can't – no matter how hard you work at it. And we reckon we are pretty good.

My simple philosophy has always been more attitudinal than prescriptive. We are in the pleasure business, I say. So always be positive, always try to say *yes* to any reasonable request. Never say *no*. Even if you mean *no*, make it sound as if you are saying *yes* by suggesting an alternative. Be enthusiastic, show a little charm, always smile, and your guests will fall into line and love you for ever. The effects of this attitude are twofold. First, your guests will believe you really care about them. And second, you will, as likely as not, sell them on an attractive idea that hadn't occurred to them. A little kindness works miracles (and is good for business). But get one stressed member of staff – especially at Christmas – and the cup of human kindness runs dry.

The other day I was passing through the hall at lunchtime when I overheard a conversation between a receptionist and a middle-aged lady weighed down with her Christmas shopping.

'Could I order some sandwiches in the bar?' asked the woman politely.

'I'm sorry, madam,' replied the receptionist. 'We don't serve sandwiches in the Rose Room, but you could go to Minstrels round the corner.'

'Well, no,' said the woman, 'I'd rather not do that. It'll be too crowded and I'm here with my elderly mother to see the Christmas tree. Surely you can serve us a sandwich?'

'No,' insisted my receptionist. 'It's not our policy.'

'Why ever not?' said the woman indignantly. 'This is the Castle Hotel. I can't believe you don't do sandwiches.'

'I know, madam, but it is management policy not to do sandwiches. That's why we've got Minstrels. The Rose Room is for lunch guests only.'

The woman gave in, picked up her carrier bags and headed for the bar where her mother was waiting. By this time I was seething. I introduced myself and apologized.

'Madam, I'm afraid it is true that we prefer not to serve sandwiches here – only to avoid a crush with people eating lunch. But if you and your mother would like to take a table in the restaurant, you do not have to choose from the main menu. At lunchtime, we also offer a terrific selection of light dishes which I think you would enjoy. A plate of smoked salmon or a nice salad. All you need have is one course. You will be comfortable and I think your mother would enjoy it. Let me show you the menu and introduce you to my restaurant manager who will look after you.'

It was an instant sale. A potential enemy became an immediate friend. Yet I despair of the thought that this brief confrontation between a guest and a member of staff was only rescued because I happened to be passing by. The receptionist had been caught off guard; she was harassed, preoccupied with other things. How often, I ask myself, does this happen? No amount of 'training' will prevent the occasional lapse in our proper devotions to our visitors. And, like the incident with Mr Seminar last week, Louise and I are as fallible as the rest of us.

Human fallibility is, at least, a forgivable sin. Theft is not. Christmas, it seems to me, is high season for taking as much as it is for giving. I was in Oxford Street yesterday where traffic wardens with megaphones were warning shoppers to beware of pickpockets. The Castle is not immune to this aspect of the festive spirit. Our Christmas decorations are a favourite target and Louise has been driven crazy repairing and restoring five trees she has installed in the hotel's function rooms and public areas. Only the big tree in the hall has been spared a mugging (so far). But the worst case of premeditated vandalism this year has been a raid on our gents loo, where the walls are hung with a set of spectacular prints of female nudes photographed by Patrick Lichfield. I am particularly proud of this collection of breathtakingly beautiful pictures, which were shot for the Unipart calendar in 1984 and given to me as a Christmas present by my brother-in-law.

At the time we were relocating our gents to another part of the hotel. It was a major refurbishment which, I felt, deserved a special effort in its decorative treatment. The Lichfield prints were a natural, so I had them mounted on silk and framed for the purpose. A grand gesture like this, I decided, called for a suitably grand loo warming party, which we held on 1 August 1984. I billed it as a celebration on the occasion of the 'First Flush' and Lord Lichfield, as guest of honour, agreed to perform this ceremonial duty. Guests included Egon Ronay, Fay Maschler, Miles Kington, Ann Leslie and Carol Thatcher (the only no-show and from whom I received no letter of apology). In all we were a party of twenty gastronomes, press and assorted diarists – the only deliberate omission being Nigel

Patrick Lichfield and me just before the 'First Flush', 1 August 1984

Dempster, who subsequently wrote a vitriolic letter to remind me, in his modest manner, that his page in the *Daily Mail* was 'the most prestigious column in English journalism'. Referring to his 'old pal Patrick Lichfield', he nevertheless wanted to stress that he was 'not angling for any invitation'. I was so flattered by Mr Dempster's interest that, for a while, I displayed his letter in one of the cubicles of the new loo.

Our guests were greeted in their bedrooms with specially commissioned miniature chamber-pots arranged with flowers. At 7.45 we mustered in the loo, where Louise had disguised the urinals with fabulous displays of sweet peas. Here was the most fragrant, the most elegant lavatory in history. And dangling over one of the cubicles was an ornate Victorian bell-pull. On cue, Lord Lichfield performed the 'First Flush'. With the aid of my general manager hidden within and primed to operate the sound system, the plumbing suddenly came alive with Handel's *Water Music*. Waiters entered with trays of champagne and the party was on its way.

The folly of this escapade inspired a rash of publicity. Good stuff, but I was also inviting trouble and within days I received letters of disgust from churchmen, feminists and bores. Worse, the first of my gorgeous pictures got nicked. Patrick kindly replaced it and we then had them all anchored to the walls. Now, thirteen Christmases on, some hooligan has succeeded in carrying off another. Once again, I have petitioned for a replacement.

My faith in humanity this Christmas, however, is not entirely lost. The one (true) symbol of this festival – ripe for the picking because it is so easy to steal – is a small wood and clay depiction of the Nativity on an old oak chest in the hall: the stable, the manger, all the dramatis personae of the Birth. We have had this collection of simple but engaging artefacts for as long as I recall. They have never been touched. This year, the scene has attracted the attention of one young waitress who told Louise that, perhaps, we should not place the Child in its crib until Christmas and that the progress of the kings and shepherds could be celebrated by moving the tiny clay characters towards the stable day by day. Hallelujah!

GHOST STORY

TUESDAY, CHRISTMAS EVE 1996

IT IS THREE IN THE AFTERNOON and the dogs have been walked. In a few hours our Christmas guests will be gathering for drinks in the hall; all candlelit, a dozen voices around the tree singing carols, Louise and I there to do our welcoming. This morning I signed sixty-five cards to the staff, enclosing a gift voucher for each one, as Louise sped from department to department giving presents. By now Andrew will have checked the arrivals list and held his final briefings. Trays of handmade chocolates and Turkish delight, wrapped in cellophane and tied with bows, will have been delivered to every bedroom with a note of greeting, the holiday menus and a wine list – the note asking guests to pre-order their wines before meals. A small but important administrative detail which avoids delay when they come to table.

Meanwhile, where would Christmas be without a ghost story? Oh yes, we have our ghosts, as one might expect of an ancient pile with a turbulent history stretching back to the age of Alfred (who burned his cakes nearby, at Athelney on the Levels) and Arthur, whose bones, with those of his Queen Guinevere, are said to be buried at Glastonbury. But the bloodiest moment in the Castle's history came in 1685 when the Duke of Monmouth, bastard son of Charles II, mustered his rebels in Taunton, proclaiming himself king on 20 June. Two weeks and two days later, at Sedgemoor, the last battle fought on English soil, the cause was lost and Monmouth was executed. Shortly after, James II despatched his Chief Justice, the murderous Judge Jeffreys, who held his 'Bloody Assizes' in the Great Hall of Taunton Castle. Thousands of Monmouth's followers were hung, their dismembered bodies publicly displayed, while the more fortunate were transported. The town became an open slaughterhouse of rotting human remains where only weeks before there had been a riotous celebration.

Walter Besant, the nineteenth-century author, tells how 'Monmouth's officers were heard roystering at the Castle Inn'. Legend has it that a fiddler entertained the men before they marched on Sedgemoor. And, like some dreadful reminder of our treachery, it is that fiddler who returns to haunt us still. Distinct feelings of a 'presence' have been more common than sightings, although night porters and maids have occasionally reported a tall figure in a long black cape appearing and vanishing in the vicinity of the bedrooms above Castle Bow, the oldest part of the hotel.

In recent years, our mysterious but perfectly benign musician seems to have become less active, while something or somebody new is taking great relish in causing mischief elsewhere – particularly on the third floor, an addition to the ancient structure built only in 1965. This presence is referred to simply as 'the poltergeist'. A strange characteristic of this new phenomenon is that he, she or it does not like change. If, for example, a room is redecorated or an item of furniture exchanged or new curtains hung, the poltergeist will show his, her or its displeasure by striking in a manner calculated to irritate and waste our time. A Hoover lying idle will rev up of its own accord and then fall silent. Lights in a room will fail irrationally, the fuse boxes intact. Water will dribble ominously from pipes bearing no evidence of leaks. Doors will slam violently on a windless day.

Last year, when Louise had completed the refurbishment of the Penthouse Suite, her most ambitious and expensive scheme, the poltergeist was livid. On the day of the Suite's first letting – to a wealthy American couple – the heavy front door closed and self-locked. The keys – to both the door and the security bolts – were nowhere to be found, neither were the spares. When the clients arrived, we made our excuses and entertained them to a cream tea in the Rose Room while our handyman and a locksmith, having failed to open the door, removed it entirely from its frame – an operation which took the best part of two hours.

Now, this Christmas, just three days ago, a Mr Jensen, a businessman visiting the hotel for the first time and occupying Room 119, reported an apparition at the end of his bed. Room 119 is on the third floor, at the end of the corridor immediately before the entrance to the Penthouse. It has not been redecorated in five years, so whether this happening was the poltergeist incarnate or whether this is an entirely new phenomenon again is open to conjecture. One thing we do know, it wasn't our seventeenth-century fiddler. Mr Jensen's vision was Regency.

On the morning after, Mr Jensen came down to breakfast, paid his bill and left. He certainly had no intention of reporting his bizarre experience and, besides, having enjoyed his visit he slipped a folder of the hotel's literature into his briefcase to read later. That evening, at home in Horsham, Mr Jensen told his wife the extraordinary events of the previous night. In the early hours of the morning, he had awakened for no apparent reason. Alert and sitting up, he glanced at his bedside clock and noted that it was 5.20 am. He then saw the figure of a young man wearing a yellow waistcoat, breeches and boots emerge from the bathroom. The youth stopped at the foot of the bed, smiled and bowed, and within seconds disappeared through the door.

When Mr Jensen finished his story, his wife started to read the literature he had brought home. An historical note running to four pages includes a description of the hotel in the early years of the nineteenth century written by a local author:

'The Castle Inn then faced the present Castle Bow. It was entered by a flight of stone steps. The courtyard was a fine specimen of olden times; it had an open gallery running partly round it, into which the bedroom doors opened. Tim Hollier, the head ostler, was usually heard halloing to the other ostlers, or talking to Best, or Lock, the waiter. Long Jim Saunders, chubby-faced Bob Miller, bandy-legged Jack Stradling and rueful-looking Bob Callard, the post-boys, *dressed in yellow jackets, buckskin breeches and boots*, were seen chatting and joking with Betty Callard, the chambermaid, or taking their morning draught of 'hot with ginger'.'

Mr Jensen, it seems, had come face to face with one of the Castle's post-boys. He called us the following morning.

Time passes swiftly – like the ghosts of our past. I must get changed. It is Christmas at last.

FRIDAY, 27 DECEMBER 1996

It's over – we are all exhausted, but there is the satisfaction of knowing that our guests are leaving happy and content this morning. The secret, although there is no magic about it, lies in careful planning and good organization. Thereafter it is a piece of cake. The menus are set – no à la carte – and everyone eats at the same time. Christmas, really, is one endless banquet running to twenty courses spread over two days and three nights, a marathon of gastronomic excess. The dishes are kept relatively simple, squarely traditional and with enough flexibility to cope with most tastes. The whole deal is packaged into one price, so no one misses the gong: even breakfast is a sell-out.

This Christmas our house guests were a particularly jolly and civilized crowd. This is not always the case. Sometimes the hotel becomes a posh refuge for the dispossessed, the lonely and the socially dysfunctional. These types, the terminally miserable, are the ones we don't need: the party-poopers and killjoys who attract attention to themselves by complaining incessantly about very little. No fun for the staff; a real pain for Andrew and me. Last year one customer accused us of serving Bernard Matthews turkey rolls on Christmas Day. I presented him with the bird's carcass and he still wouldn't believe me.

Not this Christmas. This year they were a grand lot; we all got along famously and over the holiday Louise and I discovered a little of their fascinating lives. Among them was Paul Bailey, the author and broadcaster, and his close companion Jeremy Trevathan, whose partner some years ago used to be the *Independent's* distinguished food writer Jeremy Round until his premature death. Jeremy Trevathan also brought his mother, Mrs Sinclair, a recent convert to the Catholic Church. 'She was High Anglican,' said Paul Bailey. 'But for the last two years, the three of us have spent Christmas in Rome. That's what did it!' Mrs Sinclair told us she had one other son who was, she said, a convert to Islam, married three times and the father of eight children.

Then there were the fruit farmers from Kent who'd taken a five-month sabbatical to drive a Land Rover from Cape Town to Cairo; and the Pepsi executive, his wife and three small children who'd just returned from a stint in Hong Kong. The family had hired the Penthouse for the holiday and to distract the kids we provided a flip chart and crayons in their room. One of their creations ended up on the kitchen's notice-board: a multi-coloured illustrated 'thank-you' to all the chefs for the delicious food they'd eaten. Indeed, to our surprise there was only one casualty amid all this happiness and contentment: a poor lady who confined herself to her room until Boxing Day and then claimed that her diamond solitaire had been stolen. After a search and a thorough investigation, she confessed that she had probably left it at home.

For Louise and me the celebration of Christmas is a mad shuttle between home and hotel. Christmas Day is especially fraught. At home I take on the cooking and we usually sit down at about 3.30. With Dominic away in New Zealand, this year we were five: the two of us, Nick – our second son – and my parents.

My first job is to light the fires in the drawing room and dining room. I then prepare the turkey following an excellent recipe (or rather 'receipt') Jennifer Paterson wrote in the *Spectator* six years ago. This involves a great deal of butter, black pepper and streaky bacon, and several yards of tin foil. Once the bird is in the oven, preheated to 220°C, I make off with Caruso and Bollinger, our two retrievers. This Christmas morning the sky was blue and cloudless, brilliant sunshine illuminating the landscape. As I walked up our deserted lane towards Kings Cliff Wood and then across the frozen fields to Farringdon, the church bells in North Petherton rang out from the valley below me. Forty minutes later, I turned the oven down to 170°C and changed. Before leaving the house, I left instructions for Nick to bring in more logs and keep the fires burning. Except for the roast potatoes, which Louise said she would see to, everything was in place.

In the hotel, a table had been set up in the hall, waiters pouring mulled wine into large tumblers. I grabbed a glass – delicious it was too: well spiced, zesty and warming – and did my rounds repeating the words 'Merry Christmas' at least a dozen times every few minutes. The atmosphere was good – I could sense it the moment I stepped through the door – the only hint of tension coming from the restaurant servery where Simon Girling seemed to be in a state of purposeful panic. In the kitchen, all was calm, a moment of quiet before the rush of the service. In his office, Phil sat back in his chair, feet on the desk, reading Jane Grigson's *English Food*: my Christmas present to him this year.

By 1.30, lunch was at full tilt: crackers pulled, paper hats balanced squiffily on heads (except Paul Bailey's) and the room overflowing with good cheer. The menu, a five-course blow-out, opened gently with gravadlax; not perhaps the most original of dishes but, at Christmas, comfort and familiarity take precedence over imagination and gastronomic risk. However, with Vickery's eye for presentation, the first course came lusciously parcelled around a soft filling of smoked salmon, crème fraîche and chives. The soup course was more daring: a pungently scented celeriac and saffron broth finished off with an ingredient the food pundits have suddenly and rudely written off in their end-of-year reports. According to the *Guardian* and the *Sunday Times*, truffle oil is 'out'! Like kiwi fruit, radicchio and sun-dried tomatoes (which are pretty loathsome), this heavenly essence has been dumped in the rogue's pantry of famous foodie clichés. In 1996, truffle oil made the mistake of becoming too conspicuous on the menus of too many fashionable London eateries.

The third course, a clementine sorbet, is unquestionably a gastronomic cliché and one I detest for its prissiness and affectation. A hundred years ago, when banquets ran to ten or twelve courses, a digestive refresher in the middle made good sense. These days it's a nonsense. So why do we do it? Because it's Christmas, why else? A dash of poncey affectation goes down a treat with the punters. However, to stretch a point, one might argue – plausibly perhaps – that an icy citrus sorbet is a useful palate primer in advance of the gastric onslaught that follows. And they are given the works: a choice of either roast turkey or roast goose, plus the traditional barrage of sauces, stuffings, bacon-wrapped chipolatas, vegetables et al – all those superfluous extras lovingly known as 'the trimmings'.

After that lot, the only sensible end to the feast is, indeed, something light, fresh and fruity, like a sorbet. Instead the festive ritual demands an intestinal knock-out. And for those who don't care for plum pudding and mince pies, what do we offer? (No, nothing light, fresh and fruity.) A hot chocolate pudding with chocolate sauce. I don't understand it. But then at Christmas a balanced menu is not the point.

I was home by 2.30: time to rip off the foil and turn up the oven to 200°C for the last half-hour. There was champagne, smoked salmon and presents. Louise burned the roast potatoes. I burned the bacon rolls. Nick kept the fires burning and the peace. My parents said how lovely it all was and that the roast potatoes and the bacon rolls were just how they liked them. Louise stuck holly in the pudding. I set it aflame with half a pint of Courvoisier. And when it was all over we settled down to watch *Babe* on video – until Caruso, thrilled to have been released from his kennel, knocked over my glass of port with his tail and sent a scalding mug of tea flying over Louise.

Boxing Day was easier. Again the frost-coated hills were cast in a radiant sun. But unlike the day before, the lane was busy with cars heading for Kings Cliff and the valley echoed to the sound of guns. In a hedgerow, Bollinger disturbed a fat cock pheasant, so fat it struggled to take flight. In the hotel at lunchtime, the sense of well-being was palpable as a jazz band played Duke Ellington in memory of Ronnie Scott.

NEW YEAR STING

FRIDAY, 3 JANUARY 1997

NEW YEAR WAS VOTED 'best ever' by the hundred-odd revellers brave
enough to turn up in the face of the Siberian chill now gripping the
country. For us, however, the party was completely upstaged by a mystery which,
as I write, remains unresolved. On the one hand we suspect we may be the victims
of an elaborate con. On the other, we may have won ourselves an eccentric but
extremely wealthy, free-spending new client. I think I smell a stinking rat whereas
Andrew, less cynical than me, is inhaling rose-buds and the scent of good business.
Either way, we are treading cautiously and the police – whose advice we have
sought – have made it quite clear that we have not a shred of evidence to support

our suspicions. All we have is an uncomfortable hunch and one very odd couple.

It began over the weekend before New Year when a Mr and Mrs Anton Bonsall checked into one of our large garden suites. Their reservation had been confirmed by a faxed purchase order from a company called Hanover Investments based at an address in Wembley. We accepted the booking and, against normal business practice, the receptionist agreed to send the bill to the company for settlement even though Hanover Investments was not an account customer. Our mistake and a bloody silly one too.

My first acquaintance with Mr and Mrs Bonsall came when Louise arrived home to tell me that we had some tricky customers in the house. They had been shown to their suite and complained it was too small, saying that they had just come from the George V in Paris and that they kept a permanent table at the Dorchester in London. (This is not unusual. Name-dropping is part of the game in this trade.) Regrettably, there was nothing larger, we explained, but we promised to move them to the Penthouse when it became available on 2 January. Mr Bonsall then wanted two suits sent for dry-cleaning. He gave them to the housekeeper with a message written on a yellow Post-it pad: 'Please take care of 'Mother of Pearl' buttons when finally pressing the suits,' it read. The housekeeper showed Louise the note and Louise, amused by the man's conceit, passed it to me. I took little notice: our dry-cleaners are first class – they would deal with the suits.

Having established their credentials as habitués of the world's grandest hotels, Mr and Mrs Bonsall lost no time in lording it over the staff and demanding the best off our menus and wine list. By New Year's Eve their bill had topped £1,500. Meanwhile, the two suits were returned from the dry-cleaners and to our horror, in spite of all the fuss made about the buttons, a couple had split. Mr Bonsall went ballistic, claiming they cost £80 a set. We ate humble pie and promised to replace them. Andrew found a supplier in Birmingham who promised to send a new set immediately at a cost of £11.85.

Then, by chance, we discovered that before their arrival, the Bonsalls had not been staying at the George V in Paris as they had claimed. The boyfriend of our wine waitress happens to be the head chef at the Mount Somerset – a small country house hotel, three miles east of Taunton – and it was from here that our brash couple had come. Andrew telephoned the manager who was rather surprised to hear that the Bonsalls were now staying at the Castle. When they checked out of the Mount Somerset, they had asked for a car to take them to Taunton station as they were catching a train to London to spend the New Year holiday at the Dorchester – or so they said. Their account at the Mount Somerset, meanwhile – a tally in excess of £10,000, including £600 for laundry and dry-cleaning, and a substantial bar bill inflated by Mr Bonsall's fondness for Dom Pérignon – was to be sent to Hanover Investments for settlement.

With a full house and a New Year's Eve dinner for a hundred to orchestrate, this was not an ideal moment to confront a suspected trickster. At seven o'clock Andrew telephoned Mr Bonsall, explaining politely that as Hanover Investments was not a regular account customer, he had already exceeded 'our credit limit of £1,000'. Andrew apologized for not advising him sooner but wondered if he would be kind enough to let us have a credit card number to guarantee his booking. Mr Bonsall was taken aback. He had *no* credit cards with him. He had left them in London. Neither did he have his cheque book, nor any cash. He told Andrew he needed to make certain arrangements and would call him back before 7.30. He didn't. When the party started and people gathered for drinks, there was no sign of the Bonsalls. Eventually they appeared as the first course of the banquet was being served at 8.45. By then, there was nothing to be done.

New Year's Day is New Year's Day: the day after the night before when everyone sleeps in. A 'Do not disturb' notice hung defiantly on the Bonsalls' door. Practically, there was little to be done other than to wait patiently for our guests to surface. They didn't. Indeed, the next contact with them did not come until 2.15 the following morning when our night porter took a telephone call from Mr Bonsall. His sister, he said, had been involved in a car accident and they had been called away to the Royal Berkshire Hospital in Reading where she had been admitted. He would telephone again later but, said Bob our night porter, Mr Bonsall seemed more concerned about his belongings than his sister. Bob assured him we would take good care of everything.

So yesterday morning – Thursday – Louise, Andrew, the housekeeper and I decided it was time to take a close look at the Bonsalls' suite. If they had walked out, we were interested to know what they had left behind. It did not take us long to conclude that they would appear to have rushed off leaving just about everything, including a Christian Dior gold watch, two Dupont cigarette lighters, a walnut-trimmed mobile telephone, a sophisticated pocket computer, shirts made by Zegna for Harrods, underwear from Hugo Boss, and a quantity of expensive designer-labelled clothes and Savile Row suits. On the desk we found a number of glossy folders with estate agents' particulars of country mansions in Devon and Somerset bearing seven-figure asking prices. Were the Bonsalls intending to become our neighbours, we wondered? We also discovered two heavy suitcases which were firmly locked. Lifting each one, the first rattled with what sounded like a load of silverware and the second, we thought, probably contained books or documents.

With the bank holiday behind us, the next step was to contact Hanover Investments. The original faxed reservation had been made on behalf of the Bonsalls by a Mr Peter Harrison who signed himself as 'Asst. to Group Managing Director' on the purchase order. Andrew sent Mr Harrison four urgent faxes in as many hours and he tried telephoning. The calls were all referred to an answering service and, eventually, he was told that Mr Harrison would not be returning to his office until Monday.

I decided to make a few discreet enquiries myself. Hanover Investments, I learned, had been founded barely two months ago, on 25 October 1996. The company's registered office is given as 88 Kingsway, Holborn, WC2 and its registered number is 3269325. But I found no details of the company's capitalization and no list of directors' names. Not much to go on, and my gut reaction was to wonder whether Hanover Investments wasn't just an empty shell. I then telephoned my friends at the Dorchester who ran a check on their guest histories for me. They have no record of a Mr Anton Bonsall, neither does Hanover Investments register on their computers. Enquiries of the concierge and the restaurant managers also proved negative. Mr Bonsall is not known at the Dorchester.

At three o'clock yesterday afternoon, and to my surprise, Mr Bonsall telephoned – exactly as he had promised Bob the night porter. Our conversation was brief and to the point. He seemed particularly concerned about his wife's Dior watch and I assured him that all their belongings had been safely stored and an inventory taken. He then enquired about his account and I told him it now stood at £2,406.65. He complained bitterly that we should have warned him about our '£1,000 credit limit' in advance of his arrival. I apologized but emphasized that we now expected to be paid. Could he not let me have his credit card number? No he could not, he said, but he would make the necessary arrangements for payment when his office reopened on Monday.

This is a rum business. All sorts of questions remain unanswered. How can a couple spend a long Christmas and New Year holiday away with, allegedly, no credit cards or other visible means of payment? How did they get up to Reading? If they were doing a runner, why would they leave behind valuable and important pieces like a watch, a mobile telephone and a small computer? If Mr Bonsall's sister had had a terrible accident, why could he not tell us immediately? Why call in the middle of the night? But if he is a fraudster, why call us at all? And twice? Why not just disappear into the ether? Who is this Mr Bonsall? And what are we to make of this outfit Hanover Investments?

SATURDAY, 11 JANUARY 1997

Ten days on and we are no nearer resolving the Bonsall affair. Meanwhile, although the account has been posted to Mr Harrison at Hanover Investments in Wembley, our man is proving to be an elusive creature in spite of numerous attempts to contact him, the latest word being that he is ill with flu. True, with this cold snap, there's a lot of it about at the moment and Andrew is sticking by his view that Bonsall is, as he puts it, 'legit'. I want to believe him but don't – this whole business stinks. Bonsall is a liar – that much we do know from my conversations with the Dorchester. If he can tell porkies on a grand scale, he is almost certainly a grandiose cheat to boot.

So be it. The awful truth of this episode is that, in the end, we have only ourselves to blame. A clear business dictum was breached, a policy laid down years ago had become blurred, and we were caught on the hop. The moral of this tale is that policies are only as good as their policing. Manuals, memos, bold posters on staff notice-boards are not enough: they get lost, forgotten or end up fading into the wallpaper. It's a common enough management problem and the Bonsall case could not have illustrated this better. By the telephones in the reception office there is a large notice, printed in heavy type, listing the names of all our bona fide account customers; there could be no easier reference. But that notice has been there for years. It may have been updated from time to time, but essentially it is the same notice. No one looks at it any more, lost as it is amid the rest of the office bric-a-brac.

So, with this irritating affair weighing on our minds, in the past few days Andrew and I have used the quiet of early January to review critically the way we work – beginning with reception. We are both agreed that the department has become sloppy. It needs a little shaking up. There is nothing wrong with the staff, far from it: all the team are bright, cheerful and capable. The problem, at its root, is an absence of leadership and we, perhaps, have expected too much of Alison, our head receptionist, who for all her virtues and abilities is too young and too soft-hearted to assert her full authority. She finds it difficult to direct and instruct because her team are all her friends and she is afraid of compromising these friendships. This is not an unusual problem. A small hotel like the Castle in a provincial town like Taunton becomes, for those who work in it, an extension of family and home. We never close, the staff work strange hours and many live in. There is no obvious separation between work and play. One spills into the other. Friendships blossom and, inevitably, a close-knit community like ours fuels a never-ending saga of rivalries, petty jealousies, gossip, mischief and anything else you might expect of the knotty weave of human relations.

Alison came up through the ranks. Having begun four years ago as a waitress, she graduated to the reception office and did well. Eventually, and still only twenty-four, she was rewarded with promotion to head of her department. But her new status demanded a mental leap, an attitude shift which she has found difficult to assimilate: to distinguish clearly between the disciplines required in her new role and the off-duty informality of friendships with work-mates. This has led to fudge and compromise, to the occasional blind eye and reprimands left unsaid. In short, a lack of grip.

The Bonsall business aside – the matter of our policy on account customers now clarified – Andrew and I pinpointed the weaknesses that we agreed needed tackling. Telephone handling has become a major problem: not in the manner in which calls are answered (all the receptionists are naturally polite and charming), but in the sheer act of lifting the receiver in the first place. With a rising tide of incoming calls, particularly now that we have seen a final end to that crippling recession, the girls are finding it increasingly difficult to cope. Our broad rule is that calls should be answered within three rings. These days that's pretty rare, certainly at peak times like the mornings. Whenever I call the hotel, I always count and it is not uncommon for the number of rings to rise well into double figures. The other day, to my total despair, I counted thirty-eight rings before my call was answered. Andrew is now investigating a new and sophisticated telephone system which, I hope, will reduce the pressure by diverting suppliers and management calls to the offices concerned and use an automatic holding system for reservations and enquiries which, after all, is the principal function of the reception desk. In the meantime, the girls have got to learn to become more agile and sensitive in responding to incoming calls. This may mean asking a guest checking in or an existing caller to wait a moment while the receptionist acknowledges the call and puts it on hold. It is a simple act of diplomacy but one which, they say, 'is not as easy as it sounds'. I suspect they are just nervous of doing it, fearful of upsetting the person they are dealing with at the time.

Another problem – and one which has cost us friends and valuable room lettings – is the time it has taken to reply to letters and faxes. Again we have a general rule: that confirmations of bookings should be turned round within twenty-four hours. With the upturn in trade, this thorny issue became particularly acute in the final months of 1996. Every year we do two big mailings to our customers: one in March and the second in late August or early September. Of the two, the autumn mailing – which advertises Christmas, New Year and our annual series of musical weekends – causes the most pressure on our ability to process reservations promptly. The moment leaflets land on doormats, we are flooded with booking requests; this time the deluge nearly drowned us. As a consequence there were embarrassingly long delays in sending out letters of confirmation, a problem which only came to light when I began to receive angry complaints from clients who had sent us their £200 deposits (which we promptly banked) but who had received no word of acknowledgement from us. This was a pretty poor show and one which made us look rude, slack and incompetent. Most irritatingly, the problem could easily have been avoided if the reception office had had the gumption to shout for help before the backlog of mail became too awesome. We have now drafted in reinforcements – in the shape of Andrew's stalwart PA Jacqui Gifford-Bennett – to provide the extra secretarial assistance needed to cope with the correspondence.

There were one or two other bad habits Andrew and I had spotted: symptoms of a malaise that has crept into the receptionist's daily routine. Computer screens, winking seductively on desks, make passive slaves of us. Sometimes, when I walk through the hall, I see the girls staring languidly into a kind of emptiness, mesmerized by those wretched machines which now consume our working lives. After a while, in thrall to their wicked masters, they become oblivious to their surroundings. For a guest checking in after three hours' tribulation on the motorway, a dreamy welcome by a young waif in a semi-hypnotic state is not exactly what's wanted. First impressions in this game are critical.

Having completed our survey of the reception office, we concluded that the best way to remedy these shortcomings was for Andrew to hold a meeting with all the members of the department rather than haul Alison in and demand she put her house in order. Her weak leadership, we felt, was a point heavily outweighed by her ability to do a good job as a senior player in a small team who, besides, all enjoyed working together. The leadership, drilling and discipline could be provided by Andrew.

Our discussion moved on to other things, among them the quality of our continental breakfast for those preferring room service in the mornings. Here was another classic example of a clear policy, an unambiguous standard which, with the passage of time, had gradually fallen into disrepair. Room service breakfasts are assembled in the restaurant servery. On the wall, there used to hang a large board – measuring 4 x 3 feet – upon which we portrayed a step-by-step guide to the content and lay-up of a Castle Hotel continental breakfast. This idiot's guide was lent extra effect by the use of 10 x 8 inch colour photographs illustrating all the items included in a continental breakfast, how they should be presented and where they should be located on the tray or trolley before its despatch to the guest's bedroom. This full-colour montage was prescriptive in the smallest detail and to the last sugar lump. It defined the precise shade of golden-brown for the croissants; the angle of teaspoons and coffee cups on saucers (cup handles at five o'clock); the correct way to arrange butter pats etc., etc. Not least, the board was a pictorial checklist for waiters to make doubly sure everything was present and correct. There is nothing more annoying to a guest, particularly one in a hurry, if for example the milk or the marmalade is missing. However, this magnificent piece of artwork is no more. I suspect it was dumped last time we repainted the servery and, of course, it was never replaced because everyone had forgotten its existence long before.

Just as first impressions matter, so do last impressions. Guests checking out should leave with warm feelings, otherwise we'll never see them again. Hence my campaign for a better breakfast on the simple strategy: deliver it fast and on time; make it crisp, clean and easy on the eye; fresh, wholesome and generous. In the good old days, the days of the great artwork, our official continental breakfast was:

A choice of various teas or coffee
Fresh orange juice or an alternative juice
A rack of brown and white toast
A basket offering croissants, brioche and wholemeal breads
Various preserves, honey and marmalade

The other day some friends came to stay and I decided to deliver their trolley myself. I should play floor waiter more often. Their continental breakfast, inter alia, included and omitted the following:

Coffee OK
Fresh orange juice OK
No toast rack
Toast in basket rendered limp by pile of other items
No brioche in basket

No wholemeal bread in basket
Croissants OK
Revolting Danish pastries in basket
No honey
Preserves OK
Marmalade OK

I am commissioning a new artwork for the servery. Maybe it will be a masterpiece. Even if it is it won't be good enough. We could hang Botticelli's *Birth of Venus* in our servery and you'd probably still end up with a Danish for your breakfast.

FRIDAY, 17 JANUARY 1997

My worst suspicions have been confirmed. We've been had and we can now wave farewell to our money – £2,400 of it – for we know that the Castle and the Mount Somerset were among two hotels in a major nationwide sting stretching from Gleneagles in Scotland to the Dorchester in London. The name of our fraudster is known to the police but, for the time being, all they will tell me is that it's *not* Bonsall and that Harrison – he of Hanover Investments – is his close associate in this game. So, for the price of a fax machine and a fancy letterhead, it appears that these two rats have been living the life of Riley for the past three months. But as DC Tony Knight of Avon and Somerset CID tells me, their fun will cost them an eighteen-month stay in less salubrious accommodation than the Castle's. While that's a very comforting thought, on balance, I think I would prefer to recover our money. Not that the police have caught these villains, but they seem to be getting close and they have accumulated more than enough evidence, much of which has been presented to them on a silver salver. By the time he checked into the Castle 'Mr Bonsall' had grown careless.

Enough was enough. Having failed to make contact with Mr Harrison and having stored the Bonsalls' belongings for two weeks, it was time to take a look inside the two locked suitcases left in their suite. For all we knew, one of them may have contained a bomb, so we called in security experts to do the deed. The contents of the suitcases instantly gave the game away, although most of what we found was pathetic: incidental bits and pieces of no real value to a professional thief. Our Mr Bonsall was a serious hotel junkie, obsessed with nicking even the most trivial of objects. There were toiletries from the Dorchester: soap bars, shampoos, a vanity kit. From the Mount Somerset, we found towels and bath robes. And from us, silver tea and coffee pots, a tea strainer, a sugar bowl and tongs, a milk jug, an ice cream coupe, and a salt and pepper set. 'Perfect surfaces for finger printing,' observed DC Knight in his Somerset burr.

But of greater interest to the police were the other items we discovered. These included a packet of documents identifying Bonsall's female companion (not his wife, of course), who turns out to be of Moroccan nationality. There was also a set of keys attached to a plastic tag bearing the name and address of a lock-up facility in Earl's Court: 'Abbey Self-storage, The Place for Space,' read the brightly coloured label. Best of all, we found two disposable cameras with used films which the police have had developed. They show a variety of engaging mug-shots of Bonsall and his girlfriend outside the Castle and the Mount Somerset.

And that's where we stand for the moment. The investigation continues with the assistance of the Met's 'hotel squad', who are also on the case.

FALLEN STAR

THURSDAY, 23 JANUARY 1997

THE 1997 EDITION of the Michelin Red Guide has just been published and, at a stroke, we have been stripped of our precious star. The news is so fresh – I only heard an hour ago – the shock of it hasn't sunk in. I feel strangely numb, in a state of disbelief, even indifferent, asking myself if I really care when I know perfectly well that I do. Perhaps it's as well that Louise and I are going away for a few days – to Spain for a long weekend – but as I sit here on a train bound for Paddington, all I can do is ruminate, wonder in a mild daze what the hell went so wrong for the Michelin Men to cashier us. Next week, I'll call them and try to find some answers but, like the Mafia, these people have their code of *omerta*. That's their style. There is no warning, no hearing, no right of appeal. Win their favour and silently they elevate you. Fall foul of their arcane judgements and silently they chop you. In the end we must turn on ourselves and ask where we went wrong.

Before catching the train, Phil called and offered me his resignation. I was so stung by this ludicrous proposition I told him to 'piss off': at that instant they were the only two words to tumble out of my angry, addled mind. But he was being serious and repeated his offer to quit. 'Over my dead body,' I tried. 'Don't ever talk like that to me again!' I told him he had my complete confidence, that this was not Armageddon and that we would talk things through together next week, by which time both of us will have had a few days to absorb the news.

That was half an hour ago. But sitting here one question keeps nagging away at me. Why? Why? Why? There may be a number of answers but even before exploring these I ask myself first, did we deserve to be chopped? Michelin inspectors are – of all the guides – the most meticulous, the most scrupulous, the most professional. They are slow to make their awards and cautious before removing them. As a venerable institution, Michelin is also deeply conservative: impervious to changing styles and tastes, reluctant to reward good cooking which may be more in tune with modern eating habits. This innate conservatism limits the value of the information in the Red Guide because its ancient grading system simply won't recognize the great diversity of cooking – regardless of its quality – that is now available to consumers. The star system tends to be absolutist and Francophile. It does not necessarily lead you to the 'best' restaurants because 'best' these days is a coat of many colours; a gastronomic kaleidoscope.

But the uncomfortable fact remains: we had a star and we lost it. Irrespective of the mysteries of Michelin's awards' system, there was a time, once, when we were good enough to qualify, when we made the grade. So did we deserve to be stripped of that distinguished little pip against the Castle's name? To be erased from the roll of honour in the front of the book? And to be wiped off the map of Britain showing the locations of the country's elite restaurants? It is a question I shall put to Phil because in spite of his bruised pride he is going to have to come to terms with the answer.

Staring out at the gloom of the Berkshire landscape racing past my window and casting my thoughts back over the events of the past twelve months, the painful truth gradually seeps into my consciousness. There were moments, certainly, when I complained to Phil about the food coming out of the kitchen; never bad, indeed usually pretty good, but there were times when I felt the edge had been lost: seasonings not quite accurate, imbalances in the assembly of ingredients, cooking times misjudged, that sort of thing. On one famous occasion, I remember confronting Phil and saying bluntly: 'If I'd been a Michelin inspector, we'd have just lost our star!'

That's the point about Michelin: consistency is all. Once you achieve the standard, the trick is to sustain it – day after day, week in week out – and, I suspect, their rigorous inspections ultimately exposed our fault lines. So if we deserve a caning, why did the standard slip? Vickery has the talent (he's proved that over the past six years). But he has more: he is an outstanding leader and manager, he is highly organized and he is an inspirational teacher to the young people who pass through his kitchen. My respect and admiration for his abilities put him on the family board and persuaded me to offer him shares in the company. Yet looking back over the past twelve to eighteen months, I also see a kitchen that has been in some turmoil. Phil went through a very unpleasant divorce which hurt him deeply. As he began to climb out of that pit, his loyal second-in-command, Keith Short, hit a turbulent patch in his own marriage, with an unfaithful wife who, having given him a baby daughter, deserted him for another man, disowning the child and then demanding the baby back after the lover had dumped her. While Keith was struggling to cope with the emotional upheaval in his life, Phil's television career took flight, with a queue of eager producers chasing him to appear on their programmes. Suddenly Phil was in demand and last year he became the new star of *Ready Steady Cook* and one of the principal presenters on the BBC's afternoon slot *Who'll do the Pudding?*

In Phil's absence, then, Keith was left in charge and it is now blindingly obvious that he was in no state to run a kitchen with the degree of precision and discipline demanded of a Michelin-starred restaurant. Although Phil was never away for more than a few days at a time, those periodic absences, I think, had a cumulative effect which resulted in a loss of continuity and stability. Television is a seductive mistress. The lure of the camera, the thrill and the glamour of filming, the flattery of the attention the medium fuels were enough not so much to turn his head but, perhaps, just enough to have him take his eye off the ball. Either way, Phil has been smacked by a large dose of hubris!

And yet, I ask myself, does it really matter that we've lost this thing? This tiny, petal-shaped speck in a funny red book filled with dozens of other strange little symbols which no one quite understands? Bizarre though it may seem to any other sane human being, Michelin wields the most extraordinary power over the lives of ambitious restaurateurs. It has nothing to do with business. The loss of our star will not ruin us. In fact it will make not the slightest dent in our trade. *The Good Food Guide* and the *AA Guide* are more readable and user-friendly, and, as such, much more influential if you are in the business of attracting diners through your front door. However, for the chef and the restaurateur, Michelin is a kind of divinity. It is to do with pride and honour, the respect it confers and the recognition it brings from one's peers. Michelin stars are like coronets: once crowned you become a princeling, you are admitted to the gastronomic aristocracy. Lose it and you are reduced to the ranks of the proletariat. This is a fairyland that has little to do with life in the real world of running restaurants, where success relies entirely on filling your tables. Yes, I've spotted the occasional weaknesses in our cooking and, yes, the Michelin Men have rumbled us. But these lapses are small technical nuances beyond the ken of the majority of our visitors, whose only purpose is to enjoy an evening out in a civilized setting with good food and congenial service rather than to sit at a table with the express intention of deconstructing every mouthful.

That's as may be. The fact remains – we have lost our star. Our shining coronet has been snatched from us and we want it back.

WEDNESDAY, 29 JANUARY 1997

Unable to shrug off the events of last week, I did not wait until our return from Spain to call Michelin. At 8.45 on Friday morning, sitting in the departures lounge at Gatwick Airport, I took a chance and telephoned Derek Bulmer, the editor of the Guide, whom I have known for nearly twenty years. I was in luck. When the switchboard put me through to his office, his voice came on the line.

'I've been expecting your call,' he said, after I announced myself.

'Look Derek,' I began, coming straight to the point, 'we're pretty gutted by the loss of our star. Are you around next week and can I call you to discuss this? I know your policy is not to comment on inspections, but I need to know. We're determined to win that star back!'

'Yes,' replied the senior Michelin Man, 'I'd be happy to talk but not on the telephone. I'd rather meet you and Phil together and I'm perfectly prepared to come to Taunton if necessary.'

We fixed a date – 11 am on 11 February – and I shot off to find Louise and Gate 63 for our flight to Malaga. At least the call made me feel better. Bulmer knows we run a serious kitchen and he trusts me enough to make an exception in our case. For him to take a day out from Michelin's HQ in Watford to drive to Taunton is an unusual step and a positive sign.

On our return to England, we decided to check into the hotel on Sunday evening rather than go home. Besides, an impromptu visit to the restaurant, I thought, might be instructive, especially as Phil was away recording another batch of TV shows. A Sunday dinner is never the most lively moment to eat in an hotel, particularly on a bleak January evening. But for this reason alone it is a good test of a kitchen which may feel inclined to wind down after a frenetic Sunday lunch service. As we walked into the restaurant just before nine, there were only six tables taken, including one occupied by a corpulent gentleman dining alone. With Simon Girling off duty, Christophe was in charge and he escorted us to a table next to the man. Both Louise and I instinctively arrived at the same conclusion: our lonely diner was an inspector. No doubt about it, he bore all the hallmarks of a Michelin Man: choosing off the à la carte menu, asking discreet questions of the staff, taking an uncommon interest in the food he ate. As I had my back to him, Louise gave me a mouthful-by-mouthful commentary on how she thought his dinner was progressing. He seemed to be enjoying it, she said, and the staff were being properly attentive.

Meanwhile, we ordered and I decided to play restaurant critic myself in preparation for my meeting with Phil later in the week. We ate a perfectly respectable dinner but, alas, many of the faults I had spotted in the past resurfaced. The potted duck – usually rich, moist and deeply flavoured – was dry and devoid of proper seasoning. The spiced pears that accompany the dish were perfect. Louise's marinated pasta with braised aubergines was overwhelmed by a heavy dousing of truffle oil and a pile of Parmesan shavings crudely plonked on top. The dish lacked the finesse and delicate balance of ingredients that is so much a mark of Vickery's talent. My steamed sea bass with a wild mushroom cream was, to my palate, ill-conceived as an idea and needs to be pulled off the menu. It doesn't work. Sea bass is a finely fleshed and nobly flavoured fish – it can't cope with a powerful fungal sauce, let alone the pungent and peculiar taste of Jerusalem artichokes dressing the plate. For pudding, we shared a rhubarb, custard and walnut crumble tart with mascarpone cream. This was delicious – indeed, a little winner and perfectly executed – but, I felt, the construction and nature of the dish was more suited stylistically to our simple table d'hôte menu than to the carte.

By now our corpulent friend was preparing to leave. Convinced that we'd exposed his true identity and egged on by Louise, I swung round to confront him.

'I do hope you've enjoyed your dinner,' I opened benignly.

'Oh, yes thank you,' he replied. 'Very good indeed.'

This wasn't good enough for me. I didn't believe him.

'You're an inspector aren't you?' I challenged, stubbing a finger at him a little too vehemently.

'I beg your pardon?' he said, looking startled.

'You're an inspector – an *hotel* inspector – aren't you?' I repeated, trying to modify my abrasive manner with a lukewarm smile.

'No I'm not,' he stammered. 'I'm a tax accountant actually! Been here all weekend.'

The expression of terror on the poor man's face persuaded me. Realizing my blunder, I apologized profusely and invited him to join us for a night-cap. Paranoia is endemic in the restaurant trade: we assume that anyone eating alone is, *ipso facto*, an inspector. (Lose a Michelin star and the condition becomes deeply pathological.) Anyway, our new friend turned out to be very good company in spite of his calling. He was a partner in a large firm of City accountants and had found himself in need of a little p and q for a weekend. Passionate about his food and wine, he chose the Castle on the strength of our high rating in the *AA Guide*. And to my relief we had more than lived up to our billing, which was a great comfort to Louise and me. We slept well that night.

Come Monday, and with Phil not expected back until Tuesday, I decided to continue my gustatory blitzkrieg with lunch, concentrating once more on the carte rather than the lunchtime staples. I began with the pan-fried brill, braised chicory, capers and candied lemon: one of Vickery's newer creations and a dish of great charm. The crystallized zest (crowning the plate) and the pickled buds (making the sauce) are a wonderful match for each other, a counterpoint of sweet and sour flavours which combine harmoniously with the fish. But when it was brought to table, the brill had been overcooked and the plate was undersauced – silly, careless errors which would have irritated Phil if he had been with me. Moreover, although I am a fan of this dish, its position on the menu (as a starter on the à la carte) is plain wrong. It would work more successfully, I decided, as a main course on the table d'hôte section of the menu. Next I chose one of Vickery's great specialities: his scallops with bubble and squeak and deep-fried basil. This is an unusual but heavenly dish and one that has been frequently rehearsed by the kitchen. But for me on Monday, they blew it. For a start the plate looked as if it had been assembled by a brickie with a spade. No sleight-of-hand, no flair, no artistic touch. Again, the kitchen was mean with the sauce – but worse, the five fat scallops had been cooked until they had assumed the texture of Durex, and I could see how just by looking at the poor things. Instead of searing the plump, fresh molluscs fast in an extremely hot pan, they had allowed them to stew on a lower heat. Another daft error. Still, they got the seasoning right this time – spot on – safe sex on a plate.

As I sat picking at my rubbery offering, I spotted Julian Stainton, the boss of the Western Provident Association, lunching with a fellow director at a table opposite me. We waved hello and continued eating. He too, I noticed, had chosen the scallops. For pudding I went for a selection of ices and sorbets – always a good test – and (yes, yes, I can be generous) they were brilliant, truly delicious: worthy of *two* Michelin Stars at least.

When I finished, I walked across to Julian's table. Not a man for mincing his words, Mr Stainton. If he has a problem you soon know about it. On Monday he was in an expansive mood and I stood silently as he raved and raved on about the sheer wondrousness of his scallops. I returned to my office shaking my head. One thing was certain: Julian Stainton would never make the grade as a Michelin inspector. But he *is* one of our best customers – and it is our *customers*, not the Michelin Guide, who really count.

Phil and I spent much of yesterday and this morning locked away in isolation. We did a lot of talking. Inevitably, he has found it more difficult to come to terms with our fall from grace. The first long session was introspective and confessional, a search for causes with a great deal of self-examination. The second session was shorter, more positive and pragmatic; Phil reasserting himself, determined to take a grip on his kitchen again and declaring his will to regain the lost star. We then set about the menus, returning to first principles and reviewing the thinking behind each section: at lunch and dinner; table d'hôte vs. à la carte; the balance and make-up of starters, main courses and puddings under each heading; the appropriateness and gastronomic value of every dish. I also gave Phil an undiluted account of my most recent impressions of the food coming out of the kitchen, which he took very well. But the most important task facing him had less to do with fine tuning the content of the menus. That's easy. Phil's real challenge is to reactivate his brigade and to persuade them to work more intelligently with their senses, to get them thinking about every dish they produce; to look, to smell, to taste, *not* to churn out the food as if they were robots on a production line. This is a common problem among chefs. They are often technically competent but quite incapable of thinking with their senses. The eyes, nose and palate are the chef's most precious assets, not his manual dexterity or his ability to knock out a recipe. Anyone can paint by numbers.

Happy Birthday Franz

Tuesday, 4 February 1997

I LOATHE THIS TIME OF YEAR – dark, cold, wet, dreary, miserable. But we have January behind us and at least with this new month the promise of spring feels a little closer. Meanwhile, the past few weeks have been blighted by flu and bronchitis as all of us flipped like dominoes – an epidemic that nearly brought the hotel to its knees. Still, we managed somehow and ended the month with an occupancy topping 60 per cent which, for a January in Taunton, is a remarkably healthy result.

The only joy amid this winter gloom – indeed the only spark that keeps the spirit burning – is our annual season of musical weekends which, this year, opened last

Friday evening, a date neatly coinciding with Franz Schubert's 200th birthday. So, appropriately, the weekend's programme – four concerts between Friday night and Sunday morning – was devoted entirely to Schubert's chamber music, with the Lindsays playing a repertoire of seven string quartets, including masterpieces like the D minor, *Death and the Maiden* and the Quartet in G major D887. At the birthday concert on Friday, they were joined after the interval by the cellist Ralph Kirshbaum for the Quintet in C – a piece of music so lovely, so exquisitely uplifting that were I to be sent to the gallows, I would happily hang to the sound of the Adagio in my ears.

The weekend was special in other ways too, for we had our own birthday to celebrate. This was the opening programme in our twenty-first season and I found myself wondering where the years had gone. It was in 1976 – the year of my return to the family firm – that I met Ivan Sutton, the founder and first artistic director of our musical weekends, and the person to whom I owe my passion for chamber music. A gentle and erudite man, he taught me everything, and after his death last May I decided we should dedicate the Schubert weekend to his memory. So we were joined by several members of the family: Ivan's daughter Jenny Salmon with her husband Ted, his son Mark, a professor at the Guildhall School of Music, and his daughter-in-law Alice, Mark's wife. Robin Young, the veteran correspondent of *The Times*, was also with us for our birthday celebrations with a brief from his editor to write a feature for the *Weekend* section of the newspaper. On Saturday, he was joined by his wife, Lailan, an author in her own right and a world authority on facial analysis! Never mind the Schubert, Louise and I had our work cut out as mindful hosts-cum-PRs with, I hope, convincingly agreeable faces to boot.

The organization of these festivals, a series of three weekends between January and March, is quite complex and although we now have twenty-one years' experience, the potential for crisis is high unless the events are administered with fanatical care. All of a sudden, the Castle has to assume the dual role of both hotel and concert hall. A stage is erected in the Monmouth Room with four to five rows of chairs arranged in a semi-circle around the platform. This creates an intimate atmosphere for both audience and artists which is, after all, the point of 'chamber' music. We can seat about 130 people in this manner. Of these about sixty will be hotel residents who have booked the inclusive package: two nights' accommodation, the four concerts, and all meals. The other seventy will be local music-lovers buying concert tickets to individual performances.

An annual festival of three weekends billing world-class musicians playing, in total, twelve concerts means a lot of work – extracurricular work not commonly associated with the everyday life of an hotel. Each season is planned at least twelve months in advance. Carolyn Humphreys, Ivan Sutton's successor, books the players, plans the programmes, negotiates the fees and manages the concerts, working closely with me at every stage. The cost of this enterprise is pretty steep (an artistic overhead alone of around £25,000 a year), which means that to maintain a distinguished line-up of artists, we need financial support if the weekends are to be remotely viable. Mercifully, thus far in the life of these festivals, I have succeeded in avoiding commercial sponsors. The money comes, instead, from one or two private benefactors whose only demand is complete anonymity.

We announce each new series in the preceding autumn with a simple notice advertising details of the programmes: a leaflet mailed to some 6,500 addresses taken from our own database and that of the Wigmore Hall. While the reception desk takes care of the residential bookings, Gill, my secretary, administers the box office for local concert-goers. Sounds simple enough – but it's not. Operating the box office is an irksome, thankless task requiring the combined gifts of a saint, a diplomat and a zealous bureaucrat. People will be people. They buy tickets, they return tickets, they lose tickets, they exchange tickets for other performances. When we're sold out, they complain bitterly, accusing us of sending them the literature after everyone else has received theirs, unfair seating allocations or foul play. In short, the box office is the battle zone and Gill is the front line.

With the onset of a weekend, Andrew Grahame issues a three-page briefing document to all departments and then chases round the hotel barking orders like a field commander before sending his troops over the top. Housekeepers operate an improvised cloakroom outside the Monmouth Room and sell programmes for £1.00. Porters man the doors and collect tickets. Waiters set up the green room and make sure the artists' drinks are replenished. A junior manager is given a check-list of things to be switched off, closed down or stopped immediately before each concert: the grandfather clock in the hall, cellar and kitchen fans, various ventilators. Silence is an imperative. But even these measures have not prevented disaster. A soft, sublime phrase in a Mozart quartet was once ruined by the distant roar of a Hoover on the floor above. Success is all in the detail, from the checking of fire exits to the precise timings of intervals and endings for porters to stand ready by the doors the moment the applause begins.

Last weekend was a triumph: I think Schubert would have been pleased. Our audiences certainly were, rising to give the Lindsays thunderous ovations for their playing. If there were any embarrassments (and there were), they had nothing to do with the music but, I suspect, they will add essential spice to Robin Young's story for *The Times*. At dinner after Friday's concert, Mark Sutton – the archetypal mad professor and music's answer to Magnus Pike – suddenly decided to sing 'Happy Birthday Franz'. For a moment the dining room fell to a hush as eighty-five heads turned to stare at our table. Out of politeness to our guest, Louise and I had little choice but to join in as lustily as we dared. Then, to my relief, the Lindsays struck up, which encouraged a few other tables to start singing. That was bad enough. But when Prof. Sutton broke into 'For he's a jolly good fellow,' this was one performance too many and I told him to shut up. 'Schubert's been dead 170 years,' I snapped across the table. 'He's not here to appreciate it.'

I suppose I should have guessed something like this might happen. Two days before the weekend, Mark Sutton telephoned to speak to me but got Gill instead. She was instructed to pass on his message, which she did. The professor decided that a birthday cake would be an extremely good idea and as we had a famous kitchen, we were the people to bake it. My reaction to this proposal was to groan deeply and dismiss it. A cake with two hundred candles was not a cake but a bonfire; the main man wasn't around to blow it out; and, besides, the Viennese Schubert, I am sure, would have preferred a sachertorte (the delicious chocolate confection created by Franz Sacher, Metternich's pastrycook, in 1815) to a beastly English fruit cake.

Throughout these distractions, Robin Young sat passively with a quizzical smile in his eyes. He could not have been more charming and there was little doubt he was enjoying his weekend – but one was also conscious that here was a journalist on assignment, and journalists have a habit of asking awkward questions, usually rhetorically. I could have done without: 'I see you've lost your Michelin star?' But the one that really made me wince was: 'Yes, lovely room, thank you. But you don't offer Radio 3 on your sound system. Only Classic FM?' This was a small detail I had forgotten – but, true, we decided to change to the more populist station some time ago for pretty obvious reasons. With the exception of three weekends a year, our guests are not exactly Radio 3 types. 'Oh, don't worry,' he said cheerily. 'It'll make good copy.' I'm sure it will, I thought.

There was one other hiccup, Sod's Law you could call it, but it exposed a weakness in our reception procedures. When a guest checks in we always ask if they'd like a call, a newspaper or a pot of tea first thing in the morning. Human beings tend to be creatures of habit and so these instructions are, invariably, carried forward to the next day unless a client asks us not to. When Mr Young arrived on Friday afternoon, he booked a 7.30 call for Saturday morning. However, his wife Lailan, who did not join him until Saturday lunchtime, is not an early riser. And on Sunday morning, I learned, she was pretty upset when the telephone rang to wake them up.

We have now refined this simple procedure to avoid the problem again. But, alas, nothing in this game is fail-safe.

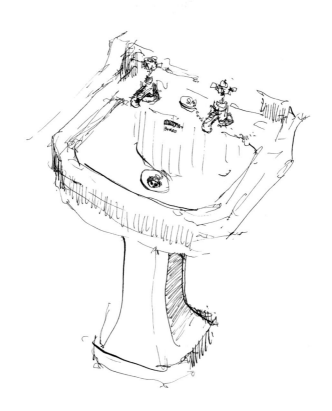

THE FRIDGE

MONDAY, 10 FEBRUARY 1997

THAT BLOODY MAN 'Bonsall' continues to play us like a fish on the end of a line. For a moment last week I thought we had him but he failed to fall into our trap. The police are convinced he doesn't know they are on to him and they are biding their time, patiently waiting for him to show up, which they expect him to do sooner or later. At this stage they do not want to spook him. Meanwhile, the dossier on our Mr Bonsall looks quite extraordinary. His real name is O'Keefe, a Londoner of no known address, whose accomplice 'Harrison' now turns out to be one and the same person. Mr O'Keefe's record as a con-artist is impressive, making our £2,400 loss look like small beer compared to some of his other scams.

He has flown to Barcelona *three* times by private jet, leaving the leasing company with an unpaid bill of £22,000. He owes a Savile Row tailor £59,000. And he very nearly persuaded BT to let him take delivery of a consignment of mobile telephones valued at £31,000. DC Knight at Taunton CID also tells me that Mr O'Keefe is 'self-delusional', he actually believes he *is* the roles he plays: a multibillionaire one day, a senior medical consultant the next. Recently, he was chased out of the Cromwell Hospital in London where he'd been doing the rounds of the private wards in a white coat posing as a Dr de Mornay.

Anyway, a week ago we got quite excited when Mr Bonsall telephoned to reconfirm his reservation for the Penthouse on Friday – a booking he had made at New Year. Simon Girling took the call and played the game perfectly. Yes, we were expecting him and Mrs Bonsall and, certainly, their suitcases were safely locked away awaiting their return. Bonsall even asked Simon if we had managed to replace the mother-of-pearl buttons which had broken when his suit was sent away to be dry-cleaned. 'Yes, Mr Bonsall,' said Simon reassuringly, 'the buttons have arrived and we've sewn them on for you.'

Thus alerted, Andrew called DC Knight, who told him that Bonsall had made a similar reservation at the Mount Somerset, the hotel he'd stayed at before coming on to us after Christmas. A plan was hatched and put into operation. The Bonsalls were to be treated as normal guests: checked in and shown to their suite. The receptionist on duty was instructed to say that the suitcases would be sent along directly. Once they were comfortably settled, we were to dial 999 and quote 'log number 76'. The police would arrive within minutes and make their arrest.

Come Friday evening, the tension mounted, all of us salivating at the prospect of Bonsall spending his weekend in a cell at the Taunton nick while he was expecting to be sipping Dom Pérignon in the Penthouse. But Mr and Mrs Bonsall did not show. Neither did they check into the Mount Somerset. However, this morning the slimy toad telephoned the Mount full of abject apologies, claiming that some business crisis had kept him in London at the weekend. We received no such call. But he has rescheduled his visit to the Mount Somerset for the twentieth. The police have been notified and I'm beginning to get very bored with this whole affair.

Tuesday, 11 February 1997

Today was the day the Michelin Man came to see us: our face-to-face with the faceless being who cashiered us, and an unusual opportunity for this secretive organization to reveal the evidence which condemned us. Such is the inscrutability of Michelin that Derek Bulmer, its editor, insists on drawing a veil of anonymity across himself – anyway as far as the media are concerned. In the absence of a name, the press have invented their own and for a reason I cannot quite fathom, he has been nicknamed 'The Fridge'. Whether this sobriquet is intended to imply a chilliness of temperament or a capacity for heroic consumption is unclear. In person, Derek Bulmer is neither cold nor fat; indeed, he is a perfectly genial and civilized human being – although his agreeable nature is stiffened by a professional veneer which keeps a safe distance between his office and the subjects of his critical palate.

As Phil and I sat before him and a thick manila file, he began by emphasizing two points. Firstly, he was not here to tell us how to run our business – we, not he, were the better judges of that. Secondly, he reminded us of Michelin's strict policy of declining to discuss the findings of individual inspections. An exception was being made in our case because of the Castle's long association with the Guide. The Fridge then opened the manila file and for the next ninety minutes we heard our indictment. For me the debriefing was entirely predictable and, in essence, an endorsement of all my own observations. For Phil the meeting was of greater value – this was his final catharsis. In all my long and often tortuous conversations with him, there had always been an element of resistance, of mild disbelief that the points and criticisms I raised were not entirely valid. He was almost in a state of denial, an unwillingness to come to terms with the raw truth. Listening to the quiet, even voice of Derek Bulmer, Vickery was getting the confirmation he needed from the horse's mouth, and although he had to sit through a catalogue of criticism based on six inspections stretching back as far as September 1995, the effect on him was invigorating rather than depressing.

As I had preached on countless occasions, cooking to Michelin star level is one thing, but to win the gong you have to sustain the standard with every dish on the menu, every time it is prepared, every day and every night of the year. Winning and keeping a Michelin star is all about consistency. Bulmer highlighted several instances where seasonings and cooking times were at fault. Leafing through his inspectors' reports, he said that starters and main courses came in for more criticism than puddings which were, generally, judged to be very good. This coincided with my own experiences, although Phil's pastry seemed to come in for some stick. On one occasion, an inspector reported that the pastry casing for a mulberry tart was so hard it 'could have bounced across the dining room floor!'

Nevertheless, the outcome of this long session was reassuring and confirmed our view there was nothing fundamentally wrong that could not be put right; nor was our culinary philosophy at odds with the values Michelin applied when making their judgements. Phil was worried that, perhaps, our menus did not conform stylistically with what the Guide or its readers might perceive as Michelin star quality – in other words, food with the frills and curlicues of French haute cuisine. The question arose as a result of one inspector's comment that our vegetables were rather crudely turned (the culinary practice of shaping potatoes, carrots, courgettes and so on into perfectly sculpted lozenges). This was a small but important detail of principle and one which Bulmer and his team may not have appreciated about our 'style'. Both Phil and I hate turned vegetables – an aspect of Gallic prissiness that is alien to the Anglo-Saxon values implicit in our kitchen. Phil's method is to cut his vegetables into wedges, creating attractive shapes with a more natural look than turned food which, in any case, is hugely wasteful.

Bulmer accepted Phil's point but dismissed it completely as a factor that may have contributed towards the loss of our star. On the contrary, he said, he welcomed the simplicity, honesty and directness of our cooking. Indeed, Michelin had been especially pleased to award us a star in the past precisely because we had evolved a culinary style – signally English in its idiom – which was unique among restaurants in this country. Phil's other great fear – that the pace of the menu's evolution is too slow – was also dismissed by Bulmer. This note of reassurance pleased me particularly because Phil's impatience to change dishes when he gets bored with them can lead to replacements which are less successful. This can also result in disappointments for visitors who come to the Castle to enjoy some of Vickery's famous 'signature' dishes like, say, the braised shoulder of lamb or the baked egg custard tart and nutmeg ice cream. 'Don't change winning dishes,' said the Fridge, 'even though they may have been on the menu a long time.'

As our meeting drew to a close, I wanted to know what our chances were of winning the star back within twelve months. Michelin are slow to give and slow to take away – my feeling was that we were probably looking at a minimum exile of two years. Realizing we were in earnest, Bulmer's response was both sanguine and cautious: 'Regaining a star in a year is very unusual,' he said, 'but it has been done. In view of your situation, you can expect a number of visits this year – more than usual.'

We stood up and I offered him lunch which he declined 'under the circumstances' … However, he did agree to a tour of the hotel to inspect Louise's latest bedrooms and, not least, to see the restaurant, which we redecorated in January: an upbeat scheme in eau-de-nil and pale pink, giving the room a bright, contemporary feel without losing any of its classical elegance. I think the Michelin Man approved. He certainly liked many of our new paintings and prints, particularly a Beryl Cook, *Two On A Stool*, which has whipped up a storm with some of our chattering regulars who think it's vulgar. The picture features the back view of a man and a woman at a bar. The man's arm, hugging the woman's waist, is colourfully tattooed, as is the woman's left shoulder. We think it's brilliant, funny and rather touching.

The other pictures – a collection of twenty, including several collages by Ron Reams, four sensuous studies of women by the Israeli artist Tarkay, and a wild, beguiling seascape by Dick Bixby – have been equally controversial. Even Phil, Andrew, Louise and I were divided in our likes and dislikes when we came to choose what to hang – a collision of tastes which generated a few heated debates. In the end, each of our preferences were represented in at least some of the works and the overall effect on the dining room is, I think, terrific – making an impact and inviting reaction which is what we wanted and exactly what has happened. This artistic mood could never have been achieved by the Karen Burgess paintings, the sensitive watercolours Louise and I bought in Plymouth last November which inspired our furious argument about their suitability for the restaurant. To my relief, these pictures have now been removed upstairs and look absolutely perfect in the peaceful setting of two garden suites.

MONDAY, 17 FEBRUARY 1997

A little weary today, drawing breath after our second musical weekend, no less a success than the first, but sometimes these do's can be very hard work. For all the pleasure the artists gave – the Chilingirian Quartet and clarinettist Andrew Marriner playing a wonderful programme of, mainly, Mozart and Brahms – this weekend produced its problems and tensions. Nothing specially dramatic, just an accumulation of incidents which ultimately send you home in a state of nervous exhaustion when it's all over.

As before we were perfectly well organized. But then you can never plan for the unexpected, neither can you legislate for silliness and error on the part of the staff, nor can you predetermine the whims, fancies and eccentricities of your punters. Our musical visitors – sensitive, cerebral souls that they are – tend to be fussy, particular and prone to complaint. Many are die-hard regulars and it is a mystery to me why some of them keep coming back year after year. A glance at the comments against each name on the arrivals list is fair warning of what to expect: 'Requires Flora, not butter', 'Allergic to cats', 'Foam pillows only', 'Room to be extra warmed with blow heater <u>before</u> arrival', 'Pouffe to be put in room as leg rest and one to be provided for concerts', 'Allergic to dairy products'. Sometimes the receptionist's comments are more prosaic, ranging from 'V. nice people' to 'Watch this one! Can be v. difficult'.

Because these occasions are as much social as musical, Louise's and my presence as hosts comes with the package – thus we are in the habit of inviting one or two guests to join our table for dinner after the concerts. Invariably, these will be our staunchest supporters and, not infrequently, they will also be our severest critics. An invitation to dine at the captain's table (where they will drink rather well) is absolutely no cause for them to modify or restrain their feelings if, for any reason, they believe we have committed some transgression. And last weekend we transgressed, not once but twice – worse, we transgressed with the very people we had invited to join our table on both Friday *and* Saturday night.

David James CBE, our guest on the first evening, is one of our oldest clients and, it must be said, one of our greatest supporters. He can also be a real pain. As Britain's most famous 'company doctor' and financial troubleshooter (minimum annual wage £1.5 million), what he wants, he expects to get. And if his demands are not precisely met, he has a tendency to become frighteningly testy. This is a fifty-nine-year-old man whose daily regime begins at 5 am with 200 press-ups, 300 sit-ups and a run round Hyde Park. Mr James, then, does not easily tolerate lesser beings. And the staff dread his visits. But over the years Louise and I have come to know and appreciate his finer qualities. Like oysters he is an acquired taste. As long as you treat him with care, he'll slip down very nicely. But just occasionally you may swallow a bad'un. And on Friday evening we did.

We were greeting our house guests at the drinks party before the first concert when David came bounding into the room at ten to seven without so much as a hello.

'I'll be serving you with a writ for £2 million on Monday morning,' he opened, fixing me with a characteristically pugnacious glare.

'Two million strikes me as fairly modest by your standards, David,' I replied jocularly.

'No, that'll do very well, having nearly cut my head open on a shelf in the bathroom, which then sent a glass tumbler smashing into the basin.'

'Well that's your fault!' observed Louise rather indelicately.

I apologized, but Mr James wasn't done yet. 'On the subject of basins,' he continued, 'you've got a blocked pipe. The water's not running out. And I haven't got my foam pillows either!'

'I'll get it fixed straight away,' I said, apologizing for a second time.

He passed into the room with his glass of fizz and I called Andrew over to alert him to the problems in Room 14. Ten minutes later he returned to confirm the basin was now running clear and that Mr James's foam pillows were in place on his bed: our error, this, and a particularly unnecessary one as every department in the hotel is well drilled in the do's and don'ts of David James. In the past, our most heinous crime has usually been committed at breakfast, where our troubleshooting music-lover has a standing order for steamed smoked haddock. Occasionally, an unwitting breakfast cook has dished this up in the company of a poached egg, which is how most people seem to like their haddock served. Not Mr James. The sight of an egg scores an eight on the DJ Richter scale. Mercifully – and after several threats of public floggings for any members of staff who so much as whispered the words 'poached egg' – Mr James was presented with his smoked haddock in its virgin state on both Saturday and Sunday morning.

But our troubles on Friday evening were far from over. As we gathered for dinner after the concert, David announced that his bathroom plumbing still wasn't functioning satisfactorily.

'How am I to shave tomorrow morning with a basin that doesn't drain properly?' he snapped. 'Come and see for yourself, if you don't believe me.'

While I chatted to our other guests, Louise followed David up to his room to inspect the delinquent U-bend. On their return, Louise had a brief word with Andrew and we moved into the dining room to find our table. Andrew decided the moment had come to abandon his dinner jacket and exchange it for an overall. Armed with a kettle, a plunger and a large dose of neat bleach, he advanced on Room 14 and attacked the obstinate plug hole like a man bent on revenge. Back in his dinner jacket, he reported to me just as the main course was being served.

'All's well,' he hissed quietly in my right ear.

'Are you *absolutely* sure?' I hissed back.

'You have my personal guarantee.'

'What was the problem?' I asked.

'Vomit!' he said and left.

Clearly, the previous occupant of Room 14 had been unwell. I made a mental note to speak to the housekeeper.

By the end of the evening – and thanks in no small measure to a couple of excellent bottles of Puligny Montrachet – David James had mellowed. He also seemed to have enjoyed his dinner, by which I mean that he did not complain. I was certainly very satisfied with the food, particularly as our numbers had topped ninety – an MGM production and no mean feat for Phil's small brigade of cooks.

While coffee was being poured, Simon Girling came over to give me a run-down on the service.

'It's gone really well tonight,' he said. 'Smooth and easy.'

'Did everyone enjoy the dinner?' I asked.

'They loved it. I've spoken to every table in the room. The only people who weren't too happy were Mr and Mrs Walsh.'

'What do you mean?' I interrupted. Only two hours earlier I had invited Philip and Jill Walsh to be our guests for dinner on Saturday.

'Well, it was Mrs Walsh really,' continued Simon. 'She said the whole menu was *white* – there was no colour. The vegetables were overcooked and, she said, she could buy better meringues in Tesco.'

Like David James, Philip and Jill Walsh have been loyal supporters of our weekends for many years. Both are retired solicitors, live in Hampshire and are good at keeping us on our toes with what Jill likes to describe as 'constructive criticism'. Unlike Mr James, the Walshes are, at least, as generous with their bouquets as they are with their brickbats. On Friday evening, however, Mrs W – who fancies herself as a bit of a gourmet – was in no mood to compliment us on a dinner which even my sensitive palate judged well-balanced and delicious.

The offendingly 'white' menu in question read as follows: spiced chicken terrine with tomato compote; roast monkfish with braised vegetables; passionfruit pavlova. The accusation of whiteness is, I suppose, moot if you start with the premise that chicken, monkfish and meringue are white ingredients. But to my eyes – and I think they were reasonably well focused on Friday night – the manner of the menu's presentation rendered Mrs Walsh's observation a touch pedantic and otiose. The terrine was assembled using the darker flesh of the thigh and drumstick to give a pleasing mottled effect – a perfect foil for the deep red globule of compote beside it. The fish came with a crisply seared surface and although the colours of the vegetables (carrots, aubergines, courgettes, fennel) were more pastel than primary, I cannot say that I was gastronomically offended by the dish's alleged pallor. As to the cooking of the vegetables, these were braised in olive oil and melted sensuously in the mouth – the flavours true and divine. The passionfruit pavlova, I thought, looked utterly serene and wonderful on its plate – the brilliant yellow of the fruit syrup dramatically highlighted by the snow white of the meringue. I confess I have never tasted a Tesco meringue so perhaps I'm missing something, but I enjoyed Mr Vickery's brand for its textural contrast of fragile/flaky exterior and chewy/gooey inside.

Still, if there are any faults with our musical weekend menus, they can be laid at my door. Phil writes them but I scrutinize them. In all, four meals are served: Friday dinner, Saturday lunch and dinner, and Sunday lunch. The menus offer no choice except on Sunday, when it is limited to two dishes at each course. This brief poses something of a challenge given the nature of the weekends and the particularities of our clientele's tastes. My method is to spread Phil's proposals on a desk and look at all four at once, keeping a pile of previous menus to hand for reference. The composition of these meals is not determinedly gastronomic. They must appeal to a sophisticated company of palates who, nevertheless, prefer fairly simple, unfussy food. There must be a proper balance and variety to the menus across each weekend and we have to beware of repetition to avoid moans from regulars. Equally, anything non-kosher or gastronomically controversial like, say, offal or pig, are out.

After Saturday night's concert and still high on the Brahms B minor Clarinet Quintet, we took our places in the dining room. As the first wine was being poured, I turned to Mrs Walsh.

'Well I hope we can do better for you tonight, Jill. Perhaps a little more Sainsbury than Tesco!'

She laughed. 'So you've heard?'

'Oh yes, I hear it all!'

Dinner, as far as I could judge, passed the rainbow test: pasta leaves with leeks and truffle oil; guinea fowl with kale; rhubarb parfait. Certainly the evening ended with a warm chord of approval from our guests, which is more than I can say about the finale the night before. As we walked out of the dining room into the hall and before allowing David James to retire to his bed, Louise – wisely – decided to escort him personally to his room to satisfy herself that everything was in perfect order. It was. But when they returned, Mr James still wasn't happy.

'It's a little better,' he said despairingly. 'But the basin's still slow to clear.'

By now I'd had enough of this game and decided to call his bluff.

'OK, David,' I said, moving towards the reception desk, 'I'll move you to another room.' He instantly declined – which was just as well because the hotel was full.

OF BANKERS AND BANQUETS

MONDAY, 3 MARCH 1997

I SEEM TO BE FLAVOUR of the moment with my bank manager. This is an unusual state of affairs, and I can't bring myself to believe the bank is being so nice to me – but then we are performing unusually well and the capital repayments on our massive loan are running twenty-four months ahead of their prescribed schedule. What was a £¾ million millstone only three years ago has halved, and the burden continues to ease with the passing of each month's successful trading. February scored a 63 per cent occupancy. The hotel's net sales of £170,000 were up 7 per cent and the relaunch of Minstrels has paid off with a 25 per cent rise in turnover: sales touching almost £40,000. For the bleakest month in our calendar, this is deeply comforting news. The 'feel-good factor' may still be eluding the high street, but just now we all feel very good indeed. So the *froideur* between us and Barclays Bank – which, during the recession, never quite dropped to freezing point thanks to the nimble diplomacy of Michael Blackwell, our chairman – has given way to a new, almost Mediterranean, warmth in our relations.

Bob Shapland, Barclays' chief honcho in these parts, keeps telephoning to congratulate us on our figures, and the other day he invited me to a big bankers' dinner – a hitherto unthinkable gesture. I accepted gracefully even though the dinner itself filled me with some dread as it was being held at the Forte Posthouse in Taunton – a chain hotel which, for me, abuses all the natural laws of good hospitality but which, regrettably, is the only local venue capable of accommodating 200 diners. However, my dread was also tempered with a good deal of professional curiosity. I had never been to a banquet at the Posthouse and this do, the annual dinner of the Chartered Institute of Bankers, was being attended by a line-up of pretty high-powered guests, who included ex-Cabinet Minister Tom King, the Chairman of Barclays, Andrew Buxton, and a host of six-figure salaried CEOs from around the region. In other words, for the host hotel this was not the annual bash of a local rugby club, this was a big-deal occasion and an opportunity to impress an audience of movers and shakers who, as part of their business routines, are in the habit of booking dinners and conferences for their own companies.

For me, this dinner proved to be a salutary lesson in market economics and modern consumer expectations. Here I am, crooning smugly about our current business performance, but as I drove away from the Forte Posthouse that evening, I was hit by a flash of despair and thought what a mug I am. Granada, the owners of this chain, know their trade better than most, but my brief experience of their style suddenly brought home the simple truth that the route to serious profits in today's hotel industry has absolutely nothing to do with the values, the standards, or even the sense of pride that lie at the heart of what I understand to be the honourable art of hospitality. Ancient principles, cardinal beliefs of the profession like the virtues of courtesy, welcome and care implicit in the word *hospitality* have been devalued and redefined thus: give the punter the minimum acceptable standard of product and charge the maximum sum of money the market will bear. Let's not be sentimental about this trade: it no longer has anything to do with giving pleasure. It is, rather, the hard-nosed game of taking as much as you dare in return for providing as little as possible. It is a cold, impersonal transaction like buying a pair of underpants.

The corporate culture of these chains is so consuming that in the end the most basic tenets of hotelkeeping – such as good manners – get lost in the race for profits. It costs *nothing* to be polite to people, to be thoughtful about their comfort, or to show a simple act of friendship by trying to make them feel at home. But these universal values – the spirit of hospitality – count for little with Granada and their like. So for me, places like the Forte Posthouse remain dismal, soulless institutions. They are an anathema. Any hotel, irrespective of its style or price, should by definition be life-enhancing. These ghastly human pens are life-depressants, cynical corporate ghettos devoid of any civilized values.

But I suppose I have to be careful here. One man's ghetto may be another man's paradise. When I drove into the Posthouse's car park it took me a while to find a space. In the lobby – a vast open plan area taking in reception, bar and restaurant – ranks of electronic games blinked wildly at young executives pumping them full of coins, and large TV screens, suspended from the ceiling, provided casual distraction to small groups of men swilling pints, while others bounced balls across a pool table. The place was jumping like a seaside amusement arcade in high season.

Bob Shapland's invitation instructed me to report to the Polden Suite for drinks before dinner – fine if I could only find the room. But there was no one to greet and direct the Institute's 200 members and guests – not even a sign – and no one to tell us where to leave our coats. Even the reception office was deserted. Eventually, I found the Polden Suite and met Bob, who introduced me to his other guests and offered me a drink. I needed it. A waitress poured me a glass of white wine which she served unchilled in a warm glass. There was worse to come.

The dread I harboured about this dinner at least pitched my expectations low. But nothing prepared me for the sheer awfulness of the meal. It was foul, seriously foul, a total disgrace, the only edible course being the starter: an avocado and bacon salad which a six-year-old child could have assembled more easily than a box of Lego bricks. The main course that followed was execrable: slices of beef like grey, twisted sheets of gun-metal dished up with a mush of mixed vegetables pre-prepped and despatched to Posthouses nationwide from some anonymous food factory. Pudding – probably from the same factory – was a disgusting sweet and synthetic citrus confection which sent waves of electric shocks ululating painfully between one's teeth. How clever, I thought. A kitchen without chefs – just a production line and a few low-paid operatives. De-skilling is what Granada would call it. Don't think pleasure, don't think quality. Think margin – no one's complaining – not even this bunch of worthies. And that's the horror of this story. Here we were, 200 reasonably well educated, middle class, moneyed thrusters and 199 of us ate up like good boys and girls. Not a word, not a grimace. Clean plates all round.

For two hours we sat, hunched in tight school lines at narrow trestles, bottles of wine plonked haphazardly for us to help ourselves. Service – or what there was of it – came from an untrained crew of scruffy teenage casuals. It was agonizing to watch. They had forgotten to lay forks for the main course, so silently, uncomplainingly, we used the small forks set for the pudding. When the moment came to clear each course, they piled the plates noisily like pallets in a warehouse. Then, to cap it all, when the chairman rose to make his speech, he congratulated the hotel at length on an 'outstanding' dinner. And he meant it. He really meant it. I cast my eyes to the ceiling and asked myself what the hell I was doing whining about Michelin stars or why I bothered to waste so much emotional energy giving my long-suffering staff grief if they failed to perform the tiniest task exactly *comme il faut*. They are an elite corps compared to the rabble at the Posthouse. But who can blame them, poor things? Throughout the evening there was not a manager to be seen anywhere, unless you count the lugubrious spectre of a pony-tailed toastmaster who carried all before him with a beer belly so large it put a cruel strain on the seams of his well-worn uniform.

One might conclude, or, more aptly, my bank manager might conclude, that I did not enjoy the evening. In fact I did. Besides, good food is not the issue at events like this. Having assuaged my professional sensibilities, I realized (after my moment of despair on the way home) that I would rather die than swap jobs with Gerry Robinson, Granada's boss. Good luck to him and his Posthouses. For me the Institute's dinner was a good opportunity to do some gentle networking and to listen to two riveting speeches: one from the Chairman of Barclays on the future of banking and the second from Tom King, who terrified his audience with the news that the biggest challenge facing Britain's security agencies no longer came from alien powers, drug barons or terrorists but from international crime syndicates who were capable of breaking into the major banks' computer systems and, thereby, spiriting away vast sums of money to secret accounts overseas. A frightening prospect that could ultimately bring our banking system to its knees, destroy our currency and ruin the nation's economy.

No sooner had I shaken off my indignation at the Posthouse's miserable efforts to stage a serious banquet than we fell into the throes of preparing for our next gastronomic dinner. The event was held last Friday evening but, unlike any before it, this party was planned with another in mind. It was to be a full dress rehearsal for my own fiftieth birthday celebration later this month.

Unusually, our bookings for the gastronomic were under par and we ended up thirty-five on the night – precisely the number of guests coming to my birthday. So I decided that we would all sit at one long table decorated with trails of flowers down its length and illuminated with the family silver: six candelabra studded with eighteen tall candles. When Phil and I sat down to discuss the food, we planned a menu principally intended for my party but one which, we felt, could safely be tested on our gastronomic guests, chief of whom was our speaker Sir Julian Critchley, himself a critical trencherman and veteran of these dinners.

The thinking we apply to these evenings is, in many respects, not dissimilar to the planning of our musical weekend menus, the difference being that gastronomics by definition must live up to their billing and the banquets run to five courses. However, the food still needs to appeal to a wide audience and if I was going to inflict the menu on thirty-five of my own chums a couple of weeks later, the restrictions on my choice of dishes would have to be even tighter. While the majority are serious eaters, the menu's construction had to appeal equally to a more sensitive minority who might be offended by the sight of anything too determinedly carnal. Eventually, Phil and I came up with this:

THE CASTLE DINING CLUB
GUEST OF HONOUR: SIR JULIAN CRITCHLEY, MP

Friday, 28 February 1997

MENU

Warm Pasta Leaves
with Braised Leeks, Olive Oil and Parmesan

Steamed Lobster and Crab Sausage
with Saffron Couscous and Caviar Dressing

Roast Cockerel with Madeira and Truffles
Rösti, Spinach, Salsify and Carrots

Wigmore
Berkswell
Wellington

Caramel Mousse with Lemon Curd Ice Cream

The cheese course has become *de rigueur* at my gastronomic evenings. People enjoy tasting new and unusual varieties, and Phil sourced three beauties from Neal's Yard Dairy in London: two delicious unpasteurized ewe's milk cheeses – the Berkswell and the Wigmore – and a magnificent golden-yellow cheese made, originally, from the milk of a Guernsey herd owned by the Duke of Wellington (hence its name) and tasting much like a mature, nutty Cheddar.

By the end of Friday evening – and even though the chefs were greeted, deservedly, with wild applause when they emerged to take their bow – I was very pleased that we had put ourselves through this rehearsal in advance of my bash on the fifteenth. Our problems were not gustatory – although I did decide, sadly, to dispense with the cheeses on the grounds that, for a birthday party, they would be excessively demanding on my friends' digestive systems, particularly as I was laying on a bit of a rave afterwards. No, our main problem was the physical assembly of one table for thirty-five people. I had a very clear idea in my own mind how I wanted it to look and in order to get the proportions right for this number, we needed a double-width table with rounded ends. This involved the linking of ten trestles ranged in two rows of five down the centre of the dining room with a half-moon attachment at each end to make what might appear to be a single, seamless table. Unfortunately, our trestles are beginning to show their age and some are decidedly ropy. Fixing the twelve sections to create one even and perfectly horizontal surface was a major test of patience and ingenuity. Beer mats, notebooks and wood chips were deployed discreetly to prop up rogue table legs; where there were gaping crevasses, trestles were bound tight with picture wire. It was all absurdly Heath Robinson, but once the table was laid, garlanded and adorned in silver, no one would have believed the trials we went through to arrive at our elegant and glittering artifice.

Come curtain-up, the show passed off successfully, although I had one minor complaint. This was a procedural detail, but one which sparked a furious debate between my managers and me. Restaurant protocol dictates that ladies be served first. However, at a formal banquet, the rule (my rule) is that the lady on the host's right is the first to be served, followed by the rest of the party moving strictly anti-clockwise round the table with the host served last. In Andrew's and Simon's opinion, my way was quite wrong. All the ladies, they insisted, should be looked after first and only then should the gentlemen be served. We are still arguing but for my party it will be played by my rules.

As for the food, the kitchen more than earned its applause. After the Michelin débâcle, Friday night demonstrated that Vickery and his brigade were back on form. The dinner was faultless. The only negative comment came from one guest who called Simon over during the main course.

'It's all superb,' said the man. 'But – and I'm really not the complaining type – look here; look at this. There's a piece of rubber on my plate.'

'No sir,' said Simon politely. 'That's not rubber. That's truffle.'

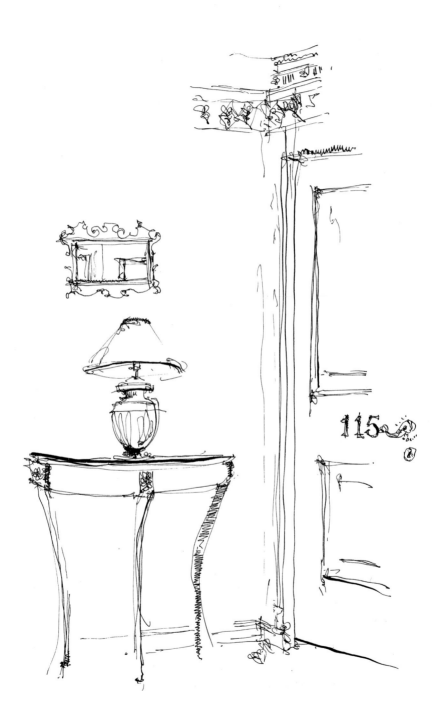

115

A POACHED EGG AND A CUP OF TEA

THURSDAY, 20 MARCH 1997

MY DIARY THIS MONTH reads like an obscene gastronomic marathon and with ten more days to go I am already suffering from peptic exhaustion (and gout). Last night, after another round of entertaining, I lay in bed actually dreading my next dinner. I just want the world to leave me in peace for a while and allow me to subsist on nothing grander than a poached egg and a cup of tea.

I love entertaining. Playing mine host is an essential and inevitable part of an hotelier's life, but it's also damned hard work, especially if the pace is dictated by an endless succession of inescapable engagements. For Louise and me, the only escape this month has been a quiet evening with Michel and Robyn Roux at the Waterside Inn, their three-star eaterie at Bray on the banks of the Thames. Not a bad way to spend a day off, but then being a guest in any company tends to be more fun than playing host. It is in the nature of hospitality, whether your guests are personal friends or paying, for the caring host to worry a little about the well-being, happiness and comfort of his visitors. Indeed, it is his duty – it's just that sometimes that duty wears you out.

Having barely recovered from my fiftieth birthday party last weekend, my appointments still look like one long rolling wave of food, drink and official merriment with brief pauses between to attend to the detail of each event. On Monday it was a group of visiting journalists from the Far East. Yesterday it was Frances Whitaker of Hawkshead (Delia Smith's producer) to discuss a television proposal with Phil Vickery. Tomorrow the Nash Ensemble arrive for the final programme in this year's season of musical weekends. On Sunday evening I'm dining with Jonathan Meades, *The Times*'s restaurant critic, Jennifer Paterson, one of the *Two Fat Ladies*, and Erica Brown, the new editor of the *Egon Ronay Guide*. All three are attending the launch of the 1997 edition of the *Trencherman's West Country* (a listing of the region's top thirty restaurants) the following day: a grand lunch for sixty, including press, senior tourist board officials, wine merchants and fellow restaurateurs. That evening it's dinner with Godfrey Smith of the *Sunday Times* and his wife, Mary, who are also attending the lunch and staying on. Then there's the company's AGM, and on Friday next week, Sheridan and Ruth Morley arrive with their troupe of players to entertain our Easter guests with a cabaret celebration of Noël Coward and his era.

It will be the greatest fun but I am planning to take Easter Monday off to sleep. And when I awake, I shall make myself a pot of tea, poach an egg and enjoy it hugely in the blissful solitude of home.

Paradoxically, one cares more – and, therefore, one worries more – about entertaining friends who do not pay than strangers who do. Celebrating that strange landmark, my half-century, five days ago, I put the entire hotel on high alert. Never before – even for visiting presidents and prime ministers – have so many memos been written, briefings held, arrangements fine tuned. Our 'rehearsal' two weeks earlier had, at least, given us a menu and a table design for Saturday's dinner; but there were still the wines to be chosen, among a few dozen other details. Although I had a broad idea of what I wanted – white burgundy, red Bordeaux – I did not intend to rely entirely on our own stocks and, besides, I decided it would be more amusing to offer my friends one glass each of a number of fine wines rather than several glasses of fewer vintages. And so – after raking through the bins in our cellar and after weeks of debate about the clarets with Corney & Barrow in London – I came up with five wines to match the four courses, kicking off with magnums of champagne before we sat down and an *eau de vie* for the toast afterwards. It was quite a line-up.

Once the wines had been fixed, I issued a detailed brief for their service. Delivery of the reds – fifteen bottles of the Talbot and a case of the Grand-Puy-Ducasse – was not expected until Thursday, little more than forty-eight hours before the dinner. These two voluptuous Médocs were to be served side-by-side with the roast cockerel. On the basis of six glasses out of a bottle, I reckoned on decanting six of each wine (we were thirty-five) to provide one generous glass for every guest. As soon as the wines arrived, the dozen bottles – six plus six – were stood upright in the cellar while the rest were racked in their bins. This would

DINNER: 15 MARCH, 1997

WINES

Apéritif:
Charles Heidsieck Brut Réserve in Magnums

Puligny-Montrachet Les Pucelles, 1990 Leflaive

Corton-Charlemagne, 1988 Drouhin

Château Talbot 1983

Château Grand-Puy-Ducasse 1982

Bonny Doon Muscat 1995

Toast
Eau de Vie, Poire

MENU

Warm Pasta Leaves
with Braised Leeks, Olive Oil
and Parmesan

Steamed Lobster and Crab Sausage
with Saffron Couscous and a Caviar Dressing

Roast Cockerel with Madeira and Truffles
Rösti, Spinach, Salsify and Carrots

Caramel Mousse
with Lemon Curd Ice Cream

Coffee

allow plenty of time for the sediment in the bottles to settle before decanting the wines on Saturday evening. The task of decanting fell to Christophe and, I told him, it had to be done between 7.00 and 7.15 – about an hour before we were called to table and no earlier. Once decanted, the stoppers were to remain out to allow a little air to bring the wines to life.

There was, of course, much more to organize: the table plan (a nightmare with thirty-five people, most of whom had never met); flowers and fruit for their bedrooms with personal notes of welcome; the band for dancing after dinner; the roulette and the baccarat; the dressing of the night club with a thousand gold and blue balloons; and much more. I had also booked a steel band for Sunday to add a touch of Caribbean spice to the farewell feast at midday … And what a feast! I wanted this to be an exuberant, spectacular finale to the weekend. A complete contrast to the black tie formality of dinner the evening before. I wanted this to be an immense picnic: a picnic on an Edwardian scale laid at one vast table, groaning with good things to eat, spilling over with a sense of abundance.

As preparations gathered pace with the approach of the weekend, there was one detail I had overlooked: the arrival of spring, and with it the consequences of a town swathed in sunshine. Suddenly, after months in hibernation, the Great Unwashed emerged from their winter squats to recolonize the centre of Taunton and, in particular, to occupy Castle Green, the leafy square in front of the hotel. Within a couple of days the daffodils had been pulverized, the grass was fouled with the droppings of their mad-eyed dogs, and the good citizens of this town were, once again, being terrorized by abuse and demands for money. Reports of harassment and unpleasantness began to filter back to me from various members of staff but, quite frankly, my mind was on other things: The Party.

Eventually, on Wednesday morning, Louise came into my office in a state of some distress. She had been in a second-floor bedroom with the housekeeper when they spotted a hairy lout on a bicycle riding out of our car park with a large bucket of lilies and roses which she had carefully stored in the garage in readiness for the weekend. My first reaction was to telephone Jefferson Horsley, the Leader of the

Council, with whom I had locked horns over the vagrancy problem last year. (Eight days on, I am still waiting for Ol' Waffles to return my call.) I then rang the *Somerset County Gazette*, knowing perfectly well that nothing helps focus the minds of our local politicians like a dose of adverse publicity. The *Gazette* duly obliged on Friday with a banner headline splashed across its front page.

Somerset County Gazette, 14 March 1997
Taunton Castle Hotel Chief Says Vagrants Back On The Green Drive Him and His Staff 'To Distraction'

WE WANT ACTION NOT JUST WORDS

Vagrants gathering on a grassy area outside Taunton's Castle Hotel are driving its managing director Kit Chapman and his staff to distraction, he claimed this week... 'I have complained before about the behaviour of these people who sit there all day drunkenly shouting and making a thorough nuisance of themselves yet the authorities do nothing... We get wonderful words of comfort from Jefferson Horsley and Taunton Deane Council about their negotiations with the Home Office over new by-laws and yet nothing happens.'
... Deane council leader Jefferson Horsley said: 'It is basically a police problem. If people are breaking the law, members of the public should report such incidents but, otherwise, what can you do?... As for by-laws against drinking in public, how does one distinguish between those drinking alcohol in a public place and those drinking outside a normal pub?'...

By 9.30, the two local radio stations and several of the region's other newspapers had picked up the story and were demanding interviews. I told them I thought Mr Horsley's response to the problem was pathetic and unhelpful. Then a terrified TV cameraman came into the hotel to ask me to provide an escort while he filmed the mob outside. If you need a bodyguard, I said, call your producer. I'm an hotelier, not a minder. At 11.30, Jenny Hoyle, the 'Taunton Town Centre Manager', telephoned me. Ms Hoyle was conciliatory and sympathetic. She suggested a meeting. I told her I was fed up with meetings but we fixed a date anyway.

In the middle of this frenzy – and to my complete surprise – our old pal Mr Bonsall called me. I could hardly believe my ears. The man is clearly quite mad. But, as the police had instructed, I behaved nonchalantly, as if it were perfectly normal for our customers to walk away without paying their bills.

'Hello, Mr Bonsall,' I said cheerily. 'How very good to hear from you again.'

'I'm sorry not to have been in touch, Mr Chapman,' he said, 'but I've been in Paris over the past month sorting out a crisis.'

'Oh dear!'

'Now I'm very conscious that I still haven't settled my account with you. Remind me, how much do I owe you?'

'£2,406.65, Mr Bonsall.'

'Right, I'll be sending one of my couriers down with the cash next week. He'll be with you no later than Wednesday.'

'Wouldn't it be more convenient for you to put it through your credit card, Mr Bonsall. If you'd just like to give me a number …'

'No, no,' he interrupted, 'the courier will deliver the cash and collect my luggage. You still have my luggage locked away safely, I hope?'

'Yes, of course,' I said. 'But a cheque would do perfectly well. If you'd like to give me your address, I'd be happy to post the account to you first.'

He wouldn't have it. Wednesday was yesterday and, of course, no courier appeared.

Fortunately it was raining on Saturday afternoon. As our dear friends arrived, they were spared a low welcome from the New Age Goths on Castle Green and the next twenty-four hours passed in a haze of happiness, high spirits and a drop or two to drink. The only anxious moment came at about 7.15 when Christophe, decanting the sixth bottle of Talbot, accidentally chipped the lip of a claret jug. The break was clean, the thin sliver of glass falling on to the table. Nevertheless, as an extra precaution, I told him to redecant the wine through muslin.

And Sunday's feast? Our Edwardian picnic? Well, Phil took over the brief, put his own spin on it and insisted I keep out of the way. 'Leave it to me! Don't interfere! And just enjoy it!' he instructed. The result was a fabulous finale to my party. When the steel band struck up and as the waiters drew back the heavy curtains separating the main dining room from the section where we had gathered for drinks, there was the table from the night before transformed into a stage set for a Peter Greenaway movie. Phil, Andrew and Christophe had rebuilt the table with a raised central platform constructed of a line of crates draped in folds of white linen loosely arranged like rolling waves. Silver wine stands – improvised pedestals – stood at each end of the line holding garlands of flowers. And woven into and around the folds of linen, they had decorated this second tier with the most dazzling display of fruits, from the obvious – apples, pears, bananas and grapes – to the exotic – mangoes, kiwi, passionfruit, pomegranates and lychees – with varieties of citrus and melon, figs, plums, pineapples, cherries, apricots and much more. I lost count after twenty.

Then, on the table surrounding this luxuriant mountain plateau was the picnic, a gastronomic patchwork quilt of unimaginable splendour. Trays of crushed ice bearing giant oysters; large flat dishes of smoked eel and smoked mackerel with pots of horseradish crème fraîche; plates of smoked salmon and gravadlax; potted ducks and spiced pears; Caesar salad and salads of mussels, cherry tomatoes, pasta ribbons, fresh tuna; bowls of marinated vegetables; couscous and peppers; lobsters split in half with potato salad in their heads; silver ovals of quails' eggs with saffron mayonnaise. For something hot, there was a sensational fish pie and a large, deep tray of magnificent beef olives in a rich, well-flavoured gravy and bowls of Vickery's unbeatable mashed potato. And for pudding, there were egg custard tarts, pecan pies, fresh fruit salads.

This was a feast like no other. An impressionist tableau never to be repeated. A memory that will return as a Proustian romance.

THURSDAY, 27 MARCH 1997

The last of this season's series of musical weekends passed harmoniously and, almost but not entirely, without incident. Philip and Jill Walsh enthused volubly about the colours in our menus and David James CBE was in a much better mood. He smiled more, complained less. The plumbing in his bedroom functioned satisfactorily but, irritatingly, the cellar was out of the Bâtard-Montrachet. 'Kit, your wine list needs sorting out!' 'Yes, David. Sorry, David!' For one reason or another, I always seem to find myself apologizing to Mr James.

For a moment, I thought we may have got off to a tricky start. Earlier in the week, David's formidable PA, Linda Thomas, telephoned Gill (my secretary) about his dining arrangements for Saturday evening, the unspoken implication of the call being that he was available for dinner at our table on Friday. As we already had guests to entertain on both evenings, Gill kept silent at Linda's discreet overture and no invitation was issued.

Come the drinks on Friday night, David did not appear. Then Andrew told me that although he had taken his seat for the first concert, he had called reception to say that he would not be dining afterwards. Oh dear, I thought. He's taken umbrage. We're in trouble. At the interval, Louise and I made a beeline for him and we chatted amiably in the bar over a glass of champagne. Honour had been restored, the niceties of our trade observed.

The following day, however, Carolyn Humphreys, our artistic director, had a bizarre exchange with him in the lift. They had just finished breakfast and as they were stepping into the lift car with a small group of other guests, Carolyn turned to him.

'What a beautiful morning, David,' she said.

'Is it?' he replied curtly. 'I hadn't noticed.' He paused for a second. 'I'd much prefer a deluge. The whole place is drying up!'

Now whether Mr James's observation referred to the Castle Hotel or to the planet Earth is unclear. Was this an arcane reference to his smoked haddock? Had it been poached dry? Or was this a profound insight on global warming? Had Hale-Bopp, the great comet now whizzing through the night sky, spoken to him? We shall never know. But I can report that when he came to leave on Sunday, he was not entirely unhappy.

'I do hope you've enjoyed the weekend, David,' I asked hopefully.

'Better than last time,' he replied.

Thank goodness, I thought. Perhaps it was the decorative company. On this occasion we seemed to attract one or two rather exotic women – the sort you can't fail to notice the moment they walk into a room. Mrs Conway – 'call me Nadia' – is Estonian and magnificently ebullient in her gold trouser suit and jewels. Her husband is quiet, English and completely in her shadow. In the past they have come as a foursome with their friends Mr and Mrs Michael Portillo, but not on this occasion as Mr Portillo has an election to fight. I offered my commiserations.

'Never mind,' I said, chatting to Nadia at Friday's drinks do. 'After May the first, Michael will have plenty of spare time to come to our concerts.'

'I doubt it,' she replied. 'He's likely to be busier than ever!'

I was about to probe the extent of Mr Portillo's ambitions to lead the Tory Party when I was distracted by the arrival of a lady who was attending one of our musicals for the first time. Her name was Adèle Leigh-Enderl and by an extraordinary coincidence she happened to be acquainted with Keith Jeffery, a retired director of the Arts Council, and his friend Adrian Carswell, who were our guests for the weekend. And so it was that Adèle Leigh-Enderl (in her time a distinguished diva and the widow of the Austrian ambassador) joined our table for dinner after the concerts on both Friday and Saturday evenings. On each occasion she sat by me, and feisty company she was too.

Unfortunately (although it could not have mattered less) Adèle had been allocated Room 116, a single on the third floor. These rooms at the top of the hotel were constructed in 1965 by an incompetent architect and a cheapjack builder, and we've been living with the consequences ever since. The problem, bluntly, is that the walls dividing each bedroom offer little protection to one's ears if the occupants next door engage in any activity louder than a silent caress. On Friday night, it seems, the couple occupying Room 115 became quite excited, indeed aroused to a degree that their bodies, heaving frantically in unison, nearly came crashing through the wall separating them from Room 116. Or so it sounded to Adèle, who lay in her bed transfixed by this impressive display of sexual gymnastics.

'My dear, it was an experience,' she said breathlessly at dinner on Saturday. 'But who are they? I have to see these people. They were fantastic.'

From the table listings on the desk by the entrance to the dining room, we identified the occupants of Room 115. Adèle could not believe her eyes (and neither could we). Our athletic lovers turned out to be a very grey item in advanced middle age: he, weedy as Douglas Hogg; she, a stout Shirley Williams look-alike.

We resumed our dinner and – more soothingly – began to discuss the Nash Ensemble's brilliant performance of the Mozart flute quartet in C.

After the final concert on Sunday, we gave lunch a miss – neither Louise nor I could face it. Besides, I needed a break before my serious binge that evening. I made a tour of the tables in the restaurant, said our goodbyes and headed home for a brisk hike over the hills with Caruso and Bollinger.

Meanwhile, with the departure of all our musical weekenders, the hotel emptied and, save my gourmet VIPs, there were precious few other arrivals. Bookings for dinner stood at five: two tables of two and a one. The atmosphere in the room would be glum and funereal – not quite the style in which to entertain the likes of Jonathan Meades, Jennifer Paterson and Erica Brown. To howls of protest from Vickery, I decided to transfer my party to the Penthouse – a distance of five floors from the kitchen. In addition, I did not want to fix the menu – my guests were to have the full run of the *carte*. With a steep flight of stairs, then a slow draughty dumb waiter connecting basement hotplate and roof-top table, Phil's objections were understandable. The point of this dinner was the food. It had to be perfect. Holding the party in the Penthouse was, in his view, an unnecessary risk. But it had to be. I needed to create the right mood – a convivial setting was essential to fulfil the promise of the food. And as there were only four of us dining, I reckoned on the dumb waiter having to make just one journey between courses.

Given the gastronomic curiosity of the company, I also knew that we would all order different dishes from the menu. There was little point, therefore, in waiting to see what people were going to eat before choosing the wine, so I pre-ordered a couple of bottles of M. Ampeau's nectar, his 1980 Meursault, and the same again of Sassicaia 1993, Tuscany's, indeed Italy's, grandest red. There was one other small detail to arrange. If I was going to survive Monday's press launch of the *Trencherman's Guide,* I would need a decent night's sleep. Past form with Meades has seen the two of us consume dangerous quantities of *alcool blanc* well into the early hours. On this occasion I could not allow myself that luxury. Come 7 am on Monday morning, I had to be alive and running, and so for Sunday evening I needed a plausible escape route. Rather than stay overnight in the hotel, I decided to go home; and as driving was out of the question, I booked a taxi to collect me at midnight.

We gathered at 7.30. When I arrived, Jonathan and Jennifer were already in the bar drinking large whiskies – he Laphroaig, she a common Bell's – an open packet of Jennifer's Woodbines on the table between them. We went upstairs where we were joined by Erica. Christophe began to pour the fizz, which Jennifer promptly refused, preferring to have her whisky tumbler recharged at frequent intervals. All of us pitched into a tray of canapés and the three marvelled at the size and fleshiness of the giant Kalamata olives.

This was a jolly, animated party of the best kind, everyone determined to eat well, drink well and make merry. The menu was well trawled of its star dishes: to start, crab tart, artichoke and mushroom salad, deep-fried sole with saffron mayo and beetroots, and smoked eel; to follow, roast turbot, shin of beef, braised shoulder of lamb, saddle of venison. Phil rose to the moment in consummate style, the dumb waiter behaved impeccably and the contentment round the table was audible. After cheese, I called for egg custard tarts and nutmeg ice cream, and the blancmange with saffron syrup, puddings that Meades lapped up greedily but which Jennifer Paterson refused to touch on the grounds that they were horrible to eat. After much persuasion, she agreed to test Vickery's way with these wonderful nursery confections.

'Disgusting! Revolting!' she cried, breaking into a loud throaty cackle.

By 11.30 Jennifer had waddled happily off to bed and shortly afterwards the night porter came to say that my driver was waiting downstairs. I left Jonathan and Erica sipping their way through an ice-cold bottle of *eau de vie de prune*. By 12.30 I was asleep.

Anyone walking into the hotel on Monday morning would never have guessed there was anything especially important going on at midday. The place was like a tired old grandfather clock that needed winding up. The restaurant staff were in a daze, zombies catching their breath after the hard labour of the musical weekend. In the kitchen, the brigade were sipping mugs of tea and gossiping while Phil leafed through a newspaper in his office. And in the hall, Andrew was wandering about with a security expert discussing panic buttons, CCTV and other precautionary installations in case of invasion by the barbarians on the Green. By ten o'clock – and with only two hours before the off – nothing was in place, nothing was happening. We hadn't even made the most fundamental decision of the day: where *exactly* to hold the Trencherman's lunch?

In all we were fifty-nine, sitting down at tables of between six and ten. This was an awkward number that did not naturally suit the spaces we had available. If we were ten more or if we were ten less, the decision would have been made for us. A larger group automatically would have meant drinks in the Monmouth Room and lunch in the whole restaurant – an L-shaped room divided by a folding glass screen and curtains. Fifty or less and we could easily hold the reception in the smaller part of the dining room, drawing the curtains back to announce lunch in the main section as we had done for my birthday. With a party of fifty-nine, the decision was moot: take the whole restaurant and there would be enough fresh air between tables to catch hypothermia; take the small section for drinks and the large section for lunch and we were risking asphyxia. To resolve our dilemma, we decided to set the tables in the large part of the room first, to see how it worked; if it was too cramped, we'd just spread the tables into the small section and move the drinks upstairs to the Monmouth Room.

At 10.30 Andrew, Phil, Louise and I gathered with Simon and Christophe to make the decision. Opinion was divided of course, but in the end Andrew and I felt that it was probably better to be cosy and intimate than airy and grand. Besides, time was running out and we still hadn't held the final briefing on the order of service.

THE TRENCHERMAN'S WEST COUNTRY:
Luncheon to launch the 1997/98 Guide
GUEST OF HONOUR: JENNIFER PATERSON

Monday, 24 March 1997

WINES
Presented by Christopher Pope
Chairman of Eldridge Pope

Aperitif:
Reynier Brut

Saumur Blanc 1995 Domaine de la Renière
René Hugues Gay

Hautes Côtes de Beaune 1993 Domaine Porcheray
Caves des Hautes Côtes

Côteaux du Layon 'Carte d'Or' 1994 Domaine Baumard

Courvoisier Napoleon
Courtesy of Allied Domecq

MENU
Seared Salt and Pepper Scallops
with Braised Tomatoes and Deep Fried Basil

Steamed Spiced Lamb Pudding
Roast Spring Vegetables and Mashed Potatoes

Caramel Mousse
Lemon Curd Ice Cream

Coffee

To get the party going, there were to be two opening speeches: one by me to welcome the press and VIPs, one by Christopher Pope, Chairman of Eldridge Pope, who had donated the wines for the occasion. He needed his moment for a sales pitch to the assembled restaurateurs.

'How long is Mr Pope speaking?' asked Phil.

'I have no idea. At least five minutes I'd say.'

'Well, you'll need to warn everybody that there'll be a delay serving the first course. I'm not starting to cook the scallops until he sits down.'

'Fair enough. I can cover that in my welcome,' I replied.

Phil's point was critical, the more so given the collection of sharp palates sitting down to lunch. Scallops need to be cooked and served immediately: leave them hanging around and they turn to rubber. We moved on to the main course.

'How exactly do you plan to serve the mashed potatoes?' I asked Vickery.

'Scoop it into the large deep bowls along with the lamb pudding and veg. That way we get it out fast and the food stays hot.'

I disagreed. 'Chef, that would be a mistake. There's enough going on in those bowls as it is. Add the mash and the dish will look overcrowded and end up eating like mush. Why not serve the potato on the side in the small oval china?'

'We can't do sixty like that,' said Simon. 'We've only got thirty-six small ovals.'

'So what?' I interrupted. 'Make up the balance by scooping the mash on to warm side plates or saucers.'

One other point was worrying Phil about the spiced lamb. 'Don't forget that the suet mould hides a prune. You'd better warn them in case someone breaks a tooth on the stone.'

'OK. I can mention that in my welcome too.'

Miraculously, by twelve o'clock we were set to go and as the final checks were being made, the first guests began to arrive. For most, the lunch was a busman's holiday; for some, a rare opportunity to snipe at the efforts of a fellow restaurateur. Like any other type that collects *en masse* for pleasure, restaurateurs can be a pretty foul lot. You'd think they'd know better. You'd think they'd behave. Fat chance. At play, they are invariably the worst breed of punter to sit at your table, and if, like the Castle, you have a high profile, a 'reputation', they treat you like a clay pigeon.

While the foodie press – Jonathan Meades, Erica Brown, Tom Jaine, Richard Binns, Godfrey Smith and others – raved enthusiastically about Vickery's robust but sensuous spiced lamb pudding, a dish the like of which they'd never quite seen before, a small coterie of my fellows got sniffy, dismissing it as inappropriately downmarket for the occasion. Bollocks to them! And to my exquisite pleasure – in spite of the health warning earlier – a couple of busmen swallowed their prune stones. 'Oh well,' I said to one, 'it'll be a happy reminder of your lunch when it plops out the other end, won't it?'

But no one enjoyed the feast more than dear Jennifer, for whom several large pre-prandial vodkas lent fire to a rush of hilarious stories about her favourite saints. By the end of lunch her hagiographies included Godfrey Smith, whose heroic frame and flowing white hair moved her deeply: 'Dress him up as a cardinal,' she boomed. 'Give him a scarlet hat and put a monkey on his shoulder!'

WEDNESDAY, 2 APRIL 1997

Peace at last! Easter is done and April's diary looks mercifully free of official entertaining and mandatory gourmandizing. For the next few days Louise and I intend to live as ascetics – hermits in our own home: she in her garden, me in my book-piled attic. I didn't even get round to poaching my promised egg on Easter Monday. The most my weary constitution could absorb was a bowl of Sainsbury's best muesli and an apple with my cup of tea.

As to the weekend, our first dip into the glamorous world of cabaret as a means of filling beds at Easter worked brilliantly. Without some unusual diversion, the hotel would have been empty. Taunton, incomprehensibly, does not rank high in people's imaginations as a great destination for a city break. Cider, cricket and cows are about as glamorous as we get. The only way I can compete with Las Vegas, London and Monte Carlo is to import my own bright lights. And this we did last Sunday night with Sheridan and Ruth Morley staging a marvellous celebration of Noël Coward with their theatrical chums Liz Robertson, who sang, and Stuart Pedlar, who played the piano, while Sheridan hosted the show, with jokes and witty tales of Coward's life.

For us, the trick was to promote a two-night Easter deal that included everything: Martini cocktails before dinner on Saturday, all meals, a talk by Sheridan about Coward and the theatre before lunch on Sunday and the performance that evening. As a result most weekenders extended their holiday either side of the package, and for the cabaret we topped up the extra space in the Monmouth Room by selling tickets to locals at a tenner a go.

The programme was a sell-out – embarrassingly so as we were selling tickets right up to the last moment and for some inexplicable reason we miscalculated the number of tickets for the available seats. This unfortunate gaffe delayed the show fifteen minutes to allow extra chairs to be ferried in by the porters, who then had to find odd spaces in the room to slot the seating in – a comic cabaret in itself which the audience took as an entertaining prelude to the main act.

What I had not anticipated was my own participation in the show, albeit a very minor part. However, Ruth decided that she needed a master of ceremonies and that I was ideally fitted for the role. To mark the start of the performance, all the lights were to be extinguished, casting the room into instant and total darkness. I was then to mount the platform swiftly and noiselessly, at which point the lights would come on to reveal my presence centre stage. I was to make a suitably burlesque introduction to the cabaret and its artistes before leaping off with a flourish as Stuart Pedlar made his entrance to take his place at the piano.

This was all very well except that by 7.15 the Monmouth Room was so full there was barely a gap you could call a gangway. How, I asked myself, am I expected to get from the door to the stage without breaking a leg? I counted the steps in my mind, estimated the height of the platform, noted the position of the piano, and threw my lot to the Fates. At Ruth's signal the room blacked out and, silently, I groped my way on to the stage. As the lights came on – and before I'd even uttered a word – the terror, relief and surprise on my hapless face tripped the audience into a wave of laughter. The show was off.

At dinner Sheridan was in full flight. The champagne flowed, toasts were proposed, the cabaret declared a triumph. In short, spirits were running high. Between stories about Robert Morley (his father), Gladys Cooper (his grandmother), Gertrude Lawrence and the two Hepburns (Katharine and Audrey), Ruth and I agreed that for Easter next year it would be worth planning a short cabaret season: a series of shows which would make our new venture more sensible commercially by spreading the costs of publicity and staging across more than one programme.

By the main course – best end of lamb – Sheridan was leading a lively debate on the nature of stardom, which then seemed to roll into a discussion about the nature of audiences and their relationship with performers. Meanwhile, on the table next door, a party of eight were celebrating a golden wedding anniversary in complete silence, the happy couple surrounded by three generations of glum-faced family. Their table looked splendid, with a golden gâteau sitting proudly on a cake stand in the centre – excuse enough, one might have thought, for a little animation from the dullest company.

'Sybil Thorndike was once asked how she felt about her audiences,' declared Sheridan, his voice rising to a crescendo. 'She replied they either felt like cold porridge or like electricity.'

At this point, a man – presumably the golden wedding couple's son – got up and approached Sheridan. 'Would you kindly address your remarks to your table and your table alone,' he said abruptly and turned on his heel.

Sheridan, struck dumb for a second, apologized – a polite gesture offered much too penitently to a dullard intent on spending good money giving himself and his family a miserable time.

'Restaurant tables are like theatre audiences,' I said. 'And that one's cold porridge.'

PAVEMENT PEOPLE

THURSDAY, 17 APRIL 1997

T HIS HAS BEEN A WEEK of tiresome people. It is beginning to dawn on me that Taunton Deane Borough Council is falling under the influence of a young nerdocracy which is driving its dozy members to new heights of folly. On Tuesday, I attended a meeting of the Taunton Town Centre Forum because the agenda promised a special presentation on plans to equip the town with a closed circuit TV system. Excellent news; action at last to combat the barbarian invader. However, item one on the agenda read 'Car Free Day, 17 June, introduced by Brendan Cleere, Environmental Co-ordinator, TDBC'. Mr Cleere's big idea is that businesses need to raise their 'awareness about transport, health and the environment' by eschewing the motor car on Tuesday, 17 June. According to the slogan in his printed propaganda, we are to 'Bus it – Bike it – Walk it', and if we do, 'TAUNTON CAR FREE DAY '97 *MEANS BUSINESS!*' The clarity of Mr Cleere's vision does not, apparently, quite extend to Hertz-borne American tourists or harassed BMW-driving execs who, I think, are unlikely to be persuaded to bus it, bike it or, for that matter, walk it from Stonehenge or Manchester for the pleasure of a bedroom at the Castle on the evening of 17 June. Never mind, Mr Cleere thinks his idea is a business winner and he wants all of us in the town centre to 'register' for Car Free Day '97 and have a lot of fun with it. In his highly original and ingenious publicity, Mr Cleere exhorts us with this message:

– Encourage all your staff to walk, cycle or use the bus.
– Organize a 'Bus vs. Bike vs. Walk' to work contest among your staff.
– Organize a 'Crazy Ways to Work' Challenge.
... the possibilities are as wide as your imagination.

Unfortunately, the meeting did not share Mr Cleere's enthusiasm and responded by bombarding his idea with undisguised contempt. 'A waste of ratepayers' money!'

'A waste of the Council's time and resources!' 'Irrelevant!' 'Stupid!' were just some of the accusations fired at the Environmental Co-ordinator and his fellow nerdocrats.

The agenda passed hurriedly to item two and the debate on proposals to equip the town centre with a CCTV system. At lunchtime only the day before, a man, perched on his scooter and eating a sandwich, had been mugged by one of the barbarians on the Green. An hysterical woman rushed into the hotel and we called the police. Everyone in the meeting room had their own stories to tell and the plans for CCTV were welcomed unanimously; although like everything else in local government, we shall probably have to wait a couple of years before we see the cameras installed. Meanwhile, here is a great new project for the environmentally-sensitive Mr Cleere. Would he, I wondered, consider organizing a Vagrant Free Day? Could his fertile imagination be engaged to:

– Encourage all staff to run down a vagrant?
– Organize a 'strap-a-vagrant-to-your-roof-rack' contest?
– Organize a 'Crazy Ways with a Vagrant' Challenge?

Sadly, as Taunton Deane Borough Council is solidly Lib-Dem, this is one idea that is unlikely to win favour among our worthy councillors, who have inflated social consciences and wear their political correctness with pride. Jenny Hoyle, the Taunton Town Centre Manager, has never been heard to utter nasty words like 'vagrant' – she prefers the sublime phrase 'pavement people'.

Nevertheless, with the general election campaign in full cry, vagrancy has become a minor party political issue locally, not least with Taunton's sitting Tory Member of Parliament, David Nicholson, who is defending a majority of little more than 3,000 votes. A modest swing in the wrong direction and, come 2 May, he will be unemployed – a prospect which, as the date approaches, seems highly probable. Mr Nicholson is the sort of chap who makes jolly company at a dinner party but, even as MPs go, he is pretty idle. He deserves to lose his seat. Ever since he succeeded Edward du Cann as the Member for Taunton, the Tory majority has shrivelled. The constituency – next door to Paddy Ashdown's Yeovil seat – is now a marginal and the Lib-Dems are scenting the prospect of victory. The only hope for Mr Nicholson is the lunar mass of his Lib-Dem opponent, a Mrs Jackie Ballard who, in this televisual, style-conscious age, may prove unelectable. But, all of a sudden, David Nicholson is trying very hard to woo us. I never hear from him from one election to the next and now, out of the blue, he is writing to me. He has even tabled a motion in the House on my behalf! This burst of energy is unprecedented; after all, there is nothing new about our problems in the town centre.

David Nicholson MP
House of Commons, London SW1A 0AA

5 April 1997

Dear Kit,

I had intended to write to you before, but as you can imagine, the last few weeks have been unusually hectic.
I <u>entirely share</u> your concern at the return of the beggars and public drinkers. You will have seen my comments in the Gazette: and just before Parliament was prorogued I tabled the enclosed motion which was one of the last to be printed in the order book. ...

Yours, David

AN EARLY DAY
708 BEGGING AND DRINKING IN PUBLIC PLACES 19:3:97

Mr David Nicholson

That this House is concerned at the growing numbers of beggars and drinkers in public places who cause nuisance and alarm ... in city and town centres; ...notes that the spring weather produces beggars and public drinkers, in, for example Castle Green, Taunton, even before the first cuckoo is heard; therefore calls on local authorities and police forces to use every opportunity given by the law to curb this nuisance, ... urges the

Home Office speedily to resolve any practical difficulties encountered in enforcing such laws and bye-laws; and calls on the political parties in their Election Addresses to give attention ... to this problem ...

It is very comforting to know that Mr Nicholson cares so much about us and has, at last, shown his eagerness to take up my comments to the local press. But I wonder if he realizes that, while my business is in Taunton, home is near Bridgwater – Tom King country – and that is where I shall be voting on 1 May.

THURSDAY, 24 APRIL 1997

There is an unwritten rule that hotelkeepers should remain firmly apolitical. To become too closely identified with one party or another is bad for business, or so it is argued by the sages of our trade. Keep your powder dry, they say. But as this election whirls furiously towards its climax, the campaign seems to create its own strange magnetic field – anyway among those who care about the hot political issues of the moment – and even I have been drawn to its fringes.

Last weekend, Westcountry Television, the region's ITV channel based in Plymouth, invited me to take part in a live debate on their early evening magazine show. The topic was 'Doomed to decline – The West Country in the Millennium', an unnecessarily gloom-laden title, I felt, but one which the producers believed would stimulate a lively discussion. My role was to speak for the tourism industry, and as Taunton has its own TV studio that's where I reported at six o'clock on Friday to be linked up with my three co-guests on the show: an environmentalist and a businessman with the programme's presenter in Plymouth, and a constitutional expert sitting in a studio in London.

Having settled into my seat in the tiny room – a sound line plugged into my left ear, the dark spectre of a remote camera lens staring at me from behind the lights – it wasn't long before I realized that a sensible debate was the last thing the producers had in mind. Stupidly, I imagined the style of the discussion to be akin to, say, David Dimbleby on *Panorama*; in other words, I expected just a soupçon of gravitas. Instead, the viewer was treated to a quick-fire barrage of tabloid hysteria punctuated by random attempts from the four studio guests to shed light on issues like education, jobs, Europe and the environment. Every few moments, the twenty-minute 'debate' was interrupted to take live telephone calls from viewers or to witness the results of a roving camera crew who had recorded the miseries of an unemployed youth, the grim prospects facing two young parents with a child to educate and the devastating consequences of the M5 and the A30 on the West Country's economy and environment.

But the big issue for most of the callers on the phone-in was Europe. Nothing you could politely describe as Euro-sceptical either. This was undiluted xenophobia. A man called Hank, choking with rage and fighting back his tears, stuttered: 'I was born British and I want to die British'. Another called Don, incensed by something I had said, let rip in his rich Devonian drawl: 'That's a load of rubbish what they're talkin' there 'bout tourism and that,' he growled. 'People won't have no money to spend and that if we stay in the Common Market. It's like I've said before, we've been tried to be conquered before over last couple of centuries by the Germans and the Spanish and that. None have done it successful-like, but they'll beat us financially in the long run if we stay in the Common Market.'

I left the studio slightly dazed and shocked. Anti-European feeling is running high in these parts, that's for sure. The farmers are angry about the beef crisis; fishermen have been demonstrating in Plymouth, and in Newlyn their vessels are flying the flag of Jimmy Goldsmith's Referendum Party. Yet the West Country is a Lib-Dem stronghold, with several Tory marginals, including Taunton, expected to fall to the advance of Paddy's thoroughly Euro-friendly forces. It makes no sense. If, on 1 May, the cries of the people translate to crosses on ballot-papers, the Lib-Dems will be routed. But somehow I think that's unlikely.

By seven I was back in the hotel and glad to be there; a quieter, more civilized place than the madness of the political circus ring. We had Gary Rhodes and his wife Jenny for the weekend and I was meeting them for a drink. Rhodes's employers, Gardner Merchant, have just opened a smart new eaterie in the City, neatly linking eponym and pun to call itself City Rhodes. Part of the reason for Gary's visit (or so I was led to believe) was to check out Simon Girling, who has applied for the post of manager. Yes, Girling has decided to leave after only a year at the Castle to pursue, he says, his career in London; a decision, I suspect, made for him by his girlfriend and one that I greeted with some irritation, although both Phil and Andrew are more than relieved to see him go. In many respects Girling has done well for us. He licked the restaurant into shape after a long period of drift; he brought in some bright new people, trained them and built a motivated, well-drilled team. He also coached Christophe hard to help him win his 'Young Waiter of the Year' award and, as a result, Christophe has blossomed into our new restaurant manager-in-waiting. But as time passed Girling's deeper weaknesses as a man began to show. His tendency to panic under pressure, to cover his errors by throwing up screens of lies, half-truths and petty deceits exposed his immaturity and lack of professionalism. By the hotplate in the kitchen, Phil now keeps an aerosol can labelled BULLSH–T REPELLANT to spray at him. In the end he lost our trust and confidence and, with Gary Rhodes's arrival, we had our final proof – not that we needed any, but it was the cherry on the icing on the cake. Girling simply lost the plot.

The first we heard about Gary's weekend booking came when Simon returned from his interview at City Rhodes. None of us could quite understand why Gary and Jenny, joined also by Bill Toner, the Managing Director of Gardner Merchant and his wife, should book a two-night stay at the Castle just to observe Simon Girling in action. Besides, they were dining out of the hotel on one evening. The booking struck us as no more sinister than any other foursome looking for a weekend break at a nice hotel in the West Country. And that is exactly what it was. If Gary or the boss of Gardner Merchant wanted an opinion on Simon Girling I'm sure they could have telephoned me. More extraordinarily, over drinks on both Friday and Saturday evenings, neither Simon Girling nor the manager's vacancy at City Rhodes were mentioned once. For such an important appointment, and if I were looking for someone to run my restaurant, I think I'd be pretty keen to ask a few questions. But not a word was said. Gary was far more interested in talking about his beloved Manchester United, who were playing Liverpool in a crucial match over the weekend.

Meanwhile Girling was in a state; running around like a headless chicken, exasperating his staff and behaving as if the delegation from Gardner Merchant were demigods whose presence meant he could ignore everyone else staying in the hotel. On Saturday morning he conscripted extra staff to cover breakfast and ordered them to report for duty at 6.30 – half an hour earlier than usual. In the event, Gary and Jenny and the Toners did not appear until 10 o'clock. That evening, after our drinks party, Louise and I took a table in a far corner of the restaurant. Christophe and the other senior staff kept quiet but their feelings were writ large in the expressions on their faces. They saw Girling's game as a ridiculous charade, ignored him and got on with their jobs while their superior flapped obsequiously around his table of VIPs.

At one point during dinner, Simon came over to see how we were. I told him to calm down, everything was fine, I said. 'If you think I'm nervous, Mr Chapman,' he replied, 'You should see what it's like in the kitchen.' This flip aside irritated me but it was characteristic of a man more expert at deceiving himself than those around him. When he left our table, I turned to Louise: 'If I were Chef I'd tell Girling to get out of my kitchen and stay out.' And that, I learned later, was exactly what Phil had done.

Gary Rhodes's visit to the Castle was his first in the seven years since his departure as my head chef, so, understandably, he was curious to test the cooking of his successor. For him, for Jenny and their friends, the food was of far greater interest than Girling's suitability as manager of City Rhodes and they ordered extravagantly from Phil's menu, choosing additional dishes to taste between courses. This habit is not unusual, particularly among visiting chefs and restaurateurs keen to sample a broad range of a colleague's repertoire at one sitting. Alas, the tactic sent Girling into a frenzy. While Vickery wanted Rhodes's table to pace their dinner with digestible pauses between dishes, Girling was harassing the kitchen to send up the food more rapidly. The fact that there were twenty other tables to serve seemed to escape the restaurant manager's notice. In the end Phil lost patience and banned him from the kitchen for the rest of the night.

I half expected the tension in the restaurant to be picked up by the antennae of Girling's prospective employers, but they were having too much fun to notice and, I think, they had already made up their minds to offer him the job.

The weekend passed. Our guests went home. But on Monday there was more debris to fall out of the atmosphere. Having lost faith in Simon a long time ago, Phil decided to cast his eye over the Gardner Merchant account and found that Saturday's dinner had been undercharged by £55. Girling had omitted to bill some of the extra items Rhodes had ordered. Phil hit the roof and Simon went into an indignant spin – a mad terrier chasing its tail – pleading ignorance and blaming everyone else other than himself. But the facts were clear. Vickery had instructed him on the charges to be made for the extras and he hadn't put them through – either because he was too busy ingratiating himself with his new employers and forgot, or because he wanted to ingratiate himself further by throwing in a few complementary dishes.

Now he has secured his new job (a position bearing the title 'General Manager', he tells us), our Mr Girling is close to becoming a liability in the hotel, and if Andrew weren't on holiday at the moment, I'd pay him off and let him go immediately. Yesterday I walked into the hotel to find myself faced with a mutiny in the staff living quarters. In his absence, Andrew had alerted Simon to the arrival of a student from Stafford College, a nineteen-year-old on five weeks' work experience in the restaurant. When the girl reported for duty, Simon had made no arrangements to accommodate her – he had forgotten – and as there were no beds to be found in the staff flat, he decided to set her up, or rather down, on the floor of the flat's kitchen. Alison Brown, the head housekeeper, objected violently to this proposal and led a delegation to my office at 8.30 in the morning. I could not believe what I was hearing. I do not expect to have to mop up after a panic-stricken manager who has been caught short, nor did I want to face the opprobrium of a well-respected institution like Stafford College. I telephoned Girling at home, hauled him out of bed and told him to get in and sort out the problem sensibly with Alison.

For a man who began so promisingly a year ago, Simon Girling's fall from favour has been surprising and a little sad. I misjudged him – but, in the end, the flaws in his character betrayed him. He is a dreamer, a twenty-nine-year-old with his head still lost in dense cloud, unsure of what he wants or where he is going. He has said that one day he intends to open his own restaurant. At the Castle we offered him the prospect of promotion, a chance to learn the business, finance, budgets, a useful stepping stone on the path towards his ultimate goal. He'll never do it now. That much is clear. Instead he has opted to make a side-step for more money; a move which, give or take a few months, will be as short-lived as the last and lead only to another glorified head waiter's job for a few extra pounds again.

In my book of protégés – led by the success of young Turks like Gary Rhodes – Simon Girling will rank among my failures. I liked him and I tried hard to open his eyes. But for all his early promise my efforts have been wasted. Instead he has been seduced by the siren call of his love. And she works in London.

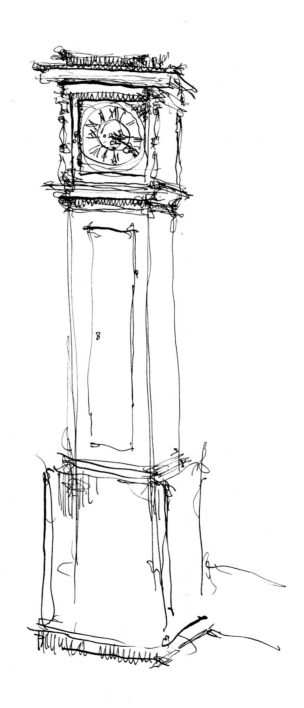

PIG POLITICS

SUNDAY, 4 MAY 1997

P OLLING DAY CAME AND WENT. And come the dawn on 2 May, as I expected, the map of the West Country was suddenly recrayoned yellow. Thanks to a few thousand Referendum Party votes and some tactical switching, the Tories were squeezed out and Ashdown's Army raised the Lib-Dem standard over seats stretching from St Ives to Somerton and Frome. In Taunton there was dancing in the streets when David Nicholson's head rolled; and as Brünnhilde, the Mighty Mrs Ballard, mounted her chariot, the crowd roared 'Long Live Paddy's Girl'! For Somerset's Tories, only Tom King in Bridgwater and David Heathcoat-Amory in Wells survived – just; their majorities so tiny that their political lives are now in intensive care.

Brünnhilde, aka Mrs Jackie Ballard, MP

Across Britain, the Conservative dead are piled high, and as the scale of New Labour's victory struck an astonished people, we all began to ask ourselves what this would mean. Auberon Waugh, a fellow Somerset man and good patron of the Castle, has begun referring to the new Prime Minister as 'the attractive-looking Tony Blair'. As much as I enjoy Mr Waugh's irony, it will turn very sour for this innkeeper if the Social Chapter, the minimum wage and the surrender of more employment policy to Brussels lead to the impoverishment of my business. I have seen it happen to my friends in France and Italy, where their hotels have been unable to sustain the high costs of employment and where, inevitably, staff cuts have led to declining standards. But who can tell what will befall us? These are private fears, vampires that visit my dreams in the small hours. For the moment we can only hope for the best and do so in the comforting knowledge that New Labour is, at least, serious about its food and drink. Unlike John Major, whose tipple is a pint or a G&T and whose favourite restaurant is a Happy Eater, Mr Blair prefers champagne and fashionable diners like the River Café. Indeed, some of our top restaurant owners are among the PM's hottest supporters, including the noble architect Richard Rogers and the ubiquitous Terence Conran. So the kitchen cabinets of the past, it seems, are giving way to a new Cabinet of Gourmets. This has to be good for the trade. A little ministerial patronage is exactly what we need and if Mr Blair runs into trouble with the hereditary peerage when he comes to his constitutional reforms, he could do worse than top up the House of Lords with a few dozen chefs. The effect of making cooks like Marco Pierre White and Nico Ladenis life peers can only be salutary for the government of this country. The quality of the catering at Westminster is bound to rise dramatically and the decisions of our leaders will be the better for eating a good lunch.

The only other crumb I can nibble in the aftermath of this election is the fate of poor Mr Portillo. Now he has been denied his chance to lead the Tory party, he will no longer be too busy to forgo our musical weekends.

In the week preceding the election, I issued my own manifesto to that hearty constituency of local gastronomes, the Castle Dining Club – a notice, signed in my name, promoting our annual Summer Party around the rose beds and within the twelfth-century remains of the Castle's keep and moat walls. This long, lazy, alfresco lunch takes place on a Sunday in mid-June. There is a bar serving champagne, chilled rosé and jugs of Pimms. Phil and his brigade take command of a rank of charcoal stoves. There is an abundance of delicious things to eat. And Hugo and the Huguenotes, Britain's greatest steel band, add a touch of Caribbean colour to the feasting and gaiety. The party-goers, dressed in their best frocks and straw hats, love it. Or so I thought until I received a sniffy letter from a Mrs Daisy Walls.

28 April 1997

Dear Mr Chapman,

With reference to your letter regarding your Midsummer Garden Party, my husband and I were thinking 'yes, this sounds rather nice, perhaps we could make up a party of eight with some of our friends' until it got to the part about the 'Magnificent Roast Suckling Pig'.
We found this insensitive, upsetting and barbaric. How offensive your letter is to animal lovers and vegetarians like ourselves.
Our circle of friends, who I must say dine at the Castle more frequently than ourselves, were equally shocked and revolted.
I know that many people will eat anything with total disregard but when you send letters to your customers I do think that you should be a little more careful and thoughtful.
Would you kindly delete us from your mailing list, I do not think we could stomach another letter like this.

Yours sincerely,

Daisy Walls

I find it impossible to take people like Mrs Walls too seriously.

29 April 1997

Dear Mrs Walls,

Thank you very much indeed for your letter of 28 April. Of course, the last thing I would wish is to offend either you or your friends. What a relief, therefore, that I mentioned the roast suckling pig in my letter. Can you imagine how dreadful it would be if you and your party arrived and actually witnessed this magnificent beast being paraded by my chefs around the Castle's rose gardens! Under the circumstances, I think I have been particularly considerate of the sensibilities of my clients.
As requested, we have deleted your name from our mailing list.

Yours sincerely,

C H G CHAPMAN
Owner of two much loved golden retrievers and one beautiful cat

WEDNESDAY, 14 MAY 1997

Andrew Grahame has fired Simon Girling. No ordinary sacking, this. This was a summary dismissal for gross misconduct. So much for the news that greeted me last night when Louise and I returned from London after a brief 24-hour visit. A day is a long time in the hotel business.

Early yesterday morning, Alison Lock, our young assistant manager, switched on her office computer to find a waiter's CV on screen. Puzzled, she showed Andrew, who began asking a few questions and before long discovered that Girling was actively recruiting several members of staff to join him at City Rhodes – waiters mostly, but also two cooks. He went to Phil and they tried contacting me in London but my mobile was turned off and I was closeted in a meeting all morning. Before confronting Girling, Andrew telephoned Clarke, Willmott & Clarke, our solicitors, to check the legal position. He and Phil then called Simon in; explained the disciplinary nature of the meeting and invited him to nominate his own witness which, after a long pause, he declined. The interview – recorded on tape – could not have lasted five minutes. Andrew instructed him to clear his desk under Alison Lock's supervision and to be off the premises within thirty minutes. He also advised Girling that he had a right to appeal to me as managing director, if he so wished. He won't. This time the fool has hanged himself.

The saddest news as I write these lines. I have just heard of Laurie Lee's death. I knew he was unwell, and has been for a long while. I knew death had to be close, but it still takes you by surprise.

I met the great man in 1986 when Chris Oakes, Gary Rhodes's predecessor here and the first of my chefs to win us a Michelin star, left Taunton to open his own eponymously named restaurant in the Slad Valley. Laurie had been invited to do the honours on the first night and I was seated next to him at the dinner. When Chris emerged to take his bow at the end of the feast, Laurie turned to me and in his wonderfully rounded Cotswold burr, he whispered: 'Look at him. Pale, pleased and exhausted. He's given birth.'

Laurie's gift with words, the lyricism of his language, always sends shivers of pleasure and envy through my body. It's the rich, sensuous texture of his imagery, the colour and beauty of his perfectly honed sentences; writing which is at once powerful, warm and utterly absorbing.

After our meeting at Oakes, we became friends, although in the eleven years that I knew him, he and Kathy, his wife, only visited the Castle once – an occasion made memorable for his wicked flirtations with Louise over dinner. An evening with Laurie was always filled with good humour, earth and spice. He was like ripe red burgundy. Indeed, wine, food and pretty women figure prominently in my memories of him. Eighteen months ago he came to my book launch at The Garrick Club. Too frail to stand, he took a seat in a corner of the room but his vigour and charm were as potent as ever. He did not have to move. The women, the wine and the food came to him, attracted like iron filings to a magnet. Among the hundreds of photographs taken that evening, the best is one of Laurie leering over a huge tray of oysters, his moist lower lip trembling with greed and his right hand, crab-like, reaching for an open shell.

He was loved by his friends and we shall miss him.

Saturday, 17 May 1997

The drama of the Girling affair seems to have overshadowed everything this week. But in other respects it has been good – indeed, rather pleasurable.

We were in London on Monday for the annual lecture of the University of Surrey Food & Wine Society, held this year at the Berkeley in Wilton Place. I created the Society twelve years ago as an antidote to the hotel school's unremitting diet of management science. Graduates of the place emerge like extruded plastic, shaped and primed to run Hilton or Marriott but incapable of distinguishing Ribena from Cabernet Sauvignon or hollandaise from béarnaise. The Society's purpose is to fill the cultural void, to persuade students that gastronomy is the heartbeat of the trade and that, like art and music, it is worthy of study. To bring the Society alive and help it function I established a Board of Friends: thirty or forty top chefs, restaurateurs and wine merchants who could be relied on to lend support to its programme. In the last twelve months members have attended five tutored wine tastings, visited Epernay in Champagne as guests of Christian Pol-Roger, and they have dined at Le Gavroche, Tante Claire and Mosimann's among other notable eateries. Each year's agenda is organized by a committee of students led by an elected chairman and the annual lecture is the final event in the Society's calendar. As president, I chair the evening, a do attracting a mixed audience of over a hundred students, tutors, Friends, industry leaders and press. And this year my speaker was Fay Maschler, the *Evening Standard*'s restaurant critic of twenty-five years and Britain's First Lady of gastronomy.

Fay has an uneasy relationship with the trade, but then all serious critics do. Inevitably, she has her enemies but, to her immense relief, none of them came to the lecture. Many chefs are frightened of her – not, I think, because of what she writes but because of what they perceive her to be. She does not smile easily (which is a shame because when she does her smile is ravishing). So some people see her as a rather cool and aloof figure. That chilly hauteur has gone now, but in the past I suspect it was her way of disguising her shyness. It took Fay fifteen years to find her soul-mate, the novelist Reg Gadney, whom she married in 1992. I first met her in the late seventies, when her marriage to Tom Maschler, the publisher, was in its terminal throes. Between husbands, Fay stepped out with a number of admirers, none of whom brought her the peace and contentment she sought – until, that is, she met Reg, whose blend of tender devotion and wicked wit won her heart.

To have persuaded Fay to deliver this year's lecture was a small coup which I owe entirely to Reg. Fay hates speaking in public and it was Reg who convinced her to do it. Come the moment, she spoke very well and, seemingly, without a trace of nervousness. Poor Reg, however, was far from at ease. It was as if he had transferred her burden of anxiety on to his own shoulders. Fay's talk, 'The Purpose of the Restaurant Critic', was illustrated with a slide presentation, and when Louise and I arrived at the Berkeley we found Reg loading the Kodak carousel while Fay sat beside him quietly sipping a glass of wine. Then a rush of irritating little problems intervened like a parade of gremlins. There were difficulties fitting the carousel on the projector, there was a problem with the focus. Some of the slides were back-to-front and had to be reloaded, and then one got jammed in the mechanism. Meanwhile, time was moving relentlessly towards the hour, people were arriving and Reg was growing increasingly agitated. Finally his anguish turned on him – a nasty jab of searing pain to a finger caught accidentally in the heavy double doors to the conference chamber. Shrugging off his agony, he composed himself and as everyone took their seats in the room, he posted himself by the projector like a guardsman on sentry duty. But he had no cause to worry – the carousel whirred smoothly through its slides casting perfectly focused images on the screen. At the end of Fay's lecture, the audience applauded enthusiastically, and for the next forty-five minutes I assumed a Dimblebyesque pose to take questions from the floor. A lively debate ensued, ranging from the ethics of tipping and attitudes towards children in restaurants to the Conranization of the London scene and the future of the capital's mega-eateries.

Later, we all dined at Zafferano in Lowndes Street, the four of us joined by Antony Worrall Thompson and Fay's sister, Beth Coventry. This place must rank among London's top three Italian restaurants. We ate magnificently. To start, my bowl of *pappardelle* with broad beans and rocket was one of the most satisfying pasta dishes I have eaten, freshness and simplicity being its principal virtues. This was followed by a main course unfamiliar to me: billed as *Involtini di Maiale alle Zucchine*, this was a pork roll (it looked like a large sausage) stuffed generously with sweet, fragrant herbs and chargrilled with fried courgettes. Utterly, meltingly delicious.

But next day, Tuesday, Louise and I enjoyed the best lunch we have eaten in a long time. At the very moment Andrew Grahame was chasing Simon Girling through the revolving door of the Castle, we were sitting innocently at the Square in Bruton Street, a restaurant which recently moved from a grand address by St James's Square to even grander premises off Berkeley Square. Regardless of the move, the Square's establishment remains intact, led by its chef, Philip Howard, a man whose low profile disguises a high talent – so much so I have noted him for my next volume of *Great British Chefs*, if and when book three comes to be written.

Among those dishes to send us into raptures were a sweetly seasoned composition of buffalo mozzarella, aubergines and anchovy vinaigrette – a variation of an old favourite reworked into a new confection I found quite sublime. Then came a spanking fresh red mullet bathing in a herbaceous olive oil broth: simple, perfectly pitched, ethereal. And again a generous chunk of glistening cod with spring vegetables and a silky buttery parsley mash that shone a phosphorescent green but tasted as if the herb had just been picked from the cottage garden.

The Square and Zafferano are two of a number of restaurants we have visited in the past few weeks, among them some well-known names: Le Petit Blanc, Raymond Blanc's brasserie in Oxford; St Petroc's, Rick Stein's bistro in Padstow; and the Carved Angel, Joyce Molyneux's famous restaurant in Dartmouth. We enjoyed them all; the staff were charming and we had a terrific time. But what strikes me about these places – and I see this time and again – is that as soon as the original inspiration has, for one reason or another, surrendered direct command of the stoves to a surrogate, the cooking loses its edge. Perhaps this is forgivable at Le Petit Blanc and St Petroc's – these restaurants are their proprietor's second strings. But then I can think of other chefs whose satellites sing with the same clarity and conviction of their master's voice. Marco Pierre White is probably the best example. The quality of the cooking at the Criterion in Piccadilly is breathtakingly high for the 200-odd punters his brasserie welcomes at any one sitting. Moreover, an evening here is better value and much more fun than dinner in the sepulchral atmosphere of MPW's three-star flagship at the Hyde Park Hotel.

Marco, I think, is an exception. He is, after all, a genius. The problem for most restaurants where the master has handed the torch to a disciple is that, no matter how long or how good the tutelage, the cloning process is rarely perfect, never exact. As a result the founder's trademark gets smudged and fault lines appear in the cooking. Of course, the good ones – those with innate talent, intelligence and acute palates of their own, don't want to be disciples for the rest of their lives. They are the ones that make the break, they become the new generation of artistic lights and the process begins all over again.

LIBERAL TENDENCIES

MONDAY, 26 MAY 1997

TO EVERY THING THERE IS A SEASON. And for us now is the season of roosting seagulls; our rooftops, flat and cosy behind the shelter of parapets, making the ideal refuge. The birds would be welcome were it not for the Penthouse roof garden which, with its magnificent views of Taunton's famous skyline, has become one of Somerset society's most sought-after venues for lunch parties and summer soirées. Regrettably, however, last year several ambitious hostesses were humiliated when posses of angry gulls dive-bombed the terrace, scattering their guests, who nearly tumbled to their deaths over the Castle's ramparts.

The trouble begins when the birds start laying and the problem has now become so acute we have set up a rota of gull patrols led by Bob, our fearless handyman. Expeditions to the roof take place in the early morning three times a week: the object of the raids being to snatch the eggs from their nests. These are dangerous missions and ones which have to be undertaken by a force of two or three agile young staff armed with broomsticks. Quietly they clamber on to the roof above the Penthouse and approach the first nest. The instant the hen spots them she takes flight and, hovering over the heads of the patrol, emits a sharp, rasping squawk. Within seconds the sky fills with dozens of flapping, cackling seagulls. Where the birds come from is a mystery, but there they are: two, three squadrons of them swooping aggressively around the handyman and his assistants. As Bob makes a dash for the nest, the others cover him and protect themselves with their broomsticks. Bounty in hand, the patrol beats a fast retreat down the ladder to the solid-walled safety of the hotel.

'What do you do with the eggs?' I asked Bob. 'Give them to Chef?'

'No,' he said, 'I chuck 'em out. What's he going to do with them?'

'At the Ritz in London,' I explained, 'they are selling at £3.50 an egg. So if it's all the same to you, Bob, they'll do nicely for my lunch!'

Very good they were too.

The annual invasion of our feathered terrorists is, at least, a threat to the peace of our guests we can control. The continued presence of the barbarian on the Green is one we cannot. The issue continues to preoccupy the local community and is faithfully reported each week by the *Somerset County Gazette*. However, with the election of the Mighty Mrs Ballard, the character of these reports has assumed a dangerously liberal tone. On election night, as poor old David Nicholson was seen blubbing in a corner ('Mr Nicholson was unable to hold back the tears,' noted the *Gaz*), the victorious Brünnhilde instantly proclaimed herself champion of the constituency's beggars and vagrants: 'Tonight the people of Taunton have lit a beacon of hope for the homeless,' she boomed.

This ridiculous statement was the starting pistol for every wishy-washy, do-gooding liberal innocent to make a quick dash for the moral high ground and a week later the *Gaz* devoted a full page to the efforts of various local groups to improve the lives of 'homeless people'. Under the provocative headline WILL YOU HELP THEM?, spokespersons for worthy agencies with worthy names like Open Door appealed to the general public to adopt a more open mind 'to the reality of life on the streets' and to recognize that we have a 'moral obligation' to help these people. The Revd Julian Smith wants us to get back to the 'Biblical vision of society'. He says the world would be a happier place if the rich became less concerned about how much money they were making. Then a very nice lady from the Taunton Association for the Homeless trotted out a few more well-worn platitudes. She told us 'to respect everyone's choice to live the way they want to live', to 'look at the problem without being judgmental' and not 'to condemn what we don't understand'.

The feature also highlighted the case of 'JJ', one 'homeless' individual whom I see regularly encamped on Castle Green. Talking to the *Gaz*'s reporter about life on the streets, JJ had this to say: 'I'm there because I choose to be there; it's what I'm accustomed to. I can survive out there but I don't know if I can survive living in a house. It's not that I can't take on board responsibility – I just don't want it'.

I decided to restore a little balance to this burning issue by asking for an interview with the *Gazette*. The debate, I felt, deserved the benefit of a few facts, a seasoning of truth and a sprinkling of reality. The editor kindly obliged and despatched Phil Hill, a senior reporter, to see me at the hotel. For twenty-five minutes Mr Hill scribbled furiously as I rehearsed a more robust view of the problems of vagrancy to that expressed by the nice people from Open Door and the Taunton Association for the Homeless. Of course, I was careful to praise the work of these worthy outfits and went out of my way to emphasize our generosity of spirit and the support the hotel has given to local charities over the years.

The article appeared last Friday: a prominent feature spread across six columns under the headline: IDLE HOMELESS DON'T DESERVE OUR SUPPORT. Mr Hill had done a thorough job, paraphrasing my arguments as direct quotations in perfect *Gazette* journalese. The intention, quite simply, was to try to draw a distinction between the provision of welfare or charitable assistance to those in genuine need, and public financing or private giving to those like JJ who had withdrawn from society by choice, opting instead for a life of idleness on the streets. I was prepared to respect their chosen lifestyle as long as they respected mine but I saw no reason to show any sympathy for their barbarian behaviour and I certainly could not see why either the state, my taxes or my kind nature should be predisposed to funding their sloth.

Finally, I issued a public invitation to Brünnhilde to join me on a walkabout round the Green to see the problem for herself. 'He has thrown down the gauntlet to Taunton MP Jackie Ballard,' proclaimed Mr Hill melodramatically in his piece. Rather rashly I also invited the Mighty One to lunch with me first. I hope she declines. I don't much care for the idea of earning a reputation as the Mohammed Al Fayed of Castle Green or for the hotel to be seen as the Paris Ritz of Taunton. Besides, she would be wise to avoid any hint of a sleazy lunch-for-vagrants scandal.

WEDNESDAY, 4 JUNE 1997

Well, I suppose it was inevitable. No matter how faithfully a newspaper reports your comments, the good old general public – incapable of reading beyond a blunt headline – will leap to their own evil conclusions. Now the dung-spreader has slipped into top gear: the letters' pages of last Friday's *Gazette* was dominated by some pretty vicious personal attacks. One correspondent, a Mr Michael Drury-Beck, even branded me a war criminal.

'What possible other alternatives are there than trying to help these folk back into society?' he ranted. 'Frog-march the homeless, the dogs and the *Big Issue* to the borders of Somerset where there is a halfway house with a cosy room with cylinder gas and incinerators in the back?

'So effusive was your indictment against Open Door and the Taunton Association for the Homeless that the good and decent people of Taunton might consider such opinions from a respected hotelier to be aligned with those attitudes normally attributed to national political parties who favour ethnic and social cleansing. You do a great dishonour to those people who share Christian and humanitarian values who live here.'

While Mr Drury-Beck relieved himself of his vitriol in public, I received a string of private messages of support: that famous force, the 'silent majority', is, I am sure, staunchly behind me, but as the attack by this man was so scurrilous, I have responded with a letter which, I hope, will be published in this Friday's paper.

2 June 1997

The Editor, Somerset County Gazette

Dear Sir,

The hysterical outbursts directed at me in last week's Postbag (30 May) deserve no reply. The problem of vagrancy in our town centre is one which troubles the whole community and merits a more serious debate. Sadly, your correspondents failed to read or understand my comments reported in the *Gazette* on 23 May. I greatly admire the selfless work of organizations like Open Door and the Taunton Association for the Homeless – indeed, the word I used was 'applaud'– and the Castle, like many other businesses in this town, has an honourable record of giving to charities, particularly to local projects. These facts were clearly highlighted in your article.

However, agencies like OD and TAH occasionally have a habit of calling upon the rest of us to fulfil what they describe as our 'moral obligation' and in the light of our experiences – right on our doorstep – I wanted to challenge the assertions they made in a full-page feature on 9 May. Moral relativism is a slippery ethic which has gained currency in this age of 'political correctness'. I don't care much for neologisms like 'street people' or 'pavement people'. They are absurd euphemisms which ultimately devalue our language and when that happens truth, reason and society's values become fogbound. Vagrant is a perfectly good English word meaning a homeless person.

My comments on the vagrancy question were not an attack on the excellent work of the aid agencies. They were, rather, an attempt to draw a distinction between public compassion and personal responsibility; between tolerance as a principle of a civilized society and that society's toleration of breaches in civilized behaviour.

These days smoking is widely considered as antisocial. Society's response has been to prohibit smoking in public places, offices and even restaurants. Vagrancy may be a more complex issue but its consequences on the quality of our lives and the culture we hold precious are profound unless robust measures are taken to defend the civilized peace of our town centre.

My views, frankly, are no different to the new Labour Government's thinking on welfare. There is a need for radical reform because the welfare state was not created for people like 'JJ' who, by choice, take a deliberate decision to pursue an alternative lifestyle. This is what JJ told the *Gazette* (9 May): 'I'm there because I choose to be there; it's what I'm accustomed to. I can survive out there but I don't know if I can survive living in a house. It's not that I can't take on board responsibility – I just don't want it'.

Harriet Harman is on record as saying that the current welfare arrangements are a disincentive to work and that the state (our taxes) can no longer be expected to finance individual idleness. This is now government policy. The Prime Minister is determined to break the dependency culture of the welfare state. And quite right too.

Clearly JJ and his friends have little respect for the concept of personal responsibility – either in the conduct of their own lives or in relation to their fellow citizens. If these 'street people' threaten and intimidate other human beings, do their reduced circumstances or deprived upbringings somehow excuse their vile behaviour? There is nothing relative about the morality of a mugging incident, whoever you are.

Before these moral mountaineers, your correspondents, hurl pious slogans from their lofty perches, they may care to consider what their lives might be like if they had a platoon of hostile vagrants camped on their doorsteps. Would they not fear for the well-being of their families and the safety of friends who came to visit them?

At the Castle I have a responsibility for the well-being of my staff and my guests. I also care passionately about Taunton, where Castle Green – a conservation area – once used to be a pleasant and agreeable place. So I shall continue my campaign until peace and civilized decency have been restored to our town centre.

Yours faithfully,

Kit Chapman

Copies of the letter have gone to Brünnhilde at the House of Commons and Ol' Waffles at the Town Council. He is especially upset with me at the moment for describing him and his fellow Liberals as 'wishy-washy' in the *Gazette* two weeks ago. Since that fateful article I have received a letter of complaint from a tour guide who recently brought a small party of Americans to the Castle and wondered if Taunton 'was a safe town to wander in'. Last weekend we had to call the police to see off another bunch of aggressive beggars. Bringing these incidents to Mr Horsley's attention seems to make no impression. All I get is a rambling letter telling me that there is nothing wishy-washy about his council and how proud they are of the actions they are taking 'to help those who are less able to look after themselves'.

Ironically, Louise, Phil, Andrew and I have just returned from Gidleigh Park in Devon where we escaped for twenty-four hours of total peace to begin thinking and planning the redevelopment of our garage block, a pile of crumbling, redundant outbuildings on the far side of our forecourt. Among the ideas we examined were a health and fitness centre, a modern bar-brasserie and a deli as well as extra bedroom accommodation for the hotel. Perhaps we should do the Christian thing and build a refuge for the homeless. There's certainly a good market for one and the location is perfect. Then Ol' Waffles and I can be friends again.

TUESDAY, 10 JUNE 1997

Strap-lined 'THE VAGRANCY DEBATE: Taunton hotelier blasts back at the "moral mountaineers",' the Postbag section of last Friday's *Gazette* devoted the best part of a whole page to readers' letters, including my own which was published in full. All except one supported my stand, the one being an advocate of Mr Drury-Beck's point of view. Indeed, Ms Angela Willes of Chard was so angry with me she inadvertently discovered a latent sense of humour. '...if I were homeless,' she fumed, 'I think I'd be hanging around the Castle too. No doubt there are rich pickings from the gourmet scrapings, pushed aside by those who know nothing of the true value of food in this world.'

Last week also brought a surprise telephone call from Brünnhilde. Speaking from her office in Westminster, I could hear Big Ben chiming five in the background. This gave our conversation a certain poignancy and an air of gravitas. Besides, I was impressed by her swift reaction to my letter. Her predecessor used to take five or six weeks to answer the appeals of his constituents. Then the Mighty One spoilt all my warm feelings by saying something very silly, in fact something so extraordinarily naïve only a Lib-Dem would suggest it.

'Have you tried *talking* to these people?' she asked.

'Mrs Ballard,' I retorted, trying hard to restrain myself, 'of course I haven't. These people can be openly hostile. They have intimidated my guests, my staff and even my wife. Nothing would be gained by talking to them.'

'But do you see where I'm coming from?' insisted Brünnhilde.

'Not exactly. If I were a sociologist, I might. But I'm not. I'm an innkeeper. My first concern is for the welfare of my staff and guests.'

In the end, we arranged to meet after her morning surgery on Saturday 21 June and I suggested that Ol' Waffles join us too. I also whispered the sweet prospect of lunch – an invitation which the new and nervous member for Taunton could neither accept nor refuse, tantalizingly torn, poor thing, between a little innocent temptation and fear of the finger of sleaze.

On the subject of politics and gastronomy, I have been riveted by the campaign strategies of the contenders for the leadership of the Conservative Party. Now that Tony Blair and his Cabinet of Gourmets have made troughing chic, these top Tories seem set on parading their own gastro-cred before the television cameras. All of them have been throwing parties as a means of winning votes. So what do we see? John Redwood being predictably nationalist (scones, cream, strawberry jam, tea); William Hague appealing to the upwardly mobile (champagne and canapés at the Carlton Club); and Ken Clarke doing his man-of-the-people number (beer and crisps). That was last night. This morning, Mr Hague, still feeling peckish, called in the media to photograph him breakfasting on bangers, beans and *mugs* of tea, thus signalling that he can be as common as Ken and as patriotic as Mr Redwood.

This was obviously a very smart move. I have just been listening to the result of the first ballot on the radio and Young William polled forty-one votes, just eight short of Ken Clarke who, until now, was the pundits' favourite for the leadership. But with Michael Howard and Peter Lilley out of the race and having thrown their lot behind the Hague campaign, the pint-swilling ex-Chancellor looks like losing the Tory crown to his junior adversary. Mr Hague is showing himself to be a proper trencherman with an eclectic palate. He is the only candidate in this bizarre election to exploit the power of the gastro-factor, knowing that no Tory leader has a hope of being effective in opposition unless he can field a shadow cabinet strong enough to match Tony and his Gourmets. Ken Clarke may be a jolly fellow; he may even be the best man for the job, but he is no use to a modern, sophisticated electorate who – as the general election proved – now prefer to be governed by a dynamic set of serious gourmandizers.

The only doubt I harbour about Young William (assuming he wins) is how convincingly he will embrace the new mood of chummy informality. His Churchillian head, Wilsonian vowels and his forthcoming marriage into the Welsh Establishment might suggest that he does not really approve of Gordon Brown's cavalier refusal to wear a black tie at the Mansion House and the Prime Minister's insistence that we all call him Tony. But, I suspect, the Young Pretender will have little choice as social conventions continue to become more unbuttoned – literally. Many hotels still insist that 'gentlemen wear a jacket and tie' in their dining rooms. We abandoned this rule fifteen years ago after the Earl of Lichfield ('call me Patrick') walked into the restaurant elegantly dressed in an immaculate open-neck white shirt and perfectly sculpted designer jeans. Before I could ask him to put on a jacket, another man walked into the room wearing a crumpled, dirty brown suit and a grease-stained tie. At that moment I realized I was on a loser: our 'house rule' had become an anachronism; it was irrelevant and meaningless. Besides, who am I to dictate how people dress as long as their manners and appearance do not offend our other guests? Restaurants are public places, open to all, every day. They cannot sensibly be bound by the sort of dress codes prescribed by a club, an officers' mess or a stiff-backed invitation to the Mansion House – on which point, incidentally, I think Gordon Brown is being plain rude to his host, the Lord Mayor of London.

But whatever I may think, it seems that New Labour's attitude to dress, manners and political style is looking to the United States and the Clinton Administration as its role model. Where dress codes are concerned, this country trails way behind American society. Last week I received a fascinating piece of information from the Savoy Hotel's archivist, Susan Scott, with whom I spent a day last October researching the life of my grandfather, Henry Prüger. When Prüger left the Savoy in 1909 to open the ill-fated *Café de l'Opéra* in New York, he took with him all those values which European society expected of its smartest and most fashionable watering holes. Within a year, my grandfather had returned to London because, I understood, he had fallen out with the unions. But this was not the real reason for his hasty departure. Ms Scott has sent me a press cutting she discovered recently, dated 9 April 1910, in which I now learn that the *Café de l'Opéra* was closed down with '£100,000 debts outstanding' (£4.6 million in today's money) because New Yorkers refused to wear evening dress. My father tells me that his father was notoriously bloody-minded, for all his brilliance as an hotelier. Although the newspaper article doesn't say so, it is pretty clear that Henry Prüger refused to compromise his standards on the question of dress. As a consequence, he was fired by his employers, who subsequently reopened the restaurant, the article says, 'under revised rules, which will relieve its free and independent patrons from the tyranny of London customs'.

MONDAY, 16 JUNE 1997

With only five days to go before the great powwow with Brünnhilde and Ol' Waffles Horsley, my campaign against the Barbarian on the Green has suffered a set-back. The dirty tricks department at Taunton Deane Borough Council has leaked a private letter written to the planners over two months ago and signed by Andrew Grahame and the managers of two neighbouring businesses. The letter raises a number of objections to the Council's proposal to dig up the cobbles on Castle Green and replace these with smooth flagstones to allow wheelchairs to pass more comfortably under Castle Bow. This work, we were told, would take six weeks and cost £16,000. We did not object to the principle of the proposal but we were concerned that work should not begin too early in the morning. The last thing we needed was for our guests to receive their wake-up calls to the sound of pneumatic drills. But, in truth, we saw this innocent plan as yet another irritation to be inflicted upon us by our local authority. After eleven months of noise, dirt and upheaval during the redevelopment of the town centre, and frustrated by the Council's complete indifference to our problems with the New Age invaders, we did not exactly welcome the prospect of the return of the diggers. In short, we had had enough aggro.

And so it is regrettable that this infamous letter ended with a few blunt and insensitively phrased words which are now being held against us: 'We feel that the money being spent on this footway,' wrote Andrew and his fellow musketeers, 'would be far better spent ridding the town of the various beggars and vagrants who continue to pollute the streets.'

The letter was dated 11 April and addressed to a Mr I Clark of Taunton Deane Environmental Services. But — two months on — it suddenly fell on to the news desks of the *Gazette*, who duly published the story last Friday under the headline: REMOVE BEGGARS BEFORE THE COBBLES. Dear Ol' Waffles is so exercised by our public campaign, he now wants to discredit us by putting a new and entirely spurious spin on the vagrancy issue. This was his chance to hit back and he went for it. Having been branded a Nazi and an ethnic cleanser, I am now accused of discriminating against the disabled. Come this morning, he lost no time in sending me an hysterical e-mail, with a copy, I noted, to jackieballard@cix.compulink.co.uk.

Date: Mon, 16 June 97 09:43 BST-1
From: jeffersonlib@cix.compulink.co.uk
To: chapman@the-castle-hotel.com

Dear Kit,

I'm looking forward to seeing you at noon on 21 June with Jackie Ballard. Can I draw your attention to how appalled I was to read the letter signed by your Andrew Grahame to the Council re the putting in of a smooth pathway for disabled wheel chair owners through Castle Bow?...

I treat with utter contempt the suggestion that the money should be used for 'ridding the town of various beggars and vagrants ... etc.'. I hope that you are going to consider disciplining your subordinate for suggesting that your firm is pro discrimination against the disabled.

Seriously, it is time that you stopped trying to conduct change through the press and worked more closely with us...

Yours sincerely,

Jefferson

FRIDAY, 20 JUNE 1997

Predictably, we were soundly caned in the correspondence columns of today's *Gazette*. Community leaders hurled their scorn and indignation in a variety of letters from local support groups. Topping them all was one from Ol' Waffles, sweetly savouring his moment of revenge.

> I was appalled when I read the comments of the three senior managers of such well-known organizations as the Castle Hotel, Next and the Ferret & Trouserleg in their letter sent to Taunton Deane Council about the proposed improvement to the footpath at Castle Bow for the benefit of disabled people. ... Would these same managers wish that we didn't put in tactile pavements to help the blind? I feel sure that their head offices do not wish for the firms to be singled out as discriminatory against the disabled. ... The Council is well aware of the [vagrancy] difficulties and is working with the police and others to bring about longer-term solutions. ... What is needed is a little less hot air, a bit more compassion and a greater understanding of the very limited powers that the authorities have to deal with anti-social behaviour.
>
> JEFFERSON HORSLEY,
>
> Leader, Taunton Deane Borough Council

The barrage of criticism from organizations representing the disabled was inevitable. We were asking for it. Andrew had shown me a draft of the original letter to Taunton Deane Environmental Services and, rushed at the time, I had glanced through it without thinking too deeply about the implications of those ill-judged words. *Mea culpa!* But for the Leader of the Borough Council to smear us publicly by suggesting our views branded us anti disabled people is outrageous. The final couple of lines in Horsley's letter also make me bloody angry. I'm all for 'less hot air' (rich coming from Ol' Waffles!) and 'more compassion', but to assert that his council has 'very limited powers' to deal with the problems on Castle Green is pathetic and betrays an absence of political will on his part.

There are now less than twenty-four hours before my summit meeting with him and Brünnhilde, and I intend to eat him alive. I have done my homework. Gill has ransacked the files in our office and produced all the evidence I need to illustrate the positive steps that might be taken by the local authority if it exercised a little imagination and leadership. The files also expose Horsley's zero record in tackling this issue since he became leader in 1991. After six frustrating years of trying to persuade him and his lot to take us seriously, he hardly has grounds to accuse me of 'trying to conduct change through the press'. Yes, I have waged a high-profile campaign – but only because my patience is exhausted and all that's left is a handy public megaphone to shake him into action.

But just at this moment I could do without a major row with the Council, particularly as tomorrow will be my first meeting with Taunton's new Member of Parliament. I want it to go well. I want it to be constructive. What's more, within the next few weeks, I hope to be presenting the town planners with an outline brief of our great Millennium Project: the scheme to redevelop the crumbling wreck of garages and outbuildings sitting idle on our forecourt by the north-east corner of the Green. In a word, I need Ol' Waffles and his Council on our side. But the omens today could not be worse. Storm clouds are gathering and just for good measure the HTV Weatherline this morning has forecast heavy showers and a risk of thunder on Sunday, the day when 130 revellers will be descending upon us for our annual Midsummer Garden Party among the rose beds within the twelfth-century stone walls of the ancient fortress. I am bracing myself for a tempestuous weekend.

SATURDAY, 21 JUNE 1997

The latest fax from the HTV Weatherline timed at 0600 gave us no comfort for tomorrow's grand barbiefest. We have been promised rain, wind and unseasonably low temperatures. By ten o'clock this morning Andrew, Phil and I finally decided to abort plan A (the Garden) and go live with plan B (bringing the whole show indoors). We telephoned Torex, the hire company, and cancelled the trestles, folding chairs, canvas parasols, charcoal grills and all the other gear essential for a big party *alfresco*. Meanwhile, people have been calling us all day to ask if we are still going ahead. 'The show goes on,' we tell them. 'Never mind the weather. We'll be throwing a fab party. Trust us!' Well, this is the official line. In fact, the whole show looks like being a logistical nightmare. For a start we don't have a room big enough to seat 130 people. The garden is a dream – masses of space – for eating, drinking and enjoying the sun-soaked rhythms of Hugo and his 'Huguenotes', probably the wackiest steel band outside the Caribbean. But restaging this great gig indoors has demanded a deep breath, a little instant improvisation and a set of new instructions to the staff.

Shortly after eleven – and with less than an hour to go before my date with Brünnhilde – we had thrashed out the detail. The two barbecue stations we had planned in the garden will now be replaced by one long buffet running the length of the dining room, with all the food cooked in the kitchen and ferried up in relays. Pre-lunch champagne and Pimms will be dispensed from three bars located in the hall, the Rose Room and the Monmouth Room, with Hugo playing by the grandfather clock in the hall to get the party going as people arrive. For better or for worse – we had no choice – the seating plan will be split: fifty-five in the restaurant, seventy-five in the Monmouth, with Hugo shuttling between the two at respectable intervals. And as a poor substitute for the riotous colours of our rose bushes, Louise telephoned Floaters, an outfit specializing in balloon displays, to see what they might do to inject a spirit of light-hearted festivity into the place.

At midday I mustered my team in the Penthouse. We were four: Louise, Phil, Andrew and me: the executive directors of the company. I wanted to create an atmosphere at once informal and businesslike; the Penthouse, I felt, struck the right note. The drawing room is arranged with two heavy sofas facing each other and a large glass-topped coffee table between. A pair of sliding doors on one wall give way to a dining room where we laid coffee, tea, mineral water and two bottles of Australian Chardonnay on the sideboard.

Shortly after 12.15, Mrs Ballard and Jefferson Horsley were ushered into the room and I introduced them to the others. As Ol'Waffles gripped Andrew's right hand, he said 'Ah! Andrew Grahame,' pompously elongating the vowels to emphasize his acknowledgement of the author of That Letter. For the next few moments we exchanged small talk as Brünnhilde admired the view across Taunton to the Quantock Hills in the distance. I invited everyone to sit down, gently but quite deliberately orchestrating each place: our guests on the sofa facing the panoramic window; Andrew and I on the opposite sofa, our backs to the light; and Louise and Phil in armchairs to one side of the coffee table. We served the refreshments: tea for our Member of Parliament; the Chardonnay for our Leader of Council, who appeared in the jolliest of moods and came dressed in a dashing check shirt open at the neck. What was he expecting? I wondered. A cosy little chat? A let's-kiss-and-make-up session?

We got down to business, my pile of files and documents spread out before me on the coffee table. But first I was determined that Ol'Waffles should be left in no two minds about our attitude to his patronizing e-mail and his outrageous statement to the press. Repeatedly, he tried to interrupt, saying that he was merely echoing the views expressed by the strategic planning committee on 5 June, when the matter of the pathway was brought before his members. I told him that his actions were nothing short of a deliberate attempt to discredit us – a move I was not prepared to tolerate from a man in his position. I also reminded him that Andrew Grahame was a colleague *not* a 'subordinate' and that it was too easy to trade in the language of contempt. What we had written was misjudged and I accepted responsibility. Equally, his retaliatory outbursts were ill-conceived and unjustified.

Throughout this exchange, the others remained silent. Then, having cleared the air, we agreed to get to grips with the meeting's original agenda: the problem of anti-social behaviour on Castle Green. For the next ten minutes – and principally for the benefit of Mrs Ballard – I presented a résumé of our dealings with the Council on this issue since 1991. There were three key points I was anxious to put across. First, in June 1991 and after a meeting with me to discuss our problems, Jefferson had set up a panel – 'The Castle Green Forum' – to explore a positive way forward. Second, in November that year, a thoughtful six-page discussion paper had been presented to the Forum in which a number of recommendations were made. These proposals were 'fully supported' by the panel and the Borough Planning Officer was asked to 'prepare options for further consideration' on specific recommendations relating to 'traffic management' and the 'redesign' of Castle Green. These and other ideas contained in the paper were, in my opinion, constructive and imaginative – moreover, they demonstrated exactly what might be done if the Council applied its mind to the problem. (So much for Horsley's constant refrain that the local authority's powers are 'limited'.) Third, and last, I showed that having reached this critical point in November 1991, no further action was taken. A meeting of the Forum scheduled for March 1992 was 'postponed'. It was never rescheduled and the initiative fizzled out.

As I spoke, Brünnhilde listened quietly and did not interrupt. When I'd finished she shot a quizzical glance across at Jefferson. I had him against the ropes, choking on his Chardonnay. What happened? she asked curtly. He didn't know. His memory was blank. He could not recall the discussion paper. He was vague about the Forum. Nothing. All gone. Spread out in front of me were the memos, the correspondence, minutes of all the meetings and a copy of the crucial document itself. I offered to copy them for him but he declined, asking instead for the exact date and references of the paper and for the dates of the Forum meetings. He made a note of them, muttering 'if I can't find these documents in our own files, something's got to be terribly wrong.' He promised to send Brünnhilde the paper and we agreed to meet again next week once he'd had a chance to review the position. I accepted and said I'd wait for his call.

Andrew then presented a report cataloguing all the incidents of anti-social behaviour we have dealt with over the past two months. We talked about police presence in the town centre and the local force's response times to calls. We outlined the measures we had taken to improve our own security: closed-circuit television, panic buttons and extra staff to mind the doors. We discussed the feasibility of new by-laws to control drinking in public places. Mrs B said she'd write to the police and promised to investigate the question of by-laws with the Home Office.

By 1.30 we were done and I offered our guests some lunch which, as I expected, they politely refused. In the end, I believe we mapped a positive way forward. Time alone will tell. But somehow I doubt I'll be looking back on this date to proclaim it the day the Castle finally made its peace with the Town Council. As for dear Brünnhilde, I'm sold. She strikes me as a thoroughly good egg, a sound lady who will work hard for her constituents. She has kind eyes and a mother-knows-best assurance without the bossiness. Her only failing is that she confesses to being a vegetarian – more evidence, if any were needed, why the Lib-Dems will never be elected to government. Unlike Tony (and now Young William), Paddy has not sussed the importance of gastro-cred in politics. Never mind, Jackie's okay and one day I'll invite her in for a bowl of Phil's delectable marinated vegetables, pasta leaves and hazelnut dressing.

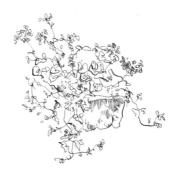

SUNDAY, 22 JUNE 1997

Thank God it's all over. We have just returned home. It was, in its way, a success. But I'm exhausted (I admit: tired and a little emotional). The HTV Weatherline proved its value and confirmed the wisdom of our decision to transfer the 'Garden' Party indoors, although by four o'clock this afternoon the sun broke through and a couple of dozen frocks and blazers poured on to the lawns, if only to parade their lovely straw hats and silk-ribboned panamas. Indeed, English sang-froid was everywhere today, the atrocious weather inspiring a Blitz mentality, all of us determined to have a jolly good time. The wind and rain did not deter the ladies from wearing their new summer frocks or the gentlemen from sporting their brightly striped blazers. And Andrew Grahame issued the staff with new uniforms for the occasion: canary yellow T-shirts branded with the hotel logo and the slogan RAIN WON'T STOP PLAY AT THE CASTLE.

The frantic preparations during the course of the morning produced their tensions. We had a full house last night. Sunday breakfast always begins late and lingers, tying up staff and delaying the *mise en place* for the party. With 130 people expected at noon, we had to move fast. As the revised instructions had only been issued yesterday, no one had read them. So when Louise and I arrived at about 10.30, a number of important details were being overlooked. While Andrew was organizing the tabling and seating plan in the restaurant and Monmouth Room, I noticed that the bar staff were stocking the three drinks stations with the wrong bottles. Yesterday I had produced a short bar list for display on each table: Pimms, Green Point (an excellent Australian fizz), Laurent Perrier and Charles Heidsieck, plus three good bottled beers, Cola and fruit juices. But for some strange reason, I found the ice buckets on the bars filled with every champagne label we stock except the ones being advertised for the party. This kind of simple stupidity makes me see red and, of course, it wastes time. I blew.

THE CASTLE AT TAUNTON
MIDSUMMER GARDEN PARTY

Sunday, 22 June 1997

Suckling pig
Lamb or beef burgers with relish
Chicken drumsticks with peanut sauce
Chorizo sausage wrapped in streaky bacon
Cold poached salmon with herb mayonnaise
Grilled fresh sardines with basil and garlic
Cold marinated vegetables
Grilled artichokes with courgette pickle
Vegetable kebabs
Chargrilled spiced aubergines with cottage cheese
Salads, dressings and breads

Pecan pie
Fresh strawberries, raspberries and cherries
Glazed lemon tart with clotted cream

Meanwhile, Phil was setting up the buffet in the restaurant, laying out all the cold food. It looked terrific: bright, colourful salads, huge bowls of fresh strawberries, cherries and raspberries, several magnificent glazed lemon tarts and trays of fine local cheeses. Looking at the tiered display, I realized that its effect would be ruined unless we organized the service in some sensible fashion. The last thing we needed was a mad crush of a hundred hungry punters overwhelming the tables, demolishing everything before them. I called Andrew and the three of us decided to get Hugo to announce lunch and to instruct our guests to take their seats, order their wines, relax, enjoy and get drinking. Christophe would then invite each group to get up and go to the buffet in turn. In the meantime, the steel band would play, while a couple of chefs whetted people's appetites by passing along the tables with vast flats bearing the two roast suckling pigs.

My last problem was Hugo himself, a man I have come to love dearly but a man whose philosophy of life is synonymous with all values Caribbean. Hugo does not understand English time; will never understand the English obsession with punctuality. I asked him to arrive at 11.30. I begged him not to be late. He promised. On his honour, he promised. 11.30 came and passed. So did 11.45. Then just as the grandfather clock was about to chime noon, Hugo's creaking, clapped-out Volvo estate rolled into the car park. By this time, the punters were streaming in. But Hugo's gentle communion with the world would not be disturbed. He and his players unloaded their drums in their own time and disappeared upstairs to change. Five minutes, he said. Twenty-five minutes later, the trio were in position and, at last, we had ourselves a party.

Now I'm going to bed.

EARLY RECOLLECTIONS

FRIDAY, 25 JULY 1997

I T'S BEEN TEN DAYS NOW since our return from Tuscany, that land of limpid light. We had a wonderful break: sixteen days of peace in a remote paradise, a medieval hill village-turned-hotel somewhere west of Siena. Any good holiday induces an element of fantasy in the spirit; lovely at the time, but painful in the homecoming when reality reasserts its cruel quotidian will.

And what did we find? A restaurant struck by an epidemic of defections to City Rhodes: the unscrupulous rat Girling having bribed a bevy of waiters to join him in London. So Christophe is, at present, short of both staff and temper. His early induction into the darker arts of restaurant management is proving tough, but this is no bad thing – it will steel his resolve. To his particular dismay, all the deserters have lied about their intentions or broken their contracts or sinned on both counts. Andrew and I have told Christophe not to authorize any wages owed to these wretched people. Let them sing for their money – and, if necessary, they can make the journey to Taunton to collect. This seems to have cheered our despondent young manager who, recalling the teaching of his parents in France, has suddenly come to appreciate the nobility of values like loyalty and honesty – and the ignobleness of the lack of them.

More promisingly, our return from *la bella Italia* heralded good news in the battle against the Barbarian. The grey-grim paper mountain rising over my desk – enough to make Everest look like a pimple – included word from Ol' Waffles and Brünnhilde. Progress appears to be in the offing. The old 'Castle Green Forum', lost and forgotten five years ago, is being dusted down and resurrected. We meet at the end of the month. The Mighty One also seems to have made an impression on the local constabulary. Andrew and the rest of the team report 'all quiet on the Green' – well, if not complete silence, peace and tranquillity, a noticeable improvement, thanks largely to a higher police profile on the turf. But, best of all, trade has been brisk, occupancies are riding high and profits for the year threaten to break new records.

Good as it is to be back in harness, I cannot recall a moment when we looked forward to a holiday more. The stresses and tribulations of the past twelve months, I think, have been no greater than at any previous time. But this year there seems to have been a profound need to escape. Perhaps age and some deeper forces were at work. Turning fifty and the subconscious anxiety of an ailing father (in spite of his miraculous recovery after the near-fatal stroke in September) may have served to remind me of my own mortality: the sudden self-realization of middle age; that you are 'not as young as you used to be'; that you are now 'past your prime' … all those dreadful, trite little mantras recited like tabloid headlines at that point of transition into mid-life.

For no obvious reason, the holiday – inspired partly by the peace and beauty of the setting, partly by this unspoken state of mind – led Louise and me to talk endlessly about our childhoods: long, reflective conversations which seemed to offer their own kind of therapy. It also occurs to me that my urgent desire to demolish and redevelop that monstrous ruin of a garage block – our great Millennium Project – may, in some way, be connected with the fact that, come the year 2000, my family will have been running the Castle for exactly a half-century. The feeling that time marches and that here is an important job left undone. One my father began and one which I must finish.

It was a Mr R G Spiller, a builder by trade and, in those days, proprietor of the Castle Hotel, who offered my father the post of manager in 1950 – an appointment he took up on 15 October at an annual salary of only £600 and on the basis that he lived in while his Greek-born wife and two children took rooms elsewhere in Taunton. The condition of the hotel in this bleak post-war period was dire – indeed, not a great deal better than our garage block today. My father had a major challenge on his hands just making the place vaguely habitable and civilized. Meanwhile, my mother, my brother Gerald (aged eleven months) and I (three-and-a-half years) were dispatched to Thessalonika to live with my grandparents. By Christmas, Spiller was sufficiently satisfied with the job his new manager was doing to agree to accommodate the family in the hotel, adjusting my father's salary accordingly – to £400. A generous man, Mr Spiller. But, at the time, my father was pretty desperate financially and in January 1951 we moved into a modest suite of rooms overlooking the garden on the second floor: a double, which was converted into a living room; two small singles – one for my parents (their double bed wedged snugly into a corner), one for Gerald and me; and a bathroom. Later, when my brother outgrew his cot, Spiller allowed us to take the remaining two rooms on the corridor – one as a bedroom for me, the other as a tiny dining room – and our wing became a self-contained flat.

The absence of a kitchen in this arrangement did not bother my mother, who never learned to cook as a child, having grown up cosseted by willing servants in her ample home in Thessalonika. In spite of the rigours of austerity – which came as a severe shock when she arrived in England as a teenage bride – living in an hotel was a pretty fair substitute for the life to which she had become accustomed in her youth. Beds were made, rooms cleaned, shoes polished – and meals were delivered from an unseen basement by rope-hauled dumb waiter.

In spite of my father's difficult circumstances, Gerald and I were, nevertheless, put under the charge of a nanny – less out of necessity, that's for sure, and more in deference to pre-war social convention. Times and attitudes had changed dramatically in Britain, but my parents, with their European backgrounds, were less pliant in their outlook. My mother and her sister had been reared by Austrian, German and French governesses, while my father and his brothers – who spent most of their boyhood in Bratislava, where their father, the indomitable Henry Prüger, owned the 250-bedroomed Savoy-Carlton Hotel – grew up under the rigid regime of various retainers and private tutors until they were sent away to be educated in England.

Our nanny was a round, ginger-haired Scot named Jenkins; she was married to a Welshman who kept a small farm in North Devon. It is to Nanny Jenkins that I owe my first serious gastronomic experience: a poignant, vivid moment; a rite of passage which still remains fixed in my memory. I suppose I could not have been more than five or six years old.

As my parents were taking a holiday – in France, I think – Gerald and I were sent to stay on the Jenkins's farm which, as I recall, was somewhere near Barnstaple. The couple lived in a tiny, primitive cottage at the foot of a steep hill. There was no electricity and at night the place reeked of paraffin. Plumbing was basic, the lavatory a shed at the back. The unfamiliarity of this isolated stone hovel inspired a mixture of fear and excitement in us – for a week or two we were living an adventure of the Famous Five. The Jenkins had no motor car: instead the Welshman's mode of transport was an old trailer drawn by a huge, slow, submissive shire horse for whose lot in life I felt acute sorrow. The poor beast would struggle desperately to haul its load up the steep track from the cottage, the farmer's only method of encouragement being to whip the wretched creature repeatedly to get us to the summit.

But the sharpest shock to the sensibilities of this tender child came when I witnessed the capture and slaughter of a proud and magnificent cockerel. One morning, I was drawn uncontrollably by the deafening sounds of domestic birds flapping, squawking and racing around the yard. Jenkins – a fit and agile man – was there, leaping and diving like a circus clown. He had selected his victim and his fattened quarry knew it. Finally, the farmer grabbed the fowl in his leather-tough hands, shook it violently and slit its throat. Wings still flailing maniacally in his grip, Jenkins made off quickly, disappearing round the back of the house. For several moments, I stood open-mouthed and awestruck. I could not understand why or for what purpose this innocent bird had been chosen for summary execution, for such a vicious and gratuitous death.

Jenkins, I decided, was a madman, a murderer. We were all in grave danger and I had to do something. I ran off to find Nanny, to warn her. Instead, I rounded the corner of a barn and found the dead chicken strung up by its legs, a large pool of fresh blood staining the hard, pale earth beneath its severed neck. The feathered corpse, hanging motionless in the warm mid-morning sunlight, froze me to the ground. Never had I seen anything so gruesome. As my mind grasped the terror before my eyes, I turned on my heel and ran for my life.

A few days later we ate that bird, and to this day it remains the most succulently flavoured, delicious chicken I have ever tasted. I can't remember when I finally exorcized my terror but clearly it didn't take long. I think the defining moment, my gastronomic epiphany, came when the smells of the roasting fowl – smells so redolent of the farmyard it was reared in – filled my nostrils as its sweet, pungent fragrance gradually consumed every nook and cranny in the cottage. Sitting at Nanny Jenkins's modest kitchen table, I suddenly realized the ambrosial pleasures of good food cooked from the freshest, most carefully nurtured raw ingredients. In my new enlightenment, Farmer Jenkins now became my hero.

Oddly, perhaps, the Castle had little part to play in my early gustatory education. There are no memories to suggest that the hotel boasted a particularly fine restaurant; no tastes I recall with a special pleasure. The bald fact is that the Castle had no creditable reputation for its food. The only reliable guide in the early and middle fifties, Raymond Postgate's pioneering *Good Food Guide*, declined to register the Castle as a place of special interest to serious gourmets. However, my father – quite properly – did make capital of two moments apparently recognizing the hotel's culinary worth. The first came in 1951 when Fanny Cradock passed through Taunton and subsequently filed a report for *Bon Viveur*, her column in the *Daily Telegraph*, in which she praised the Castle's cooking. 'And saving best for last,' she enthused, 'a luxurious large hotel which sets the standard I have long sought.' The second accolade came two years later when an obscure outfit called the *Cercle Gastronomique de Belgique* awarded the hotel its *Grand Prix*. The prize, a handsomely engraved eighteen-inch silver goblet, was publicly and prominently displayed in a glass cabinet for the next twenty years. As a child I was led to believe that this honour had now elevated us into the top rankings worldwide. We were now among the Greats. In fact, no one had ever heard of the *Cercle Gastronomique de Belgique*, nor have we since. *Tant pis!* My father milked the prize for all its worth and attracted acres of publicity. In those days foodie awards were rare – now, of course, they are a devalued currency.

But although the Castle's kitchen made little impression on my infant taste-buds, the killing of the cockerel seemed to awaken my gastronomic curiosity. Strangely, bizarrely, it was a ravaged post-war Thessalonika that introduced me to some of the more sophisticated pleasures of good food. In England, rationing and austerity bequeathed a grey, dull and dreadful diet. Elizabeth David had just published her classic *Mediterranean Food* but we had to wait awhile – for George Perry-Smith, the sixties and beyond – to begin to appreciate its fruits. Yet, in the fifties, within the rubble and remains of Greece's second city, I discovered the flavours and colours and unimaginable splendours of a gastronomic treasure chest denied us at home: an abundance of fish and seafood; exotic fruits like melons and figs; olive oil, garlic and lemons; aubergines and bright, fleshy, distorted tomatoes; oregano, basil and thyme; and the sweetest, most tempting of eastern European pastries.

It took two decades or more for Salonika to recover from occupation and war. Reconstruction was painfully slow. As young children in those early years, Gerald and I spent our summers with our mother's family, and the memories of her birthplace remain scarred on my mind. The city was a wreck, its people broken.

Riding down its parched, burnt streets, all I saw were beggars in rags and crippled children. It was a painful, unpleasant sight which made me feel uncomfortable, frightened. You could almost touch the fear – and you could smell the decay on those streets. I could not understand why. Five, six, seven, eight – every year we came and it was still the same.

Our grandparents lived on Queen Olga Street, a wide boulevard running parallel to the bay, trimmed by a line of once-gracious, now-faded Victorian villas: two-storey mansions of elegant proportions, large windows and cool verandahs. Each was built in its own garden which gave on to the sea. Athanasius and Fifi Rosis lived at number twenty-eight. He was a banker, philanthropist and wise owl. During the occupation he had assisted the escapes of several Jewish families and after the war a grateful country honoured him with the title of Norwegian Consul in Thessalonika. Fifi was descended from ancient and noble Macedonian stock. She was short, plump and adored. Her hair jet-black. Her eyes bright, glistening olives. Her skin pale, smooth, translucent like the finest porcelain. When she wrapped you in her arms it was like falling on soft silk pillows. Her hands, with their carefully manicured and varnished fingers, betrayed her status in that cushioned, privileged society. She was a generous and accomplished hostess, and her talents as an embroiderer are framed on the walls of my parents' home in Somerset.

As I recall, the villa on Queen Olga Street – distinguished by its Consul's oval plaque suspended from a first-floor balcony – was in grave need of repair. The grand iron railings surrounding the property were flaked, rusted like charred matchsticks, and the garden was a wilderness of scrub, weed and dead earth. For all its lost grandeur, at least the place limped in sympathy with its tattered city. But once we had run the gauntlet of dust and decay, breathed the stench of the streets, raced by the beggars and bent bodies; once we had closed the front door behind us and entered the cool of the house, a new world opened before us. One of polished wood, delicate lace and old silver; soft furnishings dressed in immaculate summer-white linens; refreshing breezes off the sea; and sweet, mysterious smells from the kitchen. Food was at the centre of this charmed universe: our grandmother, 'yaya', always pressing something delicious into our tiny mouths, gaping like fledglings in a nest.

Unlike England, where rationing had become a way of life, self-denial a good habit and drabness a state of mind, here in this wrecked city, in my grandparents' home, there was not the remotest sense of scarcity or deprivation. Here was only plenty, prepared and served by a small retinue of cackling peasant women who had the infuriating habit of pinching our cheeks (the traditional Greek custom of showing affection towards children). It was worth the pain. We ate wonderfully – the seafood, I think, making the most lasting impact, the glorious sight of *whole* fish coming to table on huge china dishes leaving me spellbound. *Barboúni* (red mullet) was an appetizing staple, while the abundant varieties of sea bream were just sensational: *tsipoúra, fagrí, lithríni* and best of all, the great *synagrída*. Whichever the variety, each would be served in the same fashion: simply grilled with *latholémono* (olive oil and lemon). There were other favourites too: the restoring chicken, egg and lemon broth, *avgolémono*; that great aromatic haricot bean stew, *fasoulia*; herby meat balls (*kephtédes*); and the three famous filo pies, *kotópitta* (chicken), *spanakópitta* (spinach) and *tirópitta* (cheese).

To finish, we would first refresh our palates with slices of watermelon before the maids brought in trays of *baklava*, that rich and sweet and magnificent flaky pastry stuffed with chopped almonds, pistachios and walnuts, then coated in honey and rose-water.

A lunchtime feast of this magnitude sent us all to sleep for the afternoon. Indeed, a siesta was mandatory throughout our childhood visits to Greece – a deeply civilized habit I grew to accept willingly. At six yaya would come to wake us (I can still remember the smooth, soft luxury of the fine linen sheets that covered our beds). No ordinary wake-up call this. Nothing as banal as a pot of tea or a lemonade. Yaya would present us with a *glyko* (a sweet). These were exotic delicacies offered on a long silver spoon; so rich that politesse and common sense dictated that a spoonful a day was quite enough. A tall glass of iced water necessarily accompanied the *glyko* to cleanse the mouth after ingesting this blissful early-evening treat. My favourite was *kerassi* (cherry), the bright red fruit glistening in a syrup which spilled slowly over the edge of the spoon to create a miniature slick of pinkness on its small china dish. I can taste the fruit now – the deepest, sweetest essence of cherry – cloying, sticking to my tongue and the roof of my mouth. I wanted more. Yaya never said no – she just chuckled with her pleasure at giving me pleasure, pinched my cheeks (more gently than her servants), and said '*Avrio, avrio, pethi mou*' – tomorrow, tomorrow my boy.

Our annual visits to Salonika were not confined to Queen Olga Street. There were other members of the family to whom we had to pay homage. The most important of these were my great-uncle Petros, my grandmother's brother, and his wife, Aunt Cleo. Cleo was enormous, rouged and so heavily powdered that when she shook her jowls, the atmosphere misted like a halo about her lunar features. Her ample frame was swathed in an ocean of silk. Her neck, wrists and fingers runkled under the weight of gold and precious stones. Uncle Petros was deaf as a diamond but lived like a pasha. He was a voluptuary, a sensualist who devoted his life to women and food. I once watched him consuming a fig, sucking the ripe flesh expertly out of the quartered skin. But whereas he made me feel uneasy, Cleo terrified me. Still, for all my misgivings, I soon learned that a visit to their opulent seventh-floor apartment high above the promenade was an occasion not to be missed. Cleo's hospitality was legendary.

In the backstreets, not a hundred yards from the apartment building, the grimmer reality of hungry children scavenging in gutters and tired old men begging for small change passed us over. Sitting on Cleo's flower-strewn balcony, gazing over the bay – the sea dotted with American warships – maids offered wine and ouzo to the grown-ups while Gerald and I practised the art of shelling pistachios, which we gobbled greedily. With the drinks came *mézéthes* – more colloquially *mezethákia* – olives, feta, *dolmádes* (stuffed vine leaves), *melzánasalata* (aubergine purée), *taramásalata*, salamis and so on. All delicious except for the *dolmádes* which, in spite of their visual promise, I decided were rather coarse and deeply uninteresting – an opinion which hasn't changed.

Lunch would see the damask-covered dining table laden with dishes of giant crawfish. For me, *astakós* was the ultimate gastronomic luxury: fatter, sweeter than any English lobster I have ever seen since. We ate them cold, with mayonnaise or olive oil and lemon juice. They were fantastic, and just thinking about them makes me salivate. Cleo would pick lustily at the thick flesh and then rinse her podgy, jewelled fingers in warm water poured into cut glass bowls, rose petals floating on their surface, which the maids had placed neatly on napkins by each table setting.

To follow, there were vast plates of fruit – melons, peaches, grapes, figs – and then a stunning selection of pastries bought that morning from Flóka, Greece's most famous patissier, with cafés in both Athens and Salonika. I would wait for this moment. Twelve months I would wait. And each time its consummation would be the most perfect, the most sublime moment of my life. The pastry of my dreams went by the unappealing moniker of *Kok*, perhaps the name of its inventor. I do not know the recipe. All I have is a distant but clear memory of a heavenly confection, a taste which lingers four decades on. It looked like a Big Mac: two round buns made of a fine, dense but airy-light sponge and filled with a delectable chantilly. The top bun was coated, éclair-like, with chocolate, and owing to its exquisite squidginess, we ate it with a small, ivory-handled pastry knife and fork. Like the *kerassi glyko*, the *Kok* was always served with a glass of iced water.

It was at Cleo's that – to my parents' displeasure – I acquired a taste for good Turkish coffee. The Greeks, of course, hate the Turks – especially in Macedonia. This is not surprising after 400 years of Ottoman hegemony – but the finest aspects of the 'Greek' table are the one civilized legacy of that violent occupation. So to refer to 'Greek' coffee as Turkish is treasonable but true.

These – like all my early gastronomical adventures – may explain the strange paradox of a gustatory passion matched, in equal measure, by an extraordinary culinary idleness. I don't cook but I know about cuisine. I see nothing anomalous here, any more than an opera buff who can't sing. Taste, eating, the pleasures of the palate have always been a consuming interest but they have never translated into a desire to practise. If you are spoilt you get lazy, and in the world of good food and wine I have been deliciously spoilt from the beginning. The kitchen was always a mysterious, unseen domain. In our tiny flat at the Castle, food appeared as if by magic out of a lift shaft. In Greece, in Queen Olga Street and at Aunt Cleo's, the kitchen was where the servants worked. I saw no kitchen. There was no reason. Good things issued forth on silver and bone china every day as naturally as the light of the rising sun on the Aegean Sea.

SUNDAY, 3 AUGUST 1997

My last file note on the notorious 'Castle Green Forum' records that the meeting set for 25 March 1992 had to be 'postponed'. So it was with a strange sense of history that I took my old seat in the black-beamed, mullion-windowed Municipal Hall on Thursday when the Forum reconvened after its extended rest. Cllr Tony Floyd, our amiable chairman, began the session by declaring that he did not want this to be a talking shop; he wanted the group to be 'action oriented' (a point I have insisted be minuted). From this auspicious opening, the meeting proceeded enthusiastically, a warm feeling of 'inclusiveness' (to use a voguish Blairite word) infusing our deliberations. We debated the impact of CCTV on crime and hooliganism. We discussed by-laws to stop drinking in public spaces and the feasibility of businesses on the Green clubbing together to pay for a security guard. A police representative offered the local force's services at a rate of £34 per hour for an off-duty officer. A quick calculation indicated that this service could cost us up to £70,000 a year, which we considered a mite excessive.

The Borough Council's dog warden then told us about his vital role in controlling the town's New Age mongrels who continue to use the Green as their favourite spot for dropping biggies. The Forum demanded action. The warden assured us that a Dogs-Fouling-of-Land by-law would take effect soon and the Council promised that it would not hesitate to prosecute at the first sighting of a dropped biggy. What about a Dogs-on-Lead by-law? asked the nice man from the Southern National Bus Company. Well, said the Council, this was a little tricky. A by-law already existed, but it was causing difficulties because its provisions failed to define the meaning of the term 'lead'. For example, if a dog were connected to a piece of string 100 feet long, could it not be fairly argued that this was, indeed, performing the function of a 'lead'? Furthermore, the by-law was vague on the point of who or what controlled the lead. A dog on a 100 ft 'lead' tethered to a lamppost could be seen technically not to be breaching the provisions of the regulation.

Cllr Floyd skilfully steered us through these and other arcane matters. Two hours later, a way forward had been agreed and the next meeting was fixed for mid-November.

The main excitement of the week was the arrival of the Australian cricketers in Taunton for their fixture with Somerset. They were a rum bunch – a parody of their national stereotype – uncouth and sporting about as much charm as a pair of wet flannels. The rain, which disrupted play, may not have helped, but this was no excuse for their oafish behaviour: mooching about the hotel in their green shell suits and silly caps, grunting like apes and swearing unnecessarily at the staff. Trying to communicate with these characters – even with so much as a 'g'day' – was next to impossible. All you got in return was a sneering glare. There was absolutely nothing of any substance between the ears, except, clearly, an ability to play cricket and, equally obvious, a healthy hatred towards us poms. They even refused to autograph three cricket bats brought in by a couple of devoted fans, although, to their credit, they did agree to sign a new bat which a local charity wanted to auction at a fund-raising gala.

The other striking thing about the Aussies is their complete disinterest in their past: perhaps because they don't have one. History just doesn't figure as an aspect of their culture – except, possibly, as an opaque, yawn-inducing primary school textbook. Theirs is a now-culture: a physical thing, stimulated by the immediacy and excitement of the quick-fix – a wicket, a woman, a Fosters – after which they just move on to the next thing. History, tradition, the past and all that are for poms and poofters.

If there were ever an icon of Australian cricket, one might expect Don Bradman to be up there among the gods of the game. But while the English still talk reverentially about the man who dominated test cricket before the war, the Aussies remain pretty unfazed. Still, the name did strike a chord with Alan Crompton, the Tourists' team manager who, unlike his players, at least fielded a smile and a friendly g'day when I introduced myself. But when I started talking about Bradman and whortleberry pie, his eyes squinted in bewilderment, struggling to understand why this pommy cove should be so insistent about baking a pie Bradman happened to fancy for supper sixty years ago.

'Well, it's a tradition,' I explained. 'When Sir Don stayed here in the thirties, we cooked him one and he loved it. Ever since, we've always presented the Australians with a pie when they've visited Taunton.'

'Whatberries?'

'Whortleberries! They're a kind of bilberry peculiar to the Quantock Hills just north of here.'

Eventually, a reluctant Mr Crompton agreed to a press call at which Phil Vickery would present the famous delicacy to Steve Waugh, the Aussie vice-captain, who was, for this match, captaining the team playing Somerset.

My next problem was to find the wretched berries which, I knew, came into season at about this time of year. But whether the fruit were freshly picked or frozen did not really bother me. The point was the publicity: sixty years of experience have shown that this is the best recyclable story the Castle has run. The media lap it up every time. I issue an emergency call which is instantly followed by appeals in the press and interviews on radio and television. Within twenty-four hours some generous soul invariably comes forward with a cache of precious berries. Phil bakes the pie, we stage the photo opportunity and our heroic whortleberry supplier scoops a few headlines. This year the credits fell to Esme Redwood, a farmer's daughter from Creech St Michael, who delivered 5 lb of fruit. Next day, over a picture of a spoonful of whorts aimed at Steve Waugh's mouth and Phil looking on smugly, one headline read 'Esme saves Aussies' pie', and another mixed – or, perhaps, missed – a metaphor with 'Esme gets chef out of a stew'.

It was my father who first introduced me to this great little stunt; I remember him performing the ritual when I was a child. There's an extraordinary press photograph in our archives which shows him presenting a monster pie to the Tourists in 1956. Traditions may live on but the picture reveals the rapid evolution of our lives over the past forty years, stark differences between now and then. For a start, chefs in those days were profane creatures who were kept firmly below stairs. They didn't get their picture taken like today's TV cooks. The pie itself looked completely inedible, covered by a thick, heavy crust that might have contained ball-bearings not berries. Phil, in contrast, bakes an open flan filled with a glistening swamp of the tiny purple fruit. The 1956 shot was also taken *outside* the hotel just after the

Phil Vickery, Alan Crompton and Steve Waugh with the Castle's whortleberry pie

Aussies had stepped off their coach – an indelicate moment which would have enraged the protective Alan Crompton – and the players are dressed neatly in suits and ties, clutching their hand-luggage. The only feature of the picture betraying no hint of change over the years lies in the expression on Ian Johnson's face (the Australian Test captain). While my father looks immensely proud of his chef's whortleberry pie, Johnson is scowling fiercely at the bloody thing.

1956 was a busy year for my father. In May, six weeks before the arrival of the Aussies, he threw a big party to celebrate the re-opening of the hotel's lounge and dining room, the final phase of a four-year programme of modernization to drag the place out of its post-war misery. Among the finer points of the renovation, the Castle was now able to offer its guests rooms with hot towel rails, electric razor plugs and bedside telephones – but visitors who wanted a bath were still expected to share with their neighbours along the corridor. Private bathrooms would come later, my father's first priority after his arrival in 1950 being to re-roof and re-wire the entire property.

My brother Gerald (on the right) and me as Tudor page boys, 1956

Gerald and I were not really aware of these works nor, for that matter, anything that went on in the hotel. Our home life was made as private as it was possible to make living over the shop. All we knew was that our daddy seemed to work cripplingly long hours. The opening party, however, was different. This was an important moment in my father's career and in the development of the hotel. He wanted all his family to be part of the show, and my brother and I were given starring roles in an elaborate ceremonial devised to mark the occasion. The party, a cocktail reception for about a hundred local worthies, took place in the new lounge (now our Monmouth Room). While the speeches were being made, Gerald and I, dressed as Tudor page boys (hose, doublet, cape, feather-trimmed cap et al), hid patiently outside with two senior members of staff decked out as beefeaters. Between them, they carried an enormous model of the Castle constructed of plywood, paper Union Jacks fluttering on tall sticks above the hotel's north and south towers.

On cue, the master of the Taunton Vale Harriers sounded his horn. The major, a veteran of the North African desert, had adopted this habit before going into battle and his bravery, I was told, had earned him the Military Cross. But at this particular moment, this nine-year-old page boy was *not* feeling in the least brave. Trembling beneath my hose and doublet, the Tudor pageant progressed solemnly into the lounge. I mounted a table, nervously unfurled a parchment manuscript and in a high treble voice intoned the cry 'Oyez! Oyez! Oyez!', proclaiming the Castle officially open. Gerald then turned towards the model suspended awkwardly on poles between the two beefeaters. He lowered the drawbridge, raised the portcullis and withdrew a bouquet of roses which he presented to Mrs Spiller, the proprietor's widow – old R G having died the year before. The room cheered and the tableau made its exit.

Whortleberries and grand proclamations aside, there is little of the ordinary workings of the hotel I recall in those early years. Our days as children were strictly ordered – we were not allowed to loiter on the premises, and during the school holidays the place was put out of bounds. Breakfast, like every other meal, was delivered by dumb waiter. There was always something cooked on the tray, but my parents, particular about our diets, would also administer a daily dose of cod-liver oil which, later on, was replaced by a thick, viscous substance called Radio Malt. Tea and coffee were *not* permitted. Instead, our Peter Rabbit mugs were filled to the brim with milk (gold top, naturally) and we were required to drink it all up before slinging our satchels over our shoulders. As we left the flat for school, there would be one final instruction, repeated religiously each day: 'Say good morning to the staff!' And so we did.

On our return, there was 'high tea', usually cold meats with a dull salad and occasionally baked beans, which was considered a treat. I ate them, but the appeal of those mealy pellets on a slice of sodden toast never struck me as terribly special. The big treat of the week was our ration of television on Sunday afternoons and then only an hour's worth. At school it annoyed me that my exposure to this exciting new medium was considerably more restricted than that of my contemporaries. I felt excluded because my knowledge of all the good programmes did not extend much beyond *Muffin the Mule*, *The Flower Pot Men* and the *Lone Ranger*. As there was no television in the flat, we would gather after tea around the hotel's one set, installed in the smoking room opposite the 'men only' public bar. Secretly, I prayed that we might not be joined by any of the hotel residents, but invariably a few wandered in and I would hate them for invading my private pleasure.

During those early years, the Castle also accommodated a number of elderly permanent residents; classic *Fawlty Towers* characters whom, in time, my father was quietly relieved to have check out for their hotel in the sky. The last to go was an old colonel by the name of Hawkes, a decent enough buffer whom I occasionally visited in his room on the first floor. Two things, particularly, stick in my mind about him: the pungent smell of his pipe tobacco and his obsession with jigsaw puzzles. There, laid on two baize-topped card tables, were these amazingly complex jigsaws, hundreds of pieces neatly spread around the puzzle's outline frame. Steam trains seemed to be his favourite and while he allowed me to watch, my presence was only tolerated as long as I didn't touch.

In 1953, after a spell at an infants' school called 'The Beehive', a Victorian institution run by two spinster sisters, Ethel and Nancy Gange, I was sent to Thone, the preparatory wing to Taunton, the public school where I remained imprisoned for the next twelve years: first as a day boy and later, at the age of twelve, as a boarder. The place was, I imagine, no different from any other school of its type: vile and uncivilized. These were the unhappiest days of my life, my problem being a simple hatred of a system that considered sport as its holiest canon. To play for the 1st XV on a Saturday afternoon made you a hero, to sing the first verse of *Once in Royal David's City* solo and unaccompanied in chapel, as I did, branded you a queer. Apart from swimming and tennis, at which I did *not* excel, I loathed games. I came last in any race, could not vault a horse, walk the beam or climb a rope (which appalled my father so much he had one suspended from the rafters in the hotel's garage to persuade me to conquer my weediness. I didn't).

Thone was run by an Arnoldian head who went by the name of Dr Headworth-Whitty. While the masters and prefects of the senior school took their pleasure chastising pupils by cane, Dr H-W's preferred instrument was an old gym shoe with a weighted toe, which he wielded with great enthusiasm. Mercifully, I escaped the tip of that shoe applied to my bum. At the prep school, I was a painfully timid child, conscientious and careful to keep my nose clean.

Rebellion at the injustices of this dreadful institution came later, with the growing self-awareness of adolescence. I suppose I must have been no more than thirteen when I committed my first act of anarchy, the object of my rage being an assistant housemaster who enjoyed stalking the dormitories at night with his cane. If he overheard a whisper of chatter outside the door, he'd burst in, throw on the lights and beat the lot of us. Bastard! So after chapel one Sunday morning, I organized a demonstration. I thought I had most of the house behind me but when it came to the moment, only two others joined the protest outside our tormentor's study window. Minutes later we were summoned and thrashed viciously, the weals on my arse refusing to heal fully for weeks afterwards. But our stand against the man was not in vain. In the end his conscience and his guilt mended his ways. He stopped creeping round the corridors at night and his attitude towards me suddenly became sickeningly amiable. (I think he was essentially straight but the abuses he inflicted on young boys clearly marked him out as a sadistic pervert.)

The cruel mores of schoolboy society often excite subtler but equally invidious emotions on the impressionable, sensitive heart. I always remember being slightly embarrassed by my father's occupation – an indefinable sense that hotelkeepers were not regarded in particularly high esteem. British attitudes to 'service', a word regularly confused with servility, are deeply enmeshed in our complex class system. But times have changed and these days to be a chef, a restaurateur or an hotel owner is immensely fashionable. Even so, I still find it almost impossible to hire decent English waiters and, as a consequence, our dining room is dominated by French staff, for whom waiting at table is perceived as a noble profession. But in the 1950s, shopkeepers – many sons of whom attended Thone Preparatory School – were held in higher esteem than hotel managers. With the nuances of social status and class difference, Gerald and I could add one other English prejudice – that of xenophobia. Not overt in its expression but nevertheless present. Again, an indefinable feeling told us that we were different from the rest. All our classmates had autochthonous parents; we had a Greek mother and a half Austro-Hungarian father, parentage that was impossible to conceal in view of my mother's immaculate dress sense and her exotic taste in hats, which outshone all the competition and attracted a great deal of ribald comment on official occasions like speech days, school plays and carol services. So, not only were we 'foreign', we also lived in rooms in an hotel, whereas proper people lived in houses. As a child, this, to me, suggested an imperfect existence. I didn't like being different.

School holidays at home were no less structured than term time. Every moment of our day was organized. With home being a busy hotel, this was probably sensible although, at times, I resented the restrictions imposed on our freedoms. There were tennis lessons with Miss Gange (Nancy of 'The Beehive'). There was riding instruction by a military dictator who forced us to assume impossible postures on the backs of ponies as they trotted round his paddock. There was swimming coaching in the municipal pool. And there were French lessons in our tiny dining room with Monsieur Trevette, a mysterious character with a white pointed beard who dressed entirely in black: black suit, heavy black cape and a wide-brimmed black fedora. As he strode into the hotel, clouds of smoke billowing from his pipe, Monsieur Trevette conjured a romantic vision of a nineteenth-century philosopher-poet. He also had impeccable manners of the kind you often find in cultured Frenchmen. My mother thought he was wonderful and always offered him a glass of sherry towards the end of our hourly sessions; Tio Pepe was his tipple. Kind, cultivated man though he was, Monsieur Trevette failed to teach us very much of his native tongue. Not because we did not pay attention to him. We did. His way inspired polite attentiveness. I think he was too highbrow to connect with a couple of children bored and irritated by their parents' insistence that they submit to these tutorials.

To my certain knowledge, none of my classmates were subjected to a regime like this during their holidays. They were much freer but, as I have explained, we were different. While our daily agenda of sports and French tuition discouraged us from interfering with the running of the business, the nature of my parents' own upbringing – a childhood of tutors and governesses – clearly influenced their decision to inflict all this expensive instruction on us. The natural scheme of domestic life among the *haute bourgeoisie* of middle-Europe translated and adapted to suit life in Taunton in the middle fifties.

There were, however, prescribed moments when the separate existences of schooling and hotel locked horns in a kind of uneasy social collision. My parents organized the most brilliant birthday parties for us (although Gerald and I had little say in either the arrangements or the guest list). As our second-floor flat was too small and too precious to accommodate a party of twenty little horrors, my father booked the Moat Room downstairs for the games and the smaller section of the dining room was set for the tea. Meanwhile, my mother took charge of the invitations – indeed, she orchestrated the entire show – and as I had no particular friends at Thone, she invited the whole class, including the boarders for whom she felt sorry but with whom we, as day boys, were in a semi-state of perpetual war.

These parties, my mother decreed, would be held in fancy dress – not a problem for day boys, who could rely on their eager mums to kit them out. But for the boarders, this was an impossible demand resolved only by their arrival half-an-hour before the 3 pm start, when my mother would fix them up herself: usually as Red Indians with a full head of feathers and war paint. This annual charade heaped deep embarrassment on me. Our mutual dislike was bad enough but for the boarders' faces to be smeared with paint by a strange lady with a foreign accent was an indignity that would be held against me at some later time. My mother, unfortunately, was oblivious to these petty rivalries and resentments; she thought it was all terrific fun. I just stood and watched, wishing they'd go away. But worse was to come. When the day boys arrived, it was immediately apparent that their outfits were better, more exciting and more imaginative than the boarders' who, of course, were wearing all my cast-off hats and head-dresses.

Through the years of our childhood, these bashes acquired a certain notoriety, possibly because they were held at the Castle, no ordinary venue for a kiddies' tea party. Some ambitious mothers went to extraordinary lengths to devise unusual costumes for their children (mainly boys, but my mother insisted on a few token girls – daughters of friends –which embarrassed me even more as my classmates *never* invited girls to their parties). The most bizarre costume to arrive at one of my parties was a giant Christmas cracker – worn by a dreadful wet called Speller. As they walked into the hotel, Speller's mum bristled with pride and my mother obliged by showering her effusively with congratulations for the brilliance of her inventiveness. The only difficulty was that Speller could neither sit down, nor could he breathe. By teatime, he was close to death by asphyxia and was forced to remove his costume: a relief for him but a terrible humiliation for his mother.

Like most things in our lives, Gerald's and my parties were run to a well-planned agenda. From arrival (at three) to departure (at six), every moment was organized. Riot and mayhem occasionally erupted at other children's parties – but *never* at ours. *Not* at the Castle Hotel. My parents were horrified when, on one occasion, I returned from a particularly good thrash where we had flicked ice cream at one another across the tea table. This disgraceful incident passed into family folklore, invoking a pet mantra which, henceforth, was repeated before all future parties to which we were invited: 'DON'T THROW ICE CREAM!'. At our birthday feasts, such lapses in politesse were avoided by close supervision and a benign but strict discipline.

On arrival, my young guests (I don't recall them particularly as 'friends') were invited to play 'The Donkey's Tail', an entertaining little curtain-raiser which seemed to get the party going. A large illustration of a tail-less donkey was propped up on an easel at the end of the room. Each child was blindfolded and given a cardboard cut-out of the tail, the object being to pin it to the illustration. The child guessing the most accurate position for the tail on the donkey's anatomy won a prize. From here my mother, in her role as mistress of ceremonies and loving every second, led the usual repertoire of party games (musical chairs, pass-the-parcel, and so on) until tea at 4.15.

Teatime in anyone else's house tended to be a chaotic free-for-all – everyone pitching straight for the cup-cakes, jellies and chocolate fingers. Not so at the Castle, where a quaint decorum was displayed with the assistance of two crisply-uniformed waiters. Cup-cakes, jellies and chocolate fingers were strictly embargoed until proper justice had been done to the daintily cut sandwiches, the buttered toast and the scones. Then a fanfare (my mother) ushered in the birthday cake, the candles were extinguished (ideally in one blow for maximum applause) and only now were we allowed to get our fingers satisfyingly sticky. After tea we would return to the Moat Room where a magician amused us until the six o'clock deadline, a time punctually observed by the good mothers and matrons of Thone Preparatory School.

For my parents, family honour (alternatively translated as keeping-up-appearances) was of supreme importance. Just as Gerald and I were instructed to say 'good morning' to all the staff as we left the hotel for school, so we were put on guard never to do anything or say anything that might cast the slightest blemish on the family's good name. Obedience and deference towards one's elders were the accepted values worn like a heavy cloak across our tiny shoulders. There was nothing wrong with having a party, having a good time – but even pleasure and fun had to be kept within bounds. To let one's hair down too far was to court dishonour and shame. If there were one watchword to recur in the manner of our upbringing, it would be my father's constant call to exercise 'self-control' in the conduct of our lives. Wise counsel indeed, but in the first two decades of my life – whether at school or at home – 'self-control' in practice never got much of a chance because direct control was being imposed from a higher authority. At times, I found this sense of being controlled oppressive. Whether it came from the institutionalized brutishness of an English public school or the beneficence and loving care of the family home, there was little room for free expression. Freedom ultimately meant rebellion, which came in its own good time.

Meanwhile, I hated being a child. It seemed a pointless state. I longed for adulthood because grown-ups had all the fun; grown-ups had power; grown-ups were free. Children, it seemed to me, lived in a state of siege.

Perhaps I was born middle-aged? Certainly the gastronomic evidence is there. When I entered Taunton School as a boarder, the contents of my tuck box differed dramatically from those of my contemporaries. Processed cheese wedges, condensed milk, baked beans, peanut butter, Bovril or Marmite and Heinz Sandwich Spread for them. A Colston Bassett Stilton, Kalamata olives, Hungarian salami, smoked salmon and Tiptree Strawberry Jam for me.

POKER GAME OF LIFE

MONDAY, 25 AUGUST 1997

TRADITIONALLY, August rates as one of our leaner months. We are not a holiday hotel: the jam on our bread and butter comes with the BMW-borne company executive. As the world of business and politics takes its annual breather this, then, is the time of year when we rely heavily on passing trade; convoys of Volvo estates en route to Cornwall and Texans 'doing' England. But while the press swells its pages with fascinating observations on the effect of *la cucina Toscana* on Tony Blair's waistline or with pictures of Diana and Dodi schmoozing sweetly on Daddy Fayed's ocean-going play-pen, the Castle in downtown Taunton is being gently rocked by its own silly season.

Andrew Grahame, my general manager and a director of this company, is in the throes of a clandestine and passionate affair with Nicola McArthur, my sales manager. He has never, he says, been so close to a woman. So close, indeed, that he cannot bring himself to acknowledge his adultery because 'it's not like that', 'nobody understands except us' and to call it an affair makes it sound 'so sordid which it's not'. Whether he is deeply in love or madly infatuated, his head has been turned and his grip on the day-to-day running of the hotel is losing its edge – a plain fact which, of course, he refuses to concede.

Meanwhile, business is booming, with occupancies for August riding at an astonishing 82 per cent – a record – and the restaurant, equally busy, bathing blissfully in the reflected beam of Phil Vickery's TV celebrity. To borrow Harold Macmillan, we have never had it so good. The only part of the business to look worryingly vulnerable at the moment is Minstrels, our pub, where trade dipped dramatically after the arrival in Taunton of a J D Wetherspoon's super-pub six weeks ago. With two more mega-openings in the town centre expected this autumn, these monster-boozers are sounding the death knell for small independents like Minstrels which, in spite of its pink and juniper green facial last December, has not been refashioned for ten years. It is now way beyond its sell-by date, forcing us to rethink our longer term strategy. So we are postponing plans to develop the garage block – my great Millennium Project (rechristened Project 2001) – to focus our minds on action to save us from imminent annihilation at the hands of the Big Boys. We have decided it is no longer worth competing with them and we intend to get out of the pub game to concentrate on what we reckon we're best at – hospitality and good food. Plans for the new financial year in October now include the construction of eight new letting bedrooms in a wing currently occupied by the live-in staff and the gutting of Minstrels to create a large, exciting space for a modern brasserie – something Taunton hasn't got but which, I think, the town may just be ready for.

Which brings me back to my lovesick general manager. With a frantically busy hotel to run on top of the pressures of launching two major initiatives for which we shall have to raise £500,000, the last thing I need is Andrew Grahame in a state of emotional turmoil, unable to fathom where his future lies: with his wife and adorable infant daughter, or with his paramour and colleague.

Twenty years ago – before public morality finally slid into its murky pond of obfuscation – the consequences of sexual entanglement at work were unambiguous. My father had a simple rule, often repeated: 'Don't shit on your own doorstep'. If you did, one half of the party was expected to resign – or was promptly fired. These days rules like this have lost their meaning. When the heir to the throne confesses his adultery on television or when the press describes the tattoos, moles and other distinguishing marks rumoured to be located in the vicinity of President 'Bonking Bill' Clinton's penis, where does this leave the rest of the universe? The notion of expecting either Andrew or Nicola (and it would have to be Nicola) to resign becomes risible and faintly quaint. Less risible, however, is the effect of their affair (unspoken but now general knowledge) on staff discipline and the equilibrium and efficiency of the hotel. Moral attitudes may have changed in two decades but the repercussions of an old-fashioned 'scandal' on a close-knit community like an hotel remain pretty much unchanged.

Andrew's standing as general manager is not exactly enhanced by this 'doorstep' liaison. His authority and the respect he has won from the staff are open to compromise. He and Nicola have become victims of gossip and innuendo. 'Where's Andrew?' I overheard someone ask at the desk. 'Having lunch with Nicola in Minstrels *as usual*,' replied the receptionist with a silly giggle. This kind of remark weakens his position and eventually erodes morale. He is blind to all this and when, last week, I confronted him with a catalogue of failings to illustrate his loss of grip, he got very heated and indignant with me. But facts speak: staff are taking extended lunch breaks; receptionists are munching snacks on duty; the bar isn't being properly secured out-of-hours. In a word, the place is getting bloody slack and it's making me very angry to boot.

Worse still, over the past ten days, I have been making a series of dawn raids on the hotel to check it out first thing in the morning. The early manager – a duty shared and assigned on the weekly management rota – is meant to report at 7.00 sharp. When he arrives his first job is to issue the safe keys to the duty receptionist and the fridge keys to the restaurant. Without these keys, reception can't check-out their guests nor is the restaurant able to offer theirs a glass of fresh orange juice with breakfast. On three occasions last week (*three!*), the early manager reported late – not merely a few minutes late but, respectively, 53, 24 and 32 minutes late. My fury was thermonuclear.

For me, the confidence and trust I hold in Andrew – key values which earned him his promotion to the Board – have been undermined. For months Louise and I have known about his marriage difficulties, but he has wilfully hidden his affair with Nicola in the naïve belief that their secret was safe. It wasn't. There were too many tell-tale signs betraying the deepening involvement of their relationship. Evidence gradually, almost casually, emerged of their trysts. He began taking an unusual interest in her work: sales meetings outside the hotel attended together where only her presence was necessary. In the end, the lid was bound to blow off the pot.

Over the past few weeks I have tried to encourage Andrew to come clean – gentle nudges to persuade him to discuss his problems – but he could not bring himself to face me with the truth. He persisted in his deception, lulling himself into a state of denial, unable to see the tremors he was causing in the hotel. The final trigger came when I wrote him a long memorandum on the subject of reception and the need to reorganize the office, a sensitive area which would have to be carefully handled – so my note was marked PRIVATE and CONFIDENTIAL.

We have a good team in the office, but Alison, our head receptionist, still lacks the clout I expect for this important department to work effectively. Her great strength lies in her administrative abilities: technically she is superb. But efficient administration, though vital, is not the prime function of this office. The memo to Andrew outlined my view that our receptionists should be looked upon as the front-line troops in the hotel's sales efforts. Their principal job is to sell our bedrooms for the best price, persuade customers to uptrade, promote our award-winning restaurant and sell our conference and banqueting facilities. At the moment, their approach is too passive, too mechanical, and we are under-performing. What I want is an injection of new vigour and enthusiasm by changing the culture in the office to make it more sales-driven. The girls need motivating and we need to invent an attractive rewards scheme for them. To achieve this I suggested that we renamed the department the Sales Office, putting Nicola in command and redefining Alison's role as head of administration. Nicola, who graduated from reception to sales manager a year ago, had, I felt, the maturity, the fire and the leadership qualities to make this plan work. The proposal, however, rehearsed a pretty radical shake-up of the status quo and before taking the idea forward, it was important to seek Andrew's opinion on its feasibility and implications.

To my dismay, in spite of the fact that my note was marked PRIVATE, he discussed it with Nicola. This, for me, was the last straw. I suspended the plan for the time being and Andrew, realizing at last that I knew everything, made his confession. His secret must have weighed heavily on his conscience; later in the day he told Louise how much better he felt after talking to me. A salved conscience and a little blunt speaking may be a healthy first step on the way to repairing lost faith in a business relationship – and, indeed, a friendship – that has taken a knocking. But Andrew's emotional dilemma and its impact on the hotel remain. I have asked him if Cécile, his wife, knows? He insists no, but I am not so sure. She is a shrewd lady who is not easily fooled. And Andrew? In the past I have admired his great courage. Here is a man who, as a terminal cancer patient, faced death and by a miracle survived. He is now playing poker with his marriage and his career. He's pushing his good fortune.

SUNDAY, 31 AUGUST 1997

The tragic death in Paris of Diana, Princess of Wales. This morning I called the hotel to make sure the staff had raised the union flag to half-mast. They had. This afternoon we listened to Elgar's E minor Cello Concerto on the BBC. And this evening we stared in disbelief at the images of her coffin at Northolt. First the shock that numbs. Then the shedding of a few tears. I don't think any of us could have realized how deeply the life of this beautiful woman touched us.

GOODBYE ENGLAND'S ROSE

SATURDAY, 20 SEPTEMBER 1997

THE PASSING OF SUMMER in this rural corner of England is commonly signalled by Keats's lyrical season of mists and mellowness; the hedgerows are brimming with berries, our orchards ache under their harvest of apples and, in his kitchen, Phil Vickery is making the most of it. But for me the messenger of autumn is usually a more prosaic life-form: this morning, as I stepped under my shower, the first spider greeted me from the bottom of the bath tub. Meanwhile,

Louise and I are recently returned from Provence – a final dose of sun to fortify ourselves before the rigours of winter and the onset of a new financial year.

The last three weeks have been frantic. Andrew's turbulent private life has been complicated by a nasty bout of bronchitis which laid him out for eight days. His new deputy, David Cole, is consummating his marriage in Kenya and Gill, my secretary and right-arm, is on holiday in Ireland. The hotel continues to ride at full tilt, a roller-coaster hitting record occupancies. There are budgets to draft, re-write and massage in the light of a heavy menu of special projects for 1998, the most ambitious of these being the brasserie and the new bedrooms. And like a pall still hanging over us, there's been the raw, lingering tragedy of Diana. In a few short weeks, the martyred princess has been elevated to some secular sainthood; a sacred icon for a godless world suddenly illuminating those parts of the human soul other religions have failed to reach.

With Andrew sick, I came into work on the morning of 6 September, the Saturday of the funeral (and the day of David Cole's wedding). The streets of Taunton – normally choked by traffic and packed with shoppers – were deserted. The stillness was eerie. Flags hung motionless and limp half-way up their poles. A sea of floral tributes blocked the entrance to the Municipal Hall. I parked and checked the notices posted outside the hotel and Minstrels announcing our closure to non-residents between eleven and three. Later I returned home and Louise and I sat in silence glued to the screen – a silence broken only when, with the rest of the nation, we cheered Earl Spencer's address.

Now here's a curious thing. In spite of the high emotion aroused by a unique moment of national mourning, when I woke up on Sunday, I was suddenly struck by how the humdrum in life, the fickleness of everyday human existence can, in an instant, wipe from the mind an event which has gripped us with such an extreme sense of loss. On Saturday evening, wearing a dark suit and a sober tie, I returned to the Castle. The hotel was full and we had seventy-two booked for dinner. With both my senior managers away and a third attending a close friend's wedding (nuptially, this was a popular weekend), I was anxious to keep an eye on the service, and just as well too. Beneath the serenity and glass-smooth veneer of the pond, the swans were paddling furiously. The problem, simply, was that regardless of the times people had reserved their tables, everyone arrived at once.

My role in this situation is not to interfere, step in or take over; to do so would undermine the professionalism of the team. Instead I act as a conduit of information between kitchen and restaurant, between restaurant manager and chef. My conspicuous presence in the dining room is important, both for the purpose of humouring my guests and to encourage the staff by being helpful in tiny ways: topping up a glass here, clearing a plate there. In short, a proprietorial visibility aimed at perpetuating the illusion of purposeful calm, effortless command and the appearance of the sheer joy of receiving people at your table.

On this night of nights, both kitchen and restaurant are stretched beyond their limits. As the orders begin to pile up on the peg-board by the hotplate, Vickery is barking at his brigade like a dog possessed: 'Two soup, one terrine, one crab tart' … 'Two shoulder, one bass, one brill'. In turn, his cooks at different stations around the kitchen acknowledge the order, snapping back 'Yes Chef!'.

Plates are scattered over the hotplate. Cooked food – the constituent parts of each dish – appears magically from nowhere: main ingredients, finished sauces, seasonings, vegetables, individual garnishes – all timed to coincide and to converge in one place at one time, perfectly, precisely. Light hands quickly, deftly, assemble the dishes: Vickery scrutinizing, tasting, fiddling with a detail, wiping a spot on the rim of a plate. Satisfied, he calls the order away, young waiters trembling, waiting for his word.

As the pace quickens, the rising temperature in the kitchen is palpable, almost oppressive. The sea bass order hits the hotplate. Vickery glances at the saffron mash and tears into the veg commis. 'Too dry. Look at it! Look! Start using your head. You're not thinking again. More cream. More! Now!'.

By 8.30, a major confrontation with the restaurant threatens like a giant storm cloud. Phil bolts up the stairs to find Christophe. The process of calling clients from the bar to their tables is slowing up and this is putting kitchen production out of synch with the service flow in the dining room. I chase after him. The last thing I need is a fight.

'Chef, hold on. I'll see Christophe. You go back to the hotplate.'

'Where the fuck are tables four and nine? They were called ages ago. We're ready to go and Christophe's screwing up. I haven't seen him all evening.'

'Look Phil, he's tied up taking orders. Let me see him and I'll get four and nine in.'

'I'll chew his bollocks off later. I'm fed up with this. He's not communicating – I just need to know what the fuck's going on. That's all.'

'I'll handle Christophe. Believe me, he's going like the clappers out there.'

Tensions still simmering, the service eventually locks into an uneasy rhythm, the minds of cooks and waiters lasered by the pressure, intent only on surviving the night. Diana is dead; buried today on her island. Tears shed are forgotten. In this basement furnace and on the stage set upstairs, the staff just want to live to see tomorrow.

That much I understand. But when I woke up on Sunday morning and considered the events of the previous evening, I wondered less about my staff – for whom I felt great pride – and more about the punters who, I concluded, were a pretty average lot of self-obsessed middle-Englanders. For all the heat and tribulation in the wings, the atmosphere in the restaurant was relaxed and upbeat. Mood is something you learn to gauge instinctively and it was obvious to me that, all in all, the vibes in the room were good-humoured – in itself a credit to Christophe's ample charm and his ability to smile convincingly and continuously when, behind the mask, his composure was threatened by the prospect of imminent meltdown.

And so mine host toured the tables – slowly, genially, my cup o'erflowing with human kindness. And, indeed, my guests were eager to respond, chatting variously about Phil's food, Louise's décor, other restaurants they had tried, pets in hotels, cricket, morris dancing, the weather and much else. Predictably, with seventy-two guests to satisfy, I also had my ration of whingers. One party complained their table was too cramped. A second was kept waiting for his wine. And a third fussed because we forgot to lock the garage in which he had installed his Range Rover.

Not one. Not one single, solitary soul out of that gathering of seventy-two whispered the name Diana. Not one felt moved to offer an opinion on Elton John's new interpretation of *Candle in the Wind*. Or a reaction to Tony Blair's embarrassingly dreadful reading of 1 Corinthians 13. Or a thought on Earl Spencer's tribute. Or a word about the dignity of the young princes as they walked behind their mother's coffin. As I lay in bed that Sunday morning, reflecting on the events of the day before, I asked myself how this extraordinary funeral, this desperately sad but brilliant pageant which, only hours earlier, had moved a whole nation so profoundly could now, apparently, be erased completely from the collective psyche of my dinner guests. Strange. But then restaurants like the Castle tend to be places of celebration, not mourning. Perhaps by offering our guests our hospitality, the pleasure of good food and wine, a little joy and conviviality, we allowed them a moment to escape the sadness of the day. It seems we succeeded.

Exactly one week later, we escaped to France and Oasis checked in for the weekend: Noel, Liam, Patsy, the other members of the band, minders, publicists and a red Ferrari bearing the registration OAS 1S. I was worried (Louise terrified) that this outfit – a mob who seem to have made a good job of persuading young people that loutish behaviour is cool, chic and acceptable – would trash the hotel. And so Andrew was under strict instruction to keep me informed, hourly if necessary, by fax and telephone. For Andrew, this was exactly the kind of challenge he loves. Back on top form, he rose to it and handled the group with considerable cunning. Mercifully, they did not trash the place, not physically that is, but Liam's vocabulary, characterized by his frequent use of four-letter punctuation marks, meant that the staff spent much of the weekend skilfully segregating the band from the rest of our guests. According to one of Liam's minders, 'attitude sells records'. This three-word philosophical statement is reason enough, it seems, for the world to abandon all civilized communication.

Andrew's faxes came through each morning as we sipped our coffee on a sunny terrace sheltered by cascades of bougainvillaea and mimosa:

'…a crowd of youngsters outside the hotel until 5 am. Bob [the night
porter] sent them packing.'

'They cut short the show by fifteen minutes to be back in time to watch *Match of the Day!* They returned at 11.15 and had 23 kebabs delivered which they ate in their rooms and then at 1 am came down to the bar where they stayed until 4.30. They were a little loud at times but no worse than a bunch of conference delegates.'

'Yesterday afternoon in the Rose Room, we had three tables of old ladies having tea and scones. On the other side of the room, Liam, Noel and Patsy, all in dark sun-glasses, sat waiting for their cars. The old ladies never even noticed. Outside, Taunton stopped to watch.'

'Today they want a traditional Sunday lunch at 2 pm. Have sold them a private dining room rather than have them in the restaurant which is busy.'

'Liam spoke to me a moment ago. He said: "Can I have some toast, bud?"'

The department that suffered most, however, was housekeeping. Poor Alison Brown – good and loyal but prone to a primness necessary in any fastidious head housekeeper – was relieved to see the back of Oasis. 'Never in all my life, Mr Chapman,' she sighed, 'have I seen rooms in such a disgusting state. Newspapers screwed up everywhere. Such a mess. And they never came out of their rooms for the girls to get in to clean.'

Although the visit of Oasis was demanding on the staff, it was a thrill to have them and a few lucky ones – our pretty receptionists – were given VIP tickets to the band's gig in Exeter.

For us now – the core team, Phil, Andrew, Louise and me – our sights are set on the coming financial year and much of our time is being consumed by plans and budgets which, in a steam of re-drafts, we send off to Michael Blackwell, our chairman and financial wiseman. At regular intervals we isolate ourselves in the Penthouse for meetings at which our figures, schemes and ideas are subjected to hours of hot debate and careful deconstruction. An essential but wearing process, particularly this year. To fulfil my goal to build the eight extra bedrooms and create a modern brasserie out of Minstrels, we shall need Barclays to lend us half a million pounds, a prospect which is making Phil and Louise nervous, their memories of the hell we endured in the early nineties still undimmed. I am more bullish, eager to move swiftly to see a healthy rush of extra profits before the next economic downturn. Andrew's opinion falls somewhere in between and Michael Blackwell keeps asking awkward questions.

Our attempts at an accurate analysis of the brasserie's potential are proving particularly elusive. The space has got to be more profitable than Minstrels, the pub, but the new concept places a greater emphasis on eating and, frankly, there's more money to be made in booze. Also, our view of the competition in Taunton indicates that while the drinking scene is hotting up, with the opening of new mega-pubs like J D Wetherspoons, the town's eateries are dead during the week and only come alive on Friday and Saturday evenings. But we enjoy a number of advantages over the rest. For a start we have Phil Vickery, star of *Ready Steady Cook*, and a growing celebrity to trade on. Secondly, we have the best location in the town centre. And thirdly, the brasserie would be a major new attraction to our hotel guests. Quite staggeringly, only 55 per cent of them dine in the restaurant; the other 45 per cent (businessmen on a limited budget or those looking for somewhere more casual) eat elsewhere in the area. The brasserie, then, should hoover up these people and help us fill tables on weekday evenings. And if they eat, they'll drink – and they'll drink with an easy conscience, knowing that their bed is only a thirty-second stroll up Castle Bow.

Justifying (or rejecting) a plan to invest in new bedrooms is more straightforward. Letting rooms – not operating fancy restaurants – is how hotels make their money. Fill those rooms and your hotel will show a decent profit. So for us, the question, simply, is will we sell these eight extra bedrooms? And if so, what occupancies might we expect? A month ago, we began to record every request for accommodation which had to be refused, either because the hotel was full, or because we were unable to accept the booking for some other reason: say if there were no double rooms and all we could offer were singles, or where a corporate client – frequently through an hotel booking agent – is looking for a block of three or four rooms and we only have one or two available.

Early results from this tracking process have been astonishing. Although the hotel is busy, with occupancies hovering around 85 per cent, the level of refusals has exceeded our first estimates. In the past twenty-seven days we have turned away 181 room nights or, more to the point, £16,662 in revenue which the business would have earned if we had those eight additional bedrooms – a figure, incidentally, which pays no account to the food and drink sales we would attract as a result of the extra rooms' income. For the time being we shall continue to monitor refusals through October and November with the hope of making a final decision before Christmas. Our architect is primed. If the project gets the green light, I shall want those new rooms on stream by the spring.

The new budget also contains a long shopping list of other items which, excluding a frightening sum (£77,000) for day-to-day maintenance and repairs, comes to a modest £128,190. This pot of money is earmarked for all sorts of goodies which the four of us and Michael Blackwell have argued over in our Penthouse conclaves. Inevitably, everyone has a pet project which is seen as absolutely essential rather than merely desirable. The debate is a ferocious but friendly tug of war. Phil wants a new larder fridge (won). Louise wants to refurbish the lift car (lost) in addition to the redecoration of seven bedrooms (won). Andrew wants to air-condition the Monmouth Room (lost) and install CCTV cameras in the car park (won).

The only item to receive immediate approval was the purchase of seventy new dining room chairs (budget figure £12,000). This is an assignment I have taken on personally as I now consider myself a world authority on the subject. Our present chairs are barely ten years old but they have been an unmitigated disaster from the beginning. They have caused us much grief and an effusion of vast sums in serial repairs. The other day I was entertaining Richard Binns, a travel writer on the *Sunday Times*, and half-way through his braised shoulder of lamb the right arm of his chair dislodged and thudded to the floor. He was very good about it. I closed my eyes and said a little prayer. These chairs are now beyond redemption.

They were bought originally by my dear mother, a woman with a peerless eye for the aesthetic but someone who is completely blind in matters of quotidian practicality. Her chairs are, possibly, the prettiest, most elegant things ever to adorn a dining room: eighteenth century in style, *bergère* backed, curved, graceful. Their only problem is that they were designed for a lady's boudoir, not a busy hotel restaurant.

My brief to three manufacturers is to come up with a wood design of contemporary but classical simplicity: the seat, but neither back nor arms, to be upholstered, thereby reducing soil and wear of the fabric. The frame itself must be robustly constructed, embrace the human form comfortably and feature splayed rears to withstand the common habit people have of persistently tilting chairs on their hind legs.

I have now seen a number of attractive designs and the manufacturers are beginning to send me prototypes to test. By this I mean that for a day I exchange my office chair for the proposed dining room chair and I sit in it for two or three hours while I get on with my work. Two samples from one eager supplier have already been subjected to this elementary test and both failed miserably. The first was an extremely well-made and handsome-looking chair with a wide trellis back. It looked the part and would last a thousand years. However, this was quite the most uncomfortable chair in which I have ever put bum to seat.

The second sample was very elegant, very stylish, indeed perfectly in tune with the mood of the restaurant, although I had doubts about its staying-power. The salesman, however, swore on his life it was every inch as robust as the first, pointing to the joists between the front and back legs. By six in the evening I thought we'd found our ideal chair. It was supremely comfortable and, like the first, it seemed to be a well-constructed piece of furniture. Finally, I got up, a whisper of a question mark still lurking in the back of my mind. I rested the tip of my right shoe on one of the joists – honestly, truthfully, I applied no more pressure than the dipping of a big toe into a bath tub to test the temperature of the water. The joist squeaked for an instant, then cracked.

One manufacturer down, two to go.

THURSDAY, 25 SEPTEMBER 1997

Inevitable as the mists of autumn, for hoteliers and restaurateurs this too is the season of guide books, as the new editions emerge to pronounce their verdicts. At the Castle we are happy to declare a good harvest; indeed it's been something of a bumper crop. The AA prescribed four rosettes, thus endorsing our place among the top two dozen eateries in the land. The RAC, with whom I had the terrible row last year, reinstated the hotel on the guide's elite list of 'Blue Ribbons' and Louise and I have been summoned to their grand premises in Pall Mall for the investiture in November. Best of all, *The Good Food Guide* includes us in its role of honour at the front of the book alongside only twenty-two other restaurants in Britain and we have been dubbed 'South West Star' for 1998, with a funny little stamp at the top of our page which looks strikingly like a car licence disc.

This great scoop of laurels is very satisfying and, for a moment at least, persuades us that all the *sturm und drang* are worthwhile. The missing pip, of course, is our lost star in the Michelin Guide which, unlike the others, delays publication until January. But, knowing the conservatism of this outfit, I am anticipating no change in our zero-status for at least another year.

And so, on a high and with only five days of our financial year left to run, this journal approaches its close. The new calendar, already in place and full of promise, comes with its annual line-up of well-rehearsed events. Christmas and New Year are almost sold, as is our twenty-second season of musical weekends scheduled for the early months of 1998. Gastronomic evenings are planned and I am working on a festival of cabaret for the Easter holiday. Hugo and his Huguenotes are already booked for next summer's garden party. These are our set-pieces, the dates in our year that add a little spice to life at the Castle. Not that I need any extra excitement. In this business, each day brings its own surprises, dramas and problems. For all the frustrations and headaches of running an hotel, life is never dull. But perhaps the greatest gift of owning a place like this is the scope it offers to improve; to develop; to create; experiment; play; and, not least I hope, to bring pleasure to others. It also allows the proprietor to indulge his own interests and passions – be they food, wine, music, theatre or anything else for that matter. This is no chain hotel, no bed factory. There are no institutions or shareholders to impress. The work may be exhausting but it can be immensely satisfying. In my experience, the best hotels are those which resound with the personality and prejudices of their custodians.

No other hotel I know organizes an annual music festival on the scale we do. The quartets and ensembles we bring to Taunton are world class; they cost us a fortune and impose a serious administrative burden on my managers and Gill, my secretary. The only reason we do them is because I enjoy good chamber music. There has to be an easier and more profitable way of filling an hotel over the dank weekends of an English winter. The same goes for the restaurant. Any sane businessman would know better than to invest in an expensive kitchen and cellar to satisfy the demands of a three-star hotel in a provincial town like Taunton. Our dining room is an indulgence because that's the way I like it. I'd rather die than hire a second-rate chef or deprive myself of the occasional bottle of decent burgundy. A visit to an hotel or restaurant should be life-enhancing and I see no reason why the experience should not accommodate the particularities of the keeper himself.

But while the guv'nor may set the pace and strike the tone, the heartbeat of any hotel is its people, the staff. They may be the innkeeper's biggest problem but they are also the inn's greatest asset. The potential for chaos in this game is dangerously high and too often we tiptoe close to the edge. Yet as Louise constantly reminds me, in the end our success lies in mutual support and teamwork. A room with a view, fine decorations, good food are all very well, but these desirable attributes are worthless unless our visitors are warmly received and cared for in a spirit of genuine giving. In our bedrooms, a letter of welcome invites our guests to comment on their stay. This is not a formal questionnaire with multiple-choice answers of the kind used by the big chains. The letter simply asks people to jot down their impressions on the reverse side of the notepaper. Every year a hundred or more are handed in. These, in addition to several dozen letters I receive, have one common thread running through them, a kind of mood barometer. All, almost without exception, highlight the friendliness of the staff: a comment often expressed with a measure of surprise, as if our act of hospitality were some rare discovery.

There have been times in this diary when I may have sounded off about various members of my staff (and indeed others!). But that is the point of a diary which, by its nature, records the moment and that moment's inflexions. To my staff, then,

I pay a special tribute. Our bulging files of notes and letters from contented guests are an extraordinary testimonial to them; to their patience and to their good nature in an age where everyday courtesies and kindnesses seem to count for less. Nothing upsets me more than when some boorish punter is rude to a waiter or receptionist. They cannot answer back (but I can and I do). Sadly, we are seeing a steady rise in prattish behaviour. The only response is to stay calm and polite, but sometimes our endurance is tested to breaking point.

Finally, a word about Taunton. There are times when I wonder whether the Castle is where it is because of this town or in spite of it. Some famous spark – I think it was Conrad Hilton – once said that for an hotel to succeed there were three fundamental priorities to bear in mind: Location. Location. And location. This well-worn aphorism always made perfectly good sense to me until, that is, I abandoned the London advertising scene to join the family firm in 1976. I soon realized that the principles of marketing I acquired in the advertising industry and my personal ambitions for the Castle did not necessarily coincide. While I wanted a hot chef and a smart restaurant, Taunton really didn't care and certainly wasn't prepared to pay the price. To compensate for this insult to civilization, I turned my back on the home turf, toured the United States and persuaded thousands of Americans to eat at my table instead. This strategy worked well until terrorist bombs and a few local wars frightened these Americans, who promptly turned their backs on me.

With the recession of the early nineties rubbing salt in the wound, it dawned on me that to ignore the principles of marketing was a bit like defying the laws of gravity. I returned to Earth, made my peace with Taunton and now there is every prospect that we may live happily ever after, especially as Tauntonians are suddenly showing signs of appreciating good food and wine. Then, to my complete surprise, this week I received a very charming letter from Brünnhilde, the Mighty Jackie Ballard MP. It was a short but unprecedented note to congratulate us on our special award in *The Good Food Guide*. Whatever next? Touched by her gesture and suppressing my admiration of her work as a political masseuse, I replied enthusiastically, inviting her to lunch at the earliest opportunity. Before signing off, I also reported 'all quiet on Castle Green' and suggested that her heroic influence may have brought about the final retreat of the barbarian invader. Meanwhile, last week's *Somerset County Gazette* announced Jefferson Horsley's resignation as Leader of Taunton Deane Council. Poor Ol' Waffles has had enough and who can blame him? He's taken a lot of stick, not least from me. I wrote him a nice letter too. *Peace for our time…peace with honour…?*

INDEX

AA restaurant guide 32, 56, 57, 91, 124, 127, 247
Ainsworth, Jim 75-6
Alfred, King 104
American Express 72, 74
Aplin, Paul 30
Armstrong, Lord and Lady 8-10, 85
Arthur, King 104
Ash, Rosie 65
Ashdown, Paddy 173, 175, 181, 206
Aspel, Michael 16, 18
Australian Tourists cricket team 221-4

Bailey, Paul 107, 108
Ballard, Jackie, MP 173, 181, 191, 193, 196, 197, 199, 200-1, 202, 204-6, 211, 249-50
Barclays Bank 145-9, 243-4
Bateman, Michael 27-8
Bazalgette, Peter 66, 78
Beehive, The, school 227
Berkeley Hotel, London 32, 71, 73-4, 81, 186-7
Besant, Walter 104
Binns, Richard 167, 245
Bixby, Dick, painting by 138
Blackwell, Michael 50-1, 54, 145, 243-4, 245
Blair, Tony 182, 197, 198, 206, 242
Blanc, Raymond 17, 188
Blue Ribbons 79-82, 247
Blunos, Martin and Sian 59
Bollinger (dog) 39, 108, 109, 162

'Bonsall, Anton' (Harrison; O'Keefe) 111-15, 119-20, 134-5, 158
Bradman, Don 221-2
Brake Bros. 89
Bratislava (Pressburg), Czechoslovakia ix-x, xi, xiii, 213
British Airways 65
British Gas 48
British Tourist Authority 56, 57
Brown, Alison 95, 178, 243
Brown, Erica 153, 162, 163, 167
Brown, Gordon 198
Brown, Mrs (accountant) 31-2, 50, 54, 65
Browning, Angela 74
Brünnhilde see Ballard, Jackie
Bulmer, Derek 57, 124-5, 136-8
Burgess, Karen 66-7, 138
Buxton, Andrew 146, 148

Café de l'Opera, New York 64, 199, 215
Caprice restaurant, London 72
Carswell, Adrian 161
Cartons Mondains 61-2
Caruso (dog) 39, 108, 109, 162
Carved Angel restaurant, Dartmouth 188
Castle Hotel, Taunton: 1950s ix, xiii, 20-61, 212, 214-15, 220, 238-48; 1971-90 xvi, 17-18, 106-7; 1996 1-2, 21, 25-46, 50-9, 65-6, 71, 75-87, 104-25; 1997 110-79, 182-5, 190-209, 210-12, 220-1, 249-66; Dining Club 182-3

Cercle Gastronomique de Belgique 215
Chapman, Anthony xi
Chapman, Dominic ix, xiv, 21, 107
Chapman, Etty: early life xiii, 20, 228-9; in Kit's childhood 212-13, 229-31, 261-2; in retirement 19-24, 30, 107, 109
Chapman, Gerald: childhood 212-13, 216, 218, 225-6, 244-8; career and death 70-1
Chapman, Kit: childhood 212-20, 241-8; education xiv, 127-8, 248; marriage xiv, 105-6; early career 14-15; on television 15-18, 41; manager of Castle Hotel 1-2, 21, 25-46, 50-9, 65-6, 71, 75-87, 104-25, 110-79, 182-5, 190-209, 210-12, 220-1, 233-50
Chapman, Louise: education 65-6; marries Kit xiv, 105-6; Kit's wife and partner ix, 2, 19, 20, 21, 25, 28, 33, 38, 42-3, 49-50, 58, 65, 66-9, 76-7, 95, 98, 100-1, 102, 103, 107-8, 109, 111, 125-7, 139-41, 144, 156-7, 167, 177, 188, 212, 237, 239, 242, 244, 245, 248
Chapman, Michael xi, xiii-xiv, 20
Chapman, Nell x-xi, xiii
Chapman, Nick ix, xiv, 21, 107, 108, 109
Chapman, Peter: early life xi-xiii, 36; manager of Castle Hotel ix, xiii, xvi, 21, 90, 212, 215, 222-5, 226, 245-8; in hospital 19-24, 46; in retirement 21, 107, 109, 211
Chewton Glen hotel, Hampshire 56
Children in Need (TV programme) 47-8, 87
Chilingirian Quartet 139
Chisholm, Douglas 13-14
Christian, Glynn 17

Christmas 12, 94-101, 102, 103-9
City Rhodes restaurant, London 176, 177, 184, 210
Clarke, Ken 197-8
Cleere, Brendan 171-2
Cleo, Aunt 218-19
Cole, David 239
Conran, Terence 182
Conway, Nadia 161
Cook, Beryl: *Two on a Stool* 138
Cooper, Gladys 64, 169
Corney & Barrow, London 154
Coward, Noël 60, 64, 154, 167-8
Cradock, Fanny 215
Critchley, Sir Julian 34, 149, 150
Criterion restaurant, Piccadilly 189
Crompton, Alan 222, 224
Cromwell Hospital 135
Cropper, Nina and Peter 14

Daily Telegraph 78
Davenport, Philippa 48-50
David, Elizabeth 215
Del Conte, Anna 48, 49, 50
Dempster, Nigel 102
Diana, Princess of Wales 233, 237, 239, 241, 242
Dorchester Hotel, London 71, 111, 112, 113, 119, 120
Drury-Beck, Michael 193-4, 196
du Cann, Edward 172
Durham University 65, 78

Ferret & Trouserleg pub, Taunton 4, 201
Flóka (patissier) 219
Floyd, Cllr Tony 220-1
Food and Drink (TV programme) 65-6, 78
Food & Wine Society, University of Surrey 186

Forte, Charles xiv
Forte Posthouse, Taunton 146-9
Fothergill, John ix
Freud, Clement 34

Gadney, Reg 187
Gage, Malcolm 79, 82
Gallagher, Noel, Liam and Patsy 242-3
Gange, Nancy 227, 229
Garbutt, Simon 88
Gardner Merchant 176-8
Garrick Club, London 64, 73, 185
Gidleigh Park Hotel, Devonshire 57,
    58, 75, 196
Gifford-Bennett, Jacqui 117
Girling, Simon 9-10, 25-6, 28, 29-30,
    32, 35, 36, 37, 38, 40, 42-3, 44, 46,
    51, 52, 74, 75, 76, 86, 108, 135, 142,
    151, 164, 166, 176-9, 210; dismissed
    184-5
Good Food Guide, The 26, 32, 75, 79,
    90, 91, 124, 215, 247, 249
Goring, George 56-7
Goring Hotel, London 56-7
Gottlieb, Mike 73-4
Grahame, Andrew 1-2, 7-8, 9, 11, 12,
    23, 30-2, 35, 36, 43, 45, 53-4, 65, 71,
    99, 103, 107, 110, 112, 113, 114-17,
    131, 140-1, 151, 159, 164, 178, 184-
    5, 204, 206, 208, 211, 242-3, 244,
    245; illness 1-2, 69-70; marriage 1-2,
    234-7, 239; letter to local paper 199-
    202
Grahame, Cécile 1, 2, 43, 45-6, 53, 71,
    237
Granada 176-8
Greece xiii, 212, 213, 215-20
Green, Emily 75-6
Green, Henrietta 75
Grey Advertising xiv, xvi
Gwynn-Jones, Patrick 72

Hague, William 197-8, 206
Hanover Investments 112, 113, 114,
    119
Harman, Harriet 195
Hawkes, Col. 226-7
Headworth-Whitty, Dr 227
Heathcoat-Amory, David 181
Hebden Bridge, Yorkshire 39, 40-1, 43
Henderson, Paul 57-8, 75
Hill, Phil 192-3
Hilton, Conrad 249
Hodge, Patricia 65
Hogg, Sarah 50
Horsley, Jefferson: August *1996* 4, 22-
    3; Nov. *1996* 93; March *1997* 173-4;
    June *1997* 196, 197, 199, 200-2,
    220-1; July *1997* 227; resigns 250
Howard, Michael 198
Howard, Philip 188
Hoyle, Jenny 157-8, 172
Hugo and the Huguenotes (steel
    band) 183, 203, 208-9, 247
Humphreys, Carolyn 12, 131, 160
Hyde Park Hotel, London 189

Imperial Hotel, Torquay xi, xiii, xiv, 20
Independent on Sunday 27-8
Ingham, Sir Bernard 29, 34-8, 39-46
Isserlis, Steven 14
Ivy restaurant, London 72

Jaine, Tom 75-6, 167
James, David 140-4, 159-60
Jeffery, Keith 64, 161
Jeffreys, Judge 104
Jenkins, Farmer 213-14
Jenkins, Nanny 213, 214
Jensen, Mr (hotel guest) 105-6
Jewels of Britain brochure 56, 57
Johansens 71
Johnson, Ian 224

Kessler, George 61-2
King, Jeremy 72, 73, 74
King, Tom 146, 148-9, 174, 181
Kington, Miles 14, 101
Kitchen, Frances 47-8, 87
Knight, Tony, DC 119, 120, 135

Ladenis, Nico 182
Lakehal, Christophe 32-3, 45, 46, 125,
    156, 158, 159, 163, 164, 176, 177,
    211, 256-7; wins Young Waiter of the
    Year competition 32, 71, 72, 73, 74
Le Petit Blanc brasserie, Oxford 188
Leaming, Mr (accountant) 50-1, 54
Lee, Laurie 13, 185
Leigh Rowley 49
Leigh-Enderl, Adèle 161
Lenkiewicz, R O (artist) 67-9
Leon, Ruth (Morley) 60, 64, 154,
    167-9
Lettonie restaurant, Bristol 59
Lichfield, Patrick, Earl of 101-2, 198
Lilley, Peter 198
Lindsays (string quartet) 14, 130, 132
Lipman, Maureen 34
Lock, Alison 29-30, 35, 51-2, 115-16,
    117, 184-5, 236-7
Lock, John 58, 76-7
Lott, Dame Felicity 14
Lumley, Mr (accountant) 65
Lynn, Mr (restaurant guest) 51, 54-5,
    83

MacIver, David 20, 22
Major, John 182
Mansfield, Arthur 90-1
Marriner, Andrew 139
Martin, James 78
Maschler, Fay 186-8
Maschler, Tom 187
Mawhinney, Brian 39

McArthur, Nicola 234-7
McKenzie, Mr (hotel inspector) 80-2
Meades, Jonathan 153, 162, 163, 167
Michelin Red Guide 56, 58-9, 91,
    121-6, 128, 133, 136-8, 185, 247
Midsummer Garden Party 202-3,
    207-9
Millennium Project, Castle Green
    202, 212, 234
Milne-Watson, Andrew 14
Minstrels pub, Taunton 116; colour
    scheme 12, 74; relaunched 88-9, 91-
    3, 116; to be gutted 234, 244
Moat, Frank 64
Monmouth, James, Duke of 104
Morgan, David and Mai 28-9
Morley, Robert 65, 169
Morley, Sheridan 34, 60, 64-5, 154,
    167-8, 169
Mosimann, Anton 91
Mount Somerset Hotel, Somerset
    111-12, 119, 120, 135
Musgrove Park Hospital, Taunton 1-2

Nash Ensemble 153, 162
National Farmers' Union 75
National Trust 51, 54-5, 83
Neal's Yard Dairy, London 38-9, 150
New York Herald 63
New York Times 71
Nicholson, David, MP 5, 172-4, 181,
    191
Nimmo, Derek 34
Nuffield hospital, Taunton 19-20, 22,
    23-4, 30

Oakes, Chris 91, 185
Oasis (music group) 242-3
Octagon Theatre, Yeovil 47-8, 87
O'Keefe see 'Bonsall, Anton'
Ol' Waffles see Horsley, Jefferson

Open Door association 192, 193, 194

Paterson, Jennifer 49, 107, 153, 162, 163, 165, 167
Pedlar, Stuart 168
Piermasters restaurant, Plymouth 67
poltergeist 104-5
Pope, Christopher 166
Portillo, Michael 161, 182
Postgate, Raymond 214
Prüger, Amelia ix-x
Prüger, Henry ix, x, xi, xiii, 60, 61-3, 199, 213
Prüger, Henry Anthony ix-x, xi

RAC Club: hotel guide 79-82, 263; Pall Mall premises xi, 61, 64
Raffael, Michael 75
Ready Steady Cook (TV programme) 2, 44, 48, 123
Ready Teddy ... Cook competition 47-8, 103
Reams, Ron, collages by 138
Redwood, Esme 222
Redwood, John 197
Reeves-Smith, Sir George, x, 64
Rhodes, Gary 13, 16-18, 91, 175-7, 179
Rhodes, Jenny 17, 175, 176, 177
Robertson, Liz 168
Robinson, Gerry 148
Ronay, Egon 91, 101
Rose, Jeffrey 80-2
Rosis, Athanasius and Fifi 216
Round, Jeremy 107
Roux, Michel 17, 153

Savoy Hotel, London 49; 1903-9 x-xi, 60, 81, 199; archives xiii, 60-4, 199
Savoy-Carlton Hotel, Bratislava xi-xiii, 213

Schubert, Franz 130, 132
Scott, Susan 60-1, 64, 199
Scrutton, Marianne 72
Shapland, Bob 36, 146, 147
Shepherd, Richard 17
Sherrin, Ned 34, 47
Short, Keith 85-6, 123
Skan, Martin 56, 57
Smith, Delia 92, 153
Smith, Godfrey 154, 167
Smith, Revd Julian 192
Somerset County Gazette: August 1996 4, 5; Nov. 1996 77; Dec. 1996 88; March 1997 136; May-June 1997 191-6, 200, 201; Sept. 1997 250
Sommerfelt, David 35, 36, 37-8, 43, 44, 46
Sondheim, Stephen 71
Spiller, R G 212, 226
Spreadeagle Hotel, Thame ix
Square restaurant, London 188
St Giles' Church, Cripplegate 12, 14
St John's garden centre, Somerset 96
St Mary's Ascot school 49-50
St Petroc's bistro, Padstow 188
Stafford College 178
Stainton, Julian 84, 85, 86, 127-8
Stein, Rick 8
Stephen Bull's Bistro, London 14
Stilgoe, Richard 14
Sutton, Ivan 12, 14-15, 130
Sutton, Mark 130, 132

Tarkay, paintings by 138
Taunton, Somerset 265; 1685 120; 19th-cent. 121-2; Castle Bow 4-5, 65, 104, 105-6, 199, 200, 260; Castle Green 156-7, 158, 172, 173-4, 191-5, 199-202, 205, 266; Castle Green Forum 205, 211, 236; parliamentary constituency 5, 172-4, 197; Town

Centre 3-7, 41, 172-4; Town Council 3-7, 41, 77, 173; *see also* Castle Hotel
Taunton Association for the Homeless 192, 193, 194
Taunton Deane Borough Council 171-2, 196, 199-202, 204-5, 206, 220-1, 250
Taunton Deane Environmental Services 171-2, 200, 202
Taunton School xiv, 227-8, 232
Taunton Town Centre Enhancement Scheme 3, 6, 77
Taunton Town Centre Forum 171-2
Thatcher, Carol 101
Thatcher, Denis 44-5
Thatcher, Margaret 39, 43, 44-5
Thessalonika, Greece xiii, 212, 213, 215-20
This Is Your Life (TV programme) 13, 15-18, 25
Thomas, Linda 159
Thone Preparatory School, Taunton 227, 228-30
Thorndike, Sybil 169
Toner, Bill 176, 177
Torbay xiv
Torquay, Imperial Hotel xi, xiii, xiv, 20
Trencherman's West Country Guide 153-4, 162, 164-6
Trevathan, Jeremy 107
Trevette, Monsieur 229
Tucker-Brown, Simon 35, 40, 41-2, 58
Turnbull & Asser, London 71-2
Tuscany 210

Unipart calendar 101
University of Surrey Hotel School xiv, 186

Vickery, Phil 2-3, 9-10, 11-12, 25-6,
26-8, 35, 38, 43-4, 50, 57, 70, 76, 88, 91, 92-3, 108, 122-4, 125, 127, 128, 143, 149-50, 151, 153, 158-9, 162, 163, 164, 166, 176, 177-8, 183, 184, 208, 222, 224, 234, 240-1, 260; meets Michelin man 136-8
Vienna ix

Walls, Daisy 183-4
Walsh, Philip and Jill 142-3, 159
Warner, Irene, letter from 91-2
Warner, Marina 50
Waterside Inn, Bray 153
Waugh, Auberon 34, 182
Waugh, Steve 222, 223
Webb, Brian and Eve 45
Wells, John 34
Westcountry Television 174-5
Western Provident Association 83-5, 127
Westminster College 71, 72-3
Wetherspoon, J D, pub 234, 244
Whatmore, Gill 3, 73, 76, 131, 132, 160, 202, 239, 248
Whitaker, Frances 153
White, Marco Pierre 182, 189
White Lane Gallery, Plymouth 66-7
Who'll do the Pudding? (TV programme) 2, 123
Willes, Angela 196
Williams, Stephen 67
Wilsey, Sir John 84, 86-7
Winner, Michael 56

Young, Lailan 130, 133
Young, Robin 130, 132, 133
Young Waiter of the Year competition 32, 71-4
Younger, Julian 57

Zafferano restaurant, London 187, 188